OXFORD STUDIES IN THEOLOGICAL ETHICS

General Editor
Oliver O'Donovan

Approaching the End

OXFORD STUDIES IN THEOLOGICAL ETHICS

The series presents discussions on topics of general concern to Christian Ethics, as it is currently taught in universities and colleges, at the level demanded by a serious student. The volumes will not be specialized monographs nor general introductions or surveys. They aim to make a contribution worthy of notice in its own right but also focused in such a way as to provide a suitable starting point for orientation.

The titles include studies in important contributors to the Christian tradition of moral thought; explorations of current moral and social questions; and discussions of central concepts in Christian moral and political thought. Authors treat their topics in a way that will show the relevance of the Christian tradition, but with openness to neighbouring traditions of thought which have entered into dialogue with it.

Approaching the End

A Theological Exploration of Death and Dying

DAVID ALBERT JONES

OXFORD
UNIVERSITY PRESS

OXFORD

UNIVERSITY PRESS

Great Clarendon Street, Oxford ox2 6DP

Oxford University Press is a department of the University of Oxford.
It furthers the University's objective of excellence in research, scholarship,
and education by publishing worldwide in

Oxford New York

Auckland Cape Town Dar es Salaam Hong Kong Karachi
Kuala Lumpur Madrid Melbourne Mexico City Nairobi
New Delhi Shanghai Taipei Toronto

With offices in

Argentina Austria Brazil Chile Czech Republic France Greece
Guatemala Hungary Italy Japan Poland Portugal Singapore
South Korea Switzerland Thailand Turkey Ukraine Vietnam

Oxford is a registered trade mark of Oxford University Press
in the UK and in certain other countries

Published in the United States
by Oxford University Press Inc., New York

British Library Cataloguing in Publication Data

Data available

Library of Congress Cataloging in Publication Data

Data available

Typeset by SPI Publisher Services Ltd, Pondicherry, India
Printed in Great Britain
on acid-free paper by
Biddles Ltd, King's Lynn, Norfolk

ISBN 978–0–19–928715–4

Dedicated to Eustace, who taught me that we should neither fear death too much nor love life too little.

Contents

List of Abbreviations

BM   Ambrose of Milan, *De bono mortis*; English trans. by M. P. McHugh, 'Death as a Good' in P. M. Peebles *et al.* (eds.) *Saint Ambrose: Seven Exegetical Works*, The Fathers of the Church: A New Translation, vol. 65, Washington: Catholic University of America Press, 1972.

CD   Augustine of Hippo, *De civitate Dei*; English trans. by H. Bettenson, *Augustine: City of God*, London: Penguin Books, 1984. All quotations reproduced by permission of Penguin Books Limited.

FR   Ambrose of Milan, *De fide resurrectionis*; English trans. by H. De Romestin, 'On the Belief in the Resurrection', in *Library of the Nicene and Post-Nicene Fathers (NPN)*, series II, vol. 10, Grand Rapids, Mich., 1887.

ST   Thomas Aquinas, *Summa Theologiae*; English trans. by the Fathers of the English Dominican Province, *Summa Theologica*, London: Burns, Oates & Washbourne, 1912–36.

QD2   Karl Rahner, *Zur Theologie des Todes*, Quaestiones Disputatae 2, 1958; English trans., *On the Theology of Death*, Quaestiones Disputatae 2, New York: Herder and Herder, 1961. All quotations reproduced by permission of Crossroad Publishing.

Introduction

At least two well-developed bodies of literature have emerged on practical questions relating to death, one the concern of psychology, the other the concern of ethics. These flow from two basic questions: how can we live well in the face of death? and when, if ever, is it legitimate deliberately to bring human life to an end? Related to both of these is a third question that seems to press ever harder in the context of modern medical advances: to what extent and in what circumstances should we strive to prolong life, given that death is inevitable? The perspective of faith can help to assess and evaluate the many sometimes conflicting claims of different schools of psychology and of philosophy on these questions. Thomas Aquinas held that one of the reasons that human beings need a revelation from God is that the most important truths of human life are grasped only by a few, only after much study and even then, not without mistakes. Furthermore, he argued that human beings need a revelation from God because the ultimate meaning of life lies beyond the natural powers of human reason.

There is then a demonstrable need for an explicitly theological approach to death. How, though, should one go about devising such an approach? Christian theology draws upon various sources: the Scriptures, the witness of the Christian tradition of faith and practice, rational argument, contemporary experience, and the authoritative voice of the Church as expressed by ecumenical councils, by the bishops collectively, and (according to Catholics) by the bishop of Rome speaking for the Church as a whole. On the subject of death each of these sources offers an overwhelming wealth of material, an embarrassment of riches. The subject of death is so basic to human existence and Christian theology that it has been spoken of by virtually every author and every sacred authority. At the same time there is no single scriptural or conciliar text that stands out as the necessary starting point.

As we are seeking a systematic theological account of death, one method that suggests itself is to consider one or more approaches that have been tried by outstanding Christian thinkers of the past. This not only saves us from the task of having to reinvent the wheel, so to speak, but also, through a critical consideration of a limited number of carefully chosen thinkers, it should be possible to see the difficulties involved in devising such an approach. Such a method will, of necessity, be selective, but by concentrating on the thought of a few it will enable us to engage in detail, and hopefully in depth, with some of the central theological questions as these thinkers have conceived them. This is the approach taken by the present study. Four theologians are introduced, each of whom developed a distinctive and influential theological account of human death: Ambrose of Milan, Augustine of Hippo, Thomas Aquinas, and Karl Rahner. Each will be considered in turn with respect to the account he provides, paying attention to the influences that have shaped it, the insights it provides and the weaknesses or gaps in the account. The aim is not primarily to make a contribution to the study of the history of theology, but rather, through engagement with the thought of theologians of the past, to reflect on a subject that is contemporary because perennial. After critically expounding the thought of each of these theologians in turn, a final chapter will draw the enquiry together, applying what has been learned to some contemporary practical questions regarding preparation for death, bereavement, suicide, euthanasia and the withdrawal of life-sustaining treatment.

Ambrose (discussed in Ch. 2) provides the starting point because he articulated a very clear and explicit theological account of death, one that will be criticized but which has much to teach because it represents such a radical position: he argued that death was, in itself, a positive human good, from the perspective both of philosophy and of theology. In his *De fide resurrectionis* (*FR*), Ambrose puts forward three deaths: death to sin so as to live to God, death as the completion of this present life, and the death of the soul due to sin. He expands on this analysis in his *De bono mortis* (*BM*) where he says that it seems on the face of it that the first is good, the last is bad, and the middle is midway, good for the good, bad for the bad. Nevertheless Ambrose maintains that bodily death is not a middle term, but rather is always a good thing in itself. The badness of death is not due to death but due to something else. Death is always a good thing as it always frees the soul from the prison of the body and sets the body at rest. It is the end of all evils and a safe harbour from the storms of this life. It was Ambrose's great achievement to unite Christian and Platonic piety and metaphysics into a single vision of the meaning of human death. However, from a Christian perspective, a fundamental problem with this approach is that, if the body is 'more of a burden than a benefit' to the soul, it would seem better for the soul if God had not united soul and body in the first place. This seems to contradict the doctrine of creation. Likewise the doctrine of the bodily resurrection, which Ambrose also holds dear, seems at best irrelevant, at worst problematic for the freedom of the soul. Ambrose's approach to death shapes his attitude to issues as diverse as virginity, martyrdom, suicide, fear of death, and care for the souls of those who have died.

Ambrose provides the necessary background for understanding the thought of Augustine of Hippo, the second of our theologians. Augustine of Hippo is widely regarded as the most influential thinker in Western Christianity after the age of the apostles. His thought continues to shape theology, both in the Catholic Church and in the churches of the Reformation, both directly—in those who have accepted his ideas—and indirectly—in those who have reacted against him (Fitzgerald 1999). His significance for this study is thus twofold. In the first place Augustine developed a clear and distinctive theological approach to death that is in stark contrast to that of Ambrose. In the second place the influence of his theology on the later tradition ensures the continued relevance of this particular approach to death.

Though by no means identical, there was a very close harmony between the thought of the early Augustine and that of Ambrose, his older contemporary. However, Augustine's thought developed significantly in the face of various pastoral challenges to a position distinct from, and in some important ways antithetical to, the sort of Platonist Christianity he had once shared with Ambrose. Augustine in *De civitate Dei* (*CD*) book XIII puts an alternative account of three deaths. His three are the death of the soul, the death of the body, and the death of both in hellfire, called in Scripture 'the second death'. Augustine agrees that bodily death seems to be midway, good for the good and bad for the bad, but he goes on to argue that bodily death is always a *bad* thing in itself. Careful consideration of the story of the fall from Eden shows it to be the very opposite of the Platonic fall myth. The Eden story sees the union of body and soul as natural and the separation as a punishment. The Platonic fall sees the separation of the soul as natural and the union with the body as a punishment. If the union of body and soul is a good then the separation is always a bad thing in itself, even if it may be the occasion of some good. Augustine's approach to death is thus in sharp contrast to that of Ambrose. A detailed examination of the effect of this contrast on a range of practical issues will be set out in Chapter 4.

The third theologian to be considered is Thomas Aquinas in the thirteenth century. Thomas sought to combine a theological vision drawn from Augustine with a philosophical approach based on the rediscovered thought of Aristotle. It was Aristotle who posed some of the most troubling questions for Thomas concerning death, particularly concerning the soul's survival after death, but it was Augustine who provided the theological perspective which shaped Thomas's response. The thought of Thomas Aquinas thus represents an attempt to build on Augustine's understanding of death. Thomas Aquinas is also a significant figure in his own right. He was one of the most influential Christian thinkers of the Middle Ages and continues to have a major role in contemporary philosophy. For Catholic theology he is perhaps the most important theologian since Augustine.

In the *Summa Theologiae* (*ST*), Thomas Aquinas argues that the soul and body are not two conjoined things ('substances') but one unified whole. The soul is 'the form of the body'. This might seem to preclude the separate existence of the soul after death, but Thomas rejects this inference, for he claims that the human soul has an activity that is exercised not by any bodily organ: thought. The question then arises: can souls know anything when they are separated from the body? Thomas's answer develops over time and he comes to stress that the power of understanding of the 'separated soul' (the soul isolated from the body) is very weak. This leads to a further question: in what sense can human death be considered natural? Death is, in one way, natural, in another way, a punishment for sin. Also it is natural as regards matter (the destructible body) but not as regards form (the indestructible soul). The separated souls of the just are immediately blessed with the vision of God, but this reward is not due to the soul's separation from the body. Death in itself (*per se*) is always a bad thing. It is only incidentally (*per accidens*) that death is, for some, the beginning of heavenly bliss. Thus homicide can be seen to be wrong because, in itself, it harms someone. Similarly suicide can be understood as a failure to love this life sufficiently, and is an act of injustice against society and against God. Thomas is therefore able to follow Aristotle in saying that death is the greatest natural evil, and so it is right to fear death and courage is needed to allow one to act well in the face of death. Thomas also holds that the desire for God, which is itself a gift of God, is able to overcome the natural love of life. Nevertheless, even in a theological perspective, remaining in this life, while God wishes it, is better than leaving this life before one's time. For the love by which someone submits to God's will and desires to serve God in this life is a greater thing than the desire to enjoy being with God in the next life. While Thomas's account of death is clear, and involves both theological and philosophical approaches, it suffers from a relative lack of integration, especially with regard to a separation between the theology of hope and the philosophical analysis of killing. This separation of theology and philosophy was exacerbated in subsequent centuries until the twentieth century, when a number of theologians attempted to address the problem.

The last thinker to be considered is the twentieth-century German theologian Karl Rahner. Like Thomas Aquinas before him, Rahner attempted to produce a synthesis of received theology with new philosophy. In his case this new philosophy was not Aristotle but post-Kantian German philosophy and perhaps especially the thought of Martin Heidegger, whose seminars Rahner attended. The dominant theological influence on Rahner was the thought of Thomas Aquinas. There is a complex relation between the thought of Karl Rahner on death and that of Thomas. At certain points he strongly re-affirms positions developed by Thomas, but he brings in quite new concerns and also, it can be argued, he affirms positions that are in tension with those of Thomas. In the late 1930s and early 1940s

Rahner, like many creative Catholic thinkers of the period, was regarded with suspicion. However, in the 1960s he was appointed as a theological adviser to the Second Vatican Council and he helped write the document on the Church in the Modern World. He was one of the outstanding Catholic theologians of the twentieth century and, among these, was the theologian most concerned with death as a theological question. He wrote an early monograph on this subject and returned to the question throughout his career. While Rahner remains a controversial figure among some Catholics, his significance for contemporary Catholic reflection on the theology of death is beyond dispute. This may be gauged from prominence given to him not only by the revisionist Jesuit bioethicist Richard McCormick in his *Health and Medicine in the Catholic Tradition* (1984) but also by the more traditionally minded Dominican bioethicists Benedict Ashley and Kevin O'Rourke in their *Healthcare Ethics a Theological Analysis* (1997). Indeed neither McCormick nor Ashley and O'Rourke mention any theological account of death other than that of Rahner, and that of Boros, a follower of Rahner.

Karl Rahner puts forward his own distinctive theological account of death in *Zur Theologie des Todes—On the Theology of Death,* published in 1958 as volume two of the deliberately speculative series Quaestiones Disputatae (QD2). The starting point for his discussion was the claim that death is an event that affects the human being as a whole—body and soul. It is not to be thought of as just affecting the body while leaving the immortal soul essentially unchanged. For Rahner, the human being is less a composite of body and soul and more a union of person and nature. 'Person' here refers to what is free, active, and spiritual; 'nature' refers to all that is necessary, given, and passive. The definition of death as 'the separation of body and soul' is inadequate because it captures only the natural aspect, but not the distinctively human aspect: as personal, death is also the end of our earthly pilgrimage, the culmination of our earthly life. Understood as the conclusion of a personal life, death must itself be construed as an act, the act by which one's whole life is disposed. By death the soul is not alienated from the world but is opened up to a richer 'pancosmic' relationship with the material cosmos. However, not every aspect of death is positive: if Adam had not fallen, he would still have reached a limit, though not a death in our sense. Since the fall this unalloyed Adamic act of completion has been veiled by the physical catastrophe and discontinuity of biological death. Yet, while the true character of death is now obscured by death-as-suffering, due to the fall, its inner essence is still good and redeemable. Death can still be an act of completion and self-realization. Rahner's thought on death seems to suffer from a similar fault to the thought of Ambrose. Both interpret fulfilment or completion as belonging to death as such. Nevertheless, as with Augustine, Rahner's thought develops over time and he moves away from the approach he took in 1958. His approach to the issue of 'the liberty of the sick', while flawed, represents an important and much needed effort to renew moral theology on end of life issues by turning to fundamental questions of philosophy and theology. Chapter 7, which is the last, revisits this issue and others discussed at the outset of this study, and seeks to illuminate them by drawing on our critical exploration of the thought of Ambrose, Augustine, Thomas, and Rahner.

Examination of the thought of Ambrose, Augustine, Thomas, and Rahner shows them to constitute a single extended argument on the theology of death. This can be set out in relation to the practical realities of grief, fear, and hope in the face of death. There is a rightful place for grief, a good grief, even for a Christian. Augustine teaches us that death is something with which we have to contend, and indeed that the difficult and painful process of contending with death is a means through which we are brought to our final joyful end. It is arguable that the Kübler-Ross stages of grief, or something analogous to them, make *more* sense in a theological context of redemptive hope than they do outside such a context. Christian hope affirms both the need and the difficulty of acknowledging one's own approaching death, even for a Christian. A key point for Thomas Aquinas is that, in itself, it is always wrong to kill a human being on account of the dignity of human nature (*ST* IIaIIae 64. 6). Rahner adds that it also stands in contradiction to the supernatural destiny of human beings. Thomas seeks to understand more deeply the reasons why suicide is prohibited: as self-destructive; as unjust to the community; and as a sin directly against God. If suicide is indeed a self-destructive project, then facilitating suicide is not assisting anyone, and still less is mercy killing. A more complex question is the withdrawal of treatment, and perhaps the most contentious example of this is the withdrawal of tube feeding from patients who are unconscious. Rahner argues that suicide and mercy killing are wrong because they cut off future opportunities for human freedom. But this rationale does not apply to the unconscious who therefore are not included in the prohibition against killing. However, Rahner is wrong to exclude the unconscious from all human care. What is wrong with self-killing and mercy killing is not primarily that they limit someone's future opportunities for freedom but more fundamentally that they attack the human goods that freedom exists to serve: the valuing of life, the acceptance of death, justice to others, gratitude to God. Rahner is at his most profound in describing how the need to surrender oneself to God in death (the need to die like a martyr) is anticipated throughout life. If, by the grace of God, death can be freely endured, and all that has been said implies that this is no easy task, then the final surrender in death will be the end of death and the preamble to our true end: eternal happiness in which death will be no more.

1

The Need for a Theological Approach to Death

DEATH, GRIEVING, AND KILLING

Death is a moment of judgment: for it is only after death that we can see someone's life as a whole, and it is in this sense that Solon declared, paradoxically, that we should count no one happy until that person was dead (Aristotle *Ethica Nicomachea* 1. 10. 1100a, referring to the story in Herodotus *Histories* 1. 30); furthermore, in at least some cases, the way someone dies constitutes a final test of fidelity to or betrayal of the values he or she has sought to live by, as is seen most clearly in those who die willingly for some great cause; lastly, for Christians, as for followers of many religious traditions, death is followed by reward or punishment, and hence in death each person's soul and the deeds of his or her life are weighed in the balance. Some of these themes of judgment in death will recur in what follows. However, the primary focus of this book is not how death judges people, but how people have judged death, and in particular, what meaning Christian theologians have found in death. This is worth exploring because, although death itself is ultimately unavoidable, the particular human meaning we attribute to death has definite practical consequences.

Death is a universal feature of human life. Human life is framed by conception and death. In the words of the book of Wisdom, 'there is for all mankind one entrance into life, and a common departure' (Wisdom 7: 6). Gods or angels may enjoy an eternal or undying life of which we know nothing, but the life we know about is lived under the shadow of death. A recognition of one's own mortality is thus distinctively human. Angels do not die, and animals without the power of reason do not reflect upon the prospect of their own death. Human beings, on the other hand, have always reflected upon death. It is ubiquitous in the literature in every age. Cultures as diverse as those of ancient Greece, medieval Europe, or early modern Japan have all held it to be part of wisdom to be mindful of death and the transience of life. Even our own age, which has been accused of denying the reality of death (Becker 1974), shows no dearth of writing on the subject. It is difficult to find a serious work of fiction that does not at least touch on the human experience of death, and the meaning of death plays a significant role in literary criticism and cultural studies, anthropology, sociology, and psychology, philosophy and ethics, not to mention science and medicine. Within twentieth-century continental philosophy, Heidegger's (1927) characterization of human life as 'being-towards-death' (*Sein zum Todes*) has left a lasting impression. Even the relatively barren and abstract discipline of analytic philosophy, as practised in the universities of English-speaking countries in the twentieth century, has not been able to dispense with consideration of death altogether. The question of how to understand and evaluate the prospect of non-existence is one that remains on the philosophical agenda (e.g. Nagel 1970; Van Evra 1971; Solomon and Malpas 1998). Reflecting on death and attempting to assign to it some definite human meaning has practical consequences. This is because, while there is a parallel between coming into existence and falling out of existence, between conception and death, there is also an important difference. Death is not only a limit to life, but it is a limit that we must face. This raises two distinct questions, one the concern of psychology, the other the concern of ethics.

In the first place, while death, as something suffered, is inevitable, the attitude we have to death, both to our own death and to the death of someone close to us, is not inevitable. It varies from person to person and from culture to culture and it can be altered, at least to an extent. Living with the near prospect of death, facing death, is something that can be done well or badly. It is in this sense that a range of cultures have held that the manner of someone's death is of great significance and that Christians have talked of 'making a good death'. Likewise someone's death will generally have a great effect on those who remain alive, and how we should live with the loss of someone close, that is, how to grieve well and how to 'move on', is also a matter for reflection of a practical kind.

In the second place, death can be the object of action more directly, in that death is something that can be deliberately brought about. Whereas everyone dies, not every death is the direct consequence of human actions. Most deaths are the result of accidents, diseases, or frailty and happen despite the best efforts of the person concerned, and of medical professionals, to keep that person alive. However, death as a deliberate human act, whether in war or in peacetime, whether by violent actions or by planned omissions, whether by another or by one's own hand, has also been a common feature of human history. Death by human hands, that is killing, is rightly the concern of ethics, law, and politics. In many cases killing is clearly an act of violence, unjust and unjustifiable, and the practical question for society is how to prevent and to punish such behaviour. However, in some cases killing appears to have some measure of justification or excuse as, for example, with unintended killing in the process of reasonable self-defence. It is a matter of great contemporary debate whether suicide, assisting suicide, and active voluntary euthanasia are excusable in this way. It is also a matter of dispute what counts as passive euthanasia, that is killing by omission, neglect, or abandonment and, in contrast, what counts as reasonable withdrawal of measures that are only postponing the inevitability of death. The case of Terri Schiavo, which captured the imagination of America and of much of the world, seemed to reveal a fault line running through society and also through the churches on precisely this issue. Does withdrawal of assisted nutrition and hydration necessarily amount to killing by omission?

Thus two well-developed bodies of literature have emerged on practical questions relating to death in modern society. These flow from two basic questions: how can we live well in the face of death? and when is it legitimate deliberately to bring human life to an end?

The first question has been taken up primarily by psychologists and psychotherapists of whom pride of place goes to Elisabeth Kübler-Ross with her work on *Death and Dying* (1969). She identified five stages in the process of coming to terms with death: denial, anger, bargaining, depression, and acceptance. Going beyond the purely descriptive, the aim of her work and that of those who followed her was to characterize a psychologically healthy pattern of accepting death in order to help people to achieve this acceptance, that is, to die well. The precise characterization of the stages of acceptance might be criticized for being too formal or idealized (Silver and Wortman 1980; De Spelder and Strickland 1995) and also, from a faith perspective, the whole schema might be criticized for promoting acceptance of death abstracted from any specific hope that comes from religious faith (Branson 1975) and for abstracting out the trials of faith for those believers who doubt in the face of death. Nevertheless, Kübler-Ross performed an important service by raising the issue of what it is to die well and her work has been used by a great number of others producing self-help books on facing death and on bereavement. Indeed, not only have many Christians used the ideas of Kübler-Ross, but her basic approach in terms of identifying stages of grief had already been anticipated by the explicitly Christian work of Granger Westberg (1962). Concern with helping people to die well in this sense has also informed the hospice movement which aims, not only to provide specialized medical care for those who are dying, but also to provide an environment within which people can attempt to make a good death. From the beginning the hospice movement has been strongly influenced by a specifically religious ethos and most such institutions explicitly aim to make provision for the spiritual needs of the dying.

Somewhat disconnected from this strand of thought is a distinct body of literature concerned with the ethics of killing, and, more specifically, with end-of-life decisions in a healthcare context (e.g. Biggar 2004; Dworkin 1994; Keown 2002; Singer 1994). In recent years the focal point of this literature has been the case for, and the case against, legalizing assisting suicide and voluntary euthanasia. Since 1984, in the Netherlands, both of these activities have been exempt from criminal prosecution, subject to certain conditions being fulfilled. In 1997 the state of Oregon in the United States legalized not euthanasia but physician-assisted suicide. In the United Kingdom a House of Lords Select Committee into the issue in 1994 came out strongly against changing the law (Walton 1994), but a more recent select committee was more ambivalent

(Mackay 2005).[1] Implicit in the legal question of euthanasia is the deeper ethical and philosophical question of suicide. It seems obvious that it is unfair to deprive someone else of his or her life, at least as a general rule, but what, if anything, is wrong with taking one's own life? Some philosophers and theologians tackle this question head on, but most skirt around it, either assuming the acceptability or unacceptability of suicide with only cursory arguments, or focusing on issues of law and enforceability: whether legalizing voluntary euthanasia would create a 'slippery slope' leading, for example, to involuntary euthanasia and euthanasia of those suffering curable depression. Perhaps the best current example of such a slippery slope argument is provided by John Keown in *Euthanasia, Ethics and Public Policy* (2002).

Related to these two questions is a third: to what extent should we strive to prolong life? Throughout the twentieth century, in the developed world, life expectancy increased dramatically. However, this has been more to do with better nutrition, better hygiene and, more recently, reduction in smoking, than to any specific medical breakthrough. Medicine has had its greatest impact on mortality in childbirth and in the early years. The ongoing battle against heart disease and cancer has had a more limited effect and morbidity in later life due to Alzheimer's and other degenerative diseases are actually on the increase. The dream of Goodwin in the eighteenth century that medicine was on the brink of delivering virtual immortality is as unrealistic today as it was two hundred years ago. Nevertheless, there are scientists and venture capitalists who believe it possible, at least in principle, to delay ageing and radically to extend the human lifespan two- or even threefold. They generally pin their hopes on developments in genetics and have expended much time and money on discovering the biological mechanisms of senescence in the hope that these could be reversed or at least retarded. At the more speculative end, developments in nano-technology promise a level of control at the micro-level that could one day correct and

---

[1] The Mackay Report (2005) rejected euthanasia but seemed more favourably disposed to the legalization of assisted suicide. Nevertheless, when this was put before the House in the form of Lord Joffe's Assisted Dying Bill, it was defeated decisively by 148 votes to 100 (Hansard, vol. 681, pt. 145, cc. 1184–1295 (12 May 2006)).

repair the damage that causes ageing. These plans and hopes are part of a movement termed transhumanism, which seeks to transform the biology of future generations to such an extent that they would no longer belong to the same species. Such superhumans, it is said, would regard us with the same condescension as present human beings regard the great apes. Unsurprisingly, not everyone is equally enthusiastic about the prospect of transforming human nature and a number have argued more specifically that the effort radically to extend life expectancy is ill-conceived. In this context thinkers such as Leon Kass (1988: 299–317) and Daniel Callahan (2003: ch. 3) have emphasized the importance of accepting the given life cycle of human beings as they are at present constituted, including the inevitability of death. Even if it were technically successful, the social and political effects of doubling the human lifespan take us into unknown territory. Consider its likely effects on population and the already looming problem of a large proportion of the population drawing the state pension. It seems, at least on the face of it, that the pursuit of longevity can be taken to extremes.

A more pressing practical expression of the question of how far to pursue the extension of life is the decision whether to continue with or whether to withdraw medical treatment from a patient when the treatment is burdensome or death is approaching. These kinds of decision are particularly troublesome because they can represent a clash between the need to accept death, as emphasized by psychologists and by philosophical reflections on longevity, and, on the other hand, the prohibition on deliberate killing, as emphasized by those philosophers and theologians who accept the principle of 'the sanctity of life' (e.g. Keown 2002: 30–52; Stith 1987; John Paul II 1995: 39–41).

In English law this tension is resolved, to an extent, by distinguishing between actions and omissions. Actions intended to bring about death are prohibited, but withdrawal of treatment is an omission, rather than an action, and omissions which cause death may be lawful. This distinction will not excuse negligence by someone who has a duty of care, for example if a carer leaves a young child unattended in the bath and that child should drown; it will, however, excuse where there is no duty of care. Furthermore, in *Bland* 1993 the judges declared that doctors have no positive duty to keep alive a patient in their care if that patient is in a 'persistent vegetative state', because, according to the court, living in this state does not constitute a benefit to the patient. Hence someone in this state can legally be starved to death even if the explicit intention, the *mens rea*, is to end the person's life. Even at the time it was recognized that this legal judgment left the English law 'morally and intellectually misshapen' (Lord Mustill in *Airedale NHS Trust* v. *Bland* [1993] AC 789 at 887).

Some philosophers have sought to resolve the tension between the legitimate acceptance of death and unethical deliberate killing by drawing a slightly different line: not between acts and omissions but between intended and unintended consequences (Watt 2000: 6–8; Keown 2002: 18–22). According to this account the deliberate starvation of someone, if it is intended to bring about death, should be prohibited. Nevertheless, treatment may be withdrawn if it has become burdensome to the patient and is only producing limited benefit, even when it is foreseen that death will thereby come sooner. The question is whether the speeding of death is the aim or whether it is an unwanted side effect of withdrawing burdensome treatment. This analysis is ethically much more robust than the confusion present in the current state of English law, but even this analysis is not without its problems. If death may be accepted as a side effect, why is it that it should never be produced deliberately? If death may sometimes be accepted, even welcomed, can this acceptance not inform the decision to withdraw treatment? At this point we encounter 'a deep matter' (Mahoney, Anscombe, et al. 1982: 48) which is not settled easily by recourse to distinctions between intended and unintended consequences of action. It shows the need for deeper reflection on the meaning of human death as an event, as an act, and as something not-done-but-willingly-accepted.

THE CONTRIBUTION OF THEOLOGY

As death is universal in human history, it is to be expected that religious believers would have considered the meaning of human death, but what specific contribution can religious reflection, and in particular Christian reflection, bring to the understanding of death? Christian doctrine may have much to say about what is in store for the soul after death, but in the practical realm, what is lacking in the disciplines of psychology and philosophy that can be remedied by theology? Death is a universal phenomenon not limited to Christians and for everyone, death brings this life to an end, whatever may lie after death. Death therefore cuts us off from the world in a radical way. Furthermore, where it is wrong to bring about death, it is surely not wrong only for Christians or only for Christian reasons. Killing is wrong as an offence against the individual and against natural justice, because of the value of human life which all in common have a duty to uphold. Certainly the wrongness of killing does not depend solely on the biblical commandment. Thus it might seem that, even for a Christian, it is psychology and philosophy that provide the best approach to the practical issues of death and dying, and that theology should follow in their wake, adding inspiration and motivation but not distinctive content or divergent guidance to these natural disciplines.

Without denying or disregarding the great value of the insights provided by psychology and philosophy there are, nevertheless, a number of reasons for believers also to seek a specifically theological account of human death.

In the first place the perspective of faith can help to assess and evaluate the many sometimes conflicting claims of different schools of psychology and of philosophy. Aristotle said that 'to attain any assured knowledge about the soul is one of the most difficult things in the world' (*De Anima* 1. 1. 402a). This seems to be borne out by the present state of the discipline of psychology. Whereas in the natural sciences there is detailed agreement on principles and on the foundational theories of the subject against which background disputes occur, in psychology and psychoanalysis there are alternative and radically divergent approaches, some of which deny to others any validity whatsoever. There is a body of empirical work on cognition which has achieved some success in modelling unconscious mental processes with the aid of computers, but the more specifically human the area of study, the more limited the use of such methods and the more important becomes environment, upbringing, development, social interaction, and culture. It is precisely at this point that psychology takes on the appearance of the social sciences or humanities and becomes a battleground of competing schools of thought. This state of affairs should not be deplored, for it reflects the need for specific methods and conceptual tools for the study of the specifically human, and also reflects the sort of precision we should expect of this area of study.[2] It would be a far greater mistake to imagine that all that we wished to know about the human mind could be discovered through the precise but narrow filter of physicalist concepts and quantitative methodology. It is, rather, through a variety of methods and of schools that psychology and psychoanalysis have so much of interest to say about human death. However, the existence of these divergent, sometimes conflicting and sometimes incommensurable schools and methods also creates a problem: it may sometimes be difficult, even for those in the field, to adjudicate fairly between rival claims.

If this is so in psychology, it is more so in philosophy. Questions of a philosophical kind, which go beyond the specific methods of any discipline and seek a more general, more comprehensive understanding, are unavoidable. Those who avoid philosophical questions simply assume a particular philosophical stance without examining their assumptions. However, there is no agreed method for criticizing philosophical assumptions or for resolving these questions. Philosophy, even more than psychology, is therefore composed of schools some of whom cannot speak to one another and do not even recognize the value of what the other does.[3] Without denying the possibility of synthesis, criticism, or dialogue between the divergent traditions represented in contemporary philosophy, it seems clear that, if theology can give some critical reflection on the claims of philosophers, this would certainly be a helpful contribution.

In addition to the tensions within the fields of psychology and philosophy there is also a significant tension between these two fields taken as a whole, and between the sort of advice offered by psychologists and that offered by philosophers. Where one concentrates on the processes of accepting death and of grieving, the other focuses on

---

[2] Bearing in mind the words of Aristotle that we should not expect of any discipline a greater degree of accuracy than the subject matter allows (*Ethica Nicomachea* 1. 3. 1094b).

[3] An influential account of the mutual incomprehension of different disciplines and approaches within the modern academy was provided by MacIntyre in *After Virtue* (1981).

questions of justice, law, and the value of life (or, increasingly, autonomy). Those more strongly influenced by psychology may criticize the attempt to apply particular ethical rules in end-of-life situations as an intrusion that detracts from the reality of the situation. Philosophers, on the other hand, may criticize those who pay attention only to the psychological aspects of dying for lacking clarity on vital distinctions and failing to grasp essential ethical principles. In some ways this echoes a tension which will be sketched out below between hope and commandment, a tension that also shows itself in a different way in a divide between spirituality and doctrinal theology going back at least to the fourteenth century.[4] If a theological account of death can help bring these two aspects together (hope and commandment; the spiritual and the doctrinal; the psychological and the ethical; that aspect concerned with preparation for death and bereavement and that concerned with killing and decisions to withdraw treatment), then it may provide a model for those who wish to reconcile and synthesize the insights of these two secular academic disciplines.

Thomas Aquinas held that one of the reasons that human beings need a revelation from God is that the most important truths of human life are grasped only by a few, only after much study, and even then, not without some mistakes (*Summa Theologiae* Prima Pars Question 1 article 1, henceforth *ST* Ia 1.1). He had in mind the great classical philosophers Socrates, Plato, and Aristotle who he thought had shown how far the human mind could go, but also how easy it was, even for the greatest thinkers, to make fundamental mistakes. Most people would never have the natural gifts or the leisure enjoyed by these thinkers, but everyone needs a share of wisdom to live his or her own life. Revelation is therefore necessary so that we can know quickly and reliably truths about the deepest questions concerning human life and death, truths which in principle are discoverable by anyone but which in practice few can discover without help.

A more fundamental reason that Thomas Aquinas gives as to why human beings need a revelation from God is that the ultimate meaning of life lies beyond the natural powers of human reason (*ST* Ia 1.1). Thomas claimed that human happiness lies ultimately in communion

---

[4] According to A. N. Williams (1997), though McCool (2000) dates the split a little later.

with God. All other goods are partial or transient, even the highest goods of human friendship, society, and the contemplation of truth and beauty. To be held securely and to be perfected these goods need to be part of a comprehensive human good that can exist only in heaven (*ST* IaIIae 1–2). However, what is in store for us after death, and even that there is any fully human life after death, is not something human beings could know had God not revealed it to them. This is because the hope of life beyond the grave relies not on the visible powers of nature but purely on the power of God. It is therefore necessary to develop an explicitly theological account of human death for only this account can include truths from revelation about the end of human life, in both the senses of that term. While for believer and unbeliever alike death brings this life to an end (terminus), it seems that an account that fails to encompass the end (purpose) of human life cannot give us the means to develop the right attitude to death in general, nor to judge the most difficult cases where people wonder if it is right to bring about death deliberately.

If believers shy away from developing an explicitly theological account of death, then they will operate according to an implicit theology that is unexamined and perhaps mistaken. Just as there is no avoiding philosophy, but those who do so operate with an implicit and unexamined philosophy, so for those who have faith, there is no avoiding theology. Not only prayer and spirituality but also Christian consideration of ethics or politics imply theological judgments which will either be explicit or implicit, either examined or unexamined. This is particularly noticeable in the area of ethical discussion where, in order to try to influence wider public policy, Christians sometimes concentrate on secular arguments that might sway non-believers. The specifically Christian rationale for a position is thus left unstated, even though many of those most actively concerned with, for example, the issues of abortion or euthanasia, are in fact motivated by religious belief.

The failure to articulate a specifically Christian account can leave Christians relying on weaker arguments that fail to move their fellow believers, and that leave secular thinkers attributing a 'hidden agenda' to believers (Paul 2004). It can also mean that when non-believers attribute specifically theological reasons to believers they get it deeply wrong. A good example of this is Glanville

Williams's allegation that the reason that early Christians condemned infanticide (a practice generally tolerated by pagans) was
because of the fear that unbaptized infants who died in this way
would be consigned to the fires of hell (1957: 193–5 see also D. A.
Jones 2004: 180). This claim is utterly implausible. In the first place
the early Christian rejection of infanticide is evident from the first
century CE,[5] whereas there is little evidence that the practice of
infant baptism was widespread until the late fourth century (neither Ambrose of Milan nor Augustine of Hippo was baptized as an
infant, even though both had Christian mothers). In the second
place, the claim that infants who died before baptism experience
the fires of hell seems to have arisen out of a fifth-century dispute
between Augustine and Pelagius. It has no explicit support before
this time and has waned in influence since, even in the Latin West
(Toner 1913). In the third place early Christian attitudes to infanticide were indistinguishable from ancient Jewish attitudes,[6] and no
one attributes to Jews the fear that uncircumcised infants are
destined to the fires of hell. Lastly, and perhaps most fundamentally, it would seem, if Williams were right, that Christians would
have had no strong objection to infanticide immediately after
baptism. However, there is no record that any Christian in any
age has advocated this practice and it is difficult to imagine a policy
more alien to the mindset of early Christianity (D. A. Jones 2004:
57–63).

Williams attributed this theological reasoning to Christians in
order to dismiss their objections to infanticide. This was part of a
larger effort to smooth the way for a social acceptance of child killing,
if done for eugenic reasons and with the agreement of the parents. If
the actual theological reasons that inspire Christians to reject infanticide are made more explicit (for example, the value of every child as
made in the image of God, the example of Christ as a child and his
sayings about children, the special consideration for the weak, the
virtue of hospitality), then it may be possible for non-believers to see
connections between these reasons and generally acknowledged secular values. If, however, the theology remains unstated, then it will

[5] e.g. 'You shall not kill a child by abortion nor kill it after it is born' (*Didache* 2: 2).
[6] e.g. Philo *Special Laws* 3. 117; Josephus, *Against Apion* 2: 202; *Mishnah Oholot* 7. 6.

remain possible for people like Williams wrongly to attribute to believers a theology that is alienating or absurd.

A related consideration is that, where Christians are not themselves accustomed to articulate the theological basis for ethical judgements, then they are more likely to make mistakes when they first attempt to do so. The implicit theology held by an individual may be overly reliant on the authority of divine commands or of Church law in a way that could lead ethical demands to be seen as external to the person and in tension with human freedom.[7] This may be a problem even for someone who wishes to accept the authoritative teaching, for without an understanding of the rationale for the teaching how will he or she know how to apply it in particular circumstances? As the philosopher Elizabeth Anscombe noted, it is impossible to aim at an unseen target (Anscombe 1981c: 50). It is still more of a problem when those who wish to reject some aspect of traditional Christian teaching seek to use theology as the basis for that rejection. An example of this is the work of Droge and Tabor (1992) who argue that both Scriptures and common Christian faith and practice prior to Augustine accepted suicide. In their argument they deliberately conflate martyrdom with suicide. However, all early Christians made this distinction (notwithstanding arguments about whether certain actions should be classified as suicide or whether they should be regarded as martyrdom). The failure adequately to analyse this fundamental distinction, which vitiates their study, can be attributed in part to the relative paucity of specifically theological material in contemporary ethical discussion. This is true especially of Catholic moral theology but it is true to a certain extent even among reformed Christians.[8]

There is a paradox at the centre of Christian attitudes to death. On the one hand the Gospel promises eternal life now and in the world to come, and seems to relativize the badness of death. The martyr, who embraces death willingly rather than betray the faith, is

---

[7] This can be due to a caricature of divine command theory of a sort often attributed to believers by non-believers. Such a view is systematically criticized in John Paul II in part I of *Veritatis Splendor* (1993).

[8] With some notable contemporary exceptions among whom should be mentioned Michael Banner, Nigel Biggar, Gilbert Meilaender, Oliver O'Donovan, and Stanley Hauerwas.

rewarded with everlasting life in the resurrection. On the other hand the Gospel contains and re-emphasizes the commandment 'you shall not kill' (Matthew 19: 18, cf. Exodus 20: 13) and demands not only that Christians should refrain from killing but, like the good Samaritan, that they should positively care for those who are in danger of death (Luke 10: 30–7; see also Matthew 25: 31–46). From the first century Christians had been known for their opposition to abortion and infanticide and for their refusal to abandon the sick and the dying. Furthermore, while Augustine is the first of the fathers of the Church to discuss suicide at length, a number of earlier writers had characterized suicide as a sin against God.[9] Thus the Christian attitude to death seems at once more positive and more negative than ancient pagan or modern secular attitudes. This is why the distinction between martyrdom and suicide is key. If Christians are to grasp the paradox that is the basis for this distinction, and are to live well in the face of death, then they require a clear and explicit *theological* articulation of the meaning of human death. This is especially so in a modern context where both the hope of the Gospel and the wisdom of the commandments are commonly disputed.

THE METHOD OF THE PRESENT STUDY

The four theologians whose views are the basis for this study are Ambrose of Milan, Augustine of Hippo, Thomas Aquinas, and Karl Rahner. Ambrose and Augustine were contemporaries and shared the same social and intellectual culture. In some of his early writings Augustine espouses views very similar to those of Ambrose. However, his mature thought on death represents a conscious critique of the approach of Ambrose.

Ambrose, Augustine, Thomas, and Rahner constitute a single intellectual tradition. Each chosen thinker exercised a profound influence on the ideas of the next, especially on the subject of

---

[9] e.g. Justin Martyr, *Apology* 2. 4; Clement of Alexandria, *Stromateis* 6. 9; Lactantius, *Divine Institutes* 3. 18; Basil, *Letters* 188. 2; Jerome, *Letters* 39. 3; Ambrose, *Concerning Virgins* 3. 7. 32; John Chrysostom, *Commentary on Galatians* 1. 4, see Amundsen 1989.

death. Thus, notwithstanding their very different intellectual and cultural situations, their approaches can and should be seen as moments in a single extended theological engagement with death. Focusing on these four theologians therefore offers an opportunity for sustained and well-focused reflection which would be more difficult to achieve if more or more divergent figures were chosen for consideration. Furthermore, each of these four thinkers is worthy of study in his own right, each remains influential, and each has written with particular clarity on the theology of death. It is therefore hoped that this consideration of the thought of Ambrose of Milan, Augustine of Hippo, Thomas Aquinas, and Karl Rahner will provide a real contribution to contemporary theological reflection on death, and thus to some of the practical and existential issues that the approach of death presents for us.

2

In Every Way a Good Thing: Death in the Thought of Ambrose of Milan

BACKGROUND TO THE THOUGHT OF AMBROSE OF MILAN

Ambrose belongs to the Christian culture of the late fourth century in the Latin West. This period followed the acceptance of Christianity as the dominant religion of the Roman Empire, subsequent to the conversion of the emperor Constantine. Ambrose was born in 339 CE, just two years after the death of Constantine, as the younger son of a high-ranking Roman official: the praetorian prefect of the Gauls.[1] Though born in Trier in Southern Germany, he was educated in Rome where the atmosphere of his upbringing was strongly Christian. In the mid-350s his sister, Marcellina, embraced the life of consecrated virginity, being veiled by Pope Liberius (Lancel 2002: 68). The family also laid claim to a Roman virgin martyr, Soteris, beside whose tomb Ambrose's mother would be buried (McLynn 1994: 34–5). The family was thus as prominent in the Church as it was in Roman society. Nevertheless, Ambrose himself was prepared for a secular career. In 372, with the help of the patronage of Petronius Probus, another prominent Christian who had risen to the level of praetorian prefect, Ambrose was appointed consul of the region which included the great northern Italian city of Milan.

---

[1] McLynn (1994) gives an excellent political biography but—self-confessedly—omits serious consideration of Ambrose's intellectual and doctrinal concerns. See also Hanson (1998), D. H. Williams (1993), B. Ramsey (1997), Moorhead (1999), Lancel (2002: 67–77), Brown (2000: 69–78), Homes Dudden (1935).

In the late fourth century the status of the Church was not yet secure, despite its great success in moving from a persecuted minority sect to a privileged position in the empire. Politically, paganism was far from a dead force and pagan senators continually pressed the emperor for the restoration of imperial funding while all the time hoping for a future emperor who would incline more to their cause. At the same time the Church herself was deeply divided. The doctrinal and political crisis of 'Arianism', which provoked the first great ecumenical council at Nicaea in 325 CE, was still far from resolved (Tanner 1990: 5; see also Hanson 1988; Barnes and Williams 1993). This weakened the claim of Christianity to be a unifying force which could be an adequate replacement for paganism in ancient Roman society. The Church of Milan was particularly divided over the acceptance of Nicaea,[2] and the election of a new bishop demanded the presence of Ambrose as the local consul to ensure order (McLynn 1994: 43). However, once inside the cathedral, he found himself acclaimed as the candidate of the pro-Nicene party, even though, like others intent on a secular career, he had not even been baptized but remained a long-term catechumen. With some apparent reluctance he accepted and, having received Christian baptism 'from a Catholic bishop', he received all the orders of ministry in turn and was duly consecrated bishop one week later.

The education Ambrose had received from childhood had suited him for a career as a relatively high-ranking Roman official. He was well read in Latin literature and also fluent in Greek and, as a bishop, would often incorporate into his writings extended passages from Greek authors if they seemed to him to be true and pertinent to his pastoral needs.[3] His response to the doctrinal and pastoral needs of the Church of his day was as much political as intellectual and he showed himself an able and a powerful adversary capable of confronting and humiliating even the emperor. However, it must not be assumed from this that his theological writings are of little

---

[2] Milan was 'one of the remaining western strongholds for anti-Nicene sympathies', (D. H. Williams 1993: 146).

[3] Leading to the charge of plagiarism from Jerome in the preface to his commentary on Didymus, *De Spiritu Sancto* cf. B. Ramsey (1997: 52–3), Moorhead (1999: 73 n. 5).

intellectual merit.[4] He was an important exponent of Christianity in the intellectual world of the late Roman Empire. In his writing and his sermons he endeavoured to present Christianity as the fulfilment not only of Jewish Scriptures, but as the fulfilment of the universal human spiritual quest as grasped, at least in part, by the classical philosophers, and most particularly by Plato.

The most obvious differences in the intellectual situations of Christians in the first century and Ambrose in the fourth were the loss of an immediate Jewish context and the increasing influence of that school of thought that began with Plato. These differences should not be thought absolute but rather as a matter of degree. The Jewish writings of the 'Old Covenant' remained essential—doctrinally and liturgically—for Catholic Christians, even though, from the second century, Christians considered themselves a third people, sociologically and culturally distinct from Jews as from pagans. Similarly, the influence of Greek thought upon Judaeo-Christian religion that is so evident in Ambrose in fact long predated the birth of Christ. The most prominent Jewish synthesizer of Jewish thought and Greek philosophy, Philo of Alexandria, was a contemporary of the apostle Paul. Nevertheless, there is little evidence for any influence of Philo upon Paul, and the extent of his influence upon any of the writings of the New Testament remains debatable.[5]

Christians began to take up ideas from Philo in the late second century of the Christian era, and in the early third century it was another Alexandrian, Origen, who attempted an analogous harmonization of the Christian Gospel with Platonic philosophy. Later in the third century the Platonic tradition was itself reinterpreted by Plotinus and by his disciple, Porphyry. Although Porphyry attacked Christianity, this new presentation of the Platonic tradition was attractive to many educated Christians. It was made available in Latin translation by a North African who taught rhetoric in Rome,

---

[4] Homes Dudden (1935: ii. 555) remarks that 'Ambrose can hardly be reckoned a theologian of the very highest rank', though he admits that he suffers perhaps unjustly by comparison with the exceptional genius of Augustine. While Homes Dudden does recognize that some important theological themes were developed by Ambrose, he presents his teaching on death without comment (1935: ii. 650–3, 676).

[5] See index references to New Testament and to Paul in Radice and Runia (1988), (2000).

Marius Victorinus, a man very sympathetic to the Christian religion, who finally embraced baptism under the influence of Simplicianus, a priest from Milan (Brown 2000: 84; Moorhead 1999: 170–1; Rist 1994: 3). Simplicianus was a spiritual mentor to Ambrose and succeeded him as bishop.

In protesting his unsuitability as a bishop, Ambrose had confessed a desire to embark upon a life of philosophy. This is an illuminating claim, for Ambrose was obviously deeply impressed by the philosophical writing of Plato and of later Platonists. In adapting this philosophy to the Christian Gospel, Ambrose was guided by the work of the Jewish theologian Philo and the Christian theologian Origen, and by the contemporary Greek-speaking Christian theologians Basil the Great and Didymus the Blind, themselves promoters of a revival of interest in the works of Origen. The effect of this was to make Ambrose an impressive and sophisticated preacher who could engage with the philosophical thought of his age (Brown 2000: 74–5). It also suited a time when immediate expectation of the end of the world had faded and when asceticism and virginity were beginning to replace martyrdom as the sign of Christian radicalism (Brown 1989). Ambrose's sister was a consecrated virgin and his brother, while active in worldly administration, remained celibate. Ambrose was extravagant in his praise for virginity, though without resorting to the detraction of marriage found in Jerome or Tertullian. His importance lay in his ability to articulate such aspirations and fuse them with a contemporary philosophical vision. This fusion of Christian faith and Platonic philosophy is seen in every area of Ambrose's thought, but it is perhaps most evident in his account of death, a subject that he returned to many times.

THREE DEATHS

Ambrose was forced to reflect on death by the loss of his brother Satyrus, to whom he was devoted, and who died in 379, a few years after Ambrose became bishop of Milan. At the funeral Ambrose preached an oration intense in the grief it expressed. A week later he preached a second sermon with the aim of moderating the excesses of his grief by appeal to the consolations of reason and the hope of resurrection. These two sermons were known by the joint title of 'Two books of St Ambrose on the decease of his brother Satyrus' (*De excessu fratris sui Satyri*). The second was also known as singly as 'On belief in the resurrection' (*De fide resurrectionis*, henceforth *FR*). This second sermon is in effect a treatise on death. Its aim is to argue that one should not mourn excessively over the death of a loved one. In support of this, in the first half of the book,[6] two prime considerations are brought forward: first it is urged that death should not be mourned as though it were some special calamity or exceptional circumstance. Death is the common lot of everyone; it is inevitable, a law of nature, a common sentence, a common debt; it is 'the measure of the flesh itself' (*FR* 4). It is through not acting 'according to nature' (*FR* 6) and resisting excessive grief that some are driven to a sort of madness. By this madness they think they can avoid enduring death by taking it themselves. In doing so they separate themselves permanently from those they wished to follow, 'that they might by that very means demonstrate their madness in not enduring death, and yet seeking it; in adopting that as a remedy which they flee from as an evil . . . But this is not common, since nature herself restrains although madness drives men on' (*FR* 11). It is unbecoming, even unnatural, to rail against what is necessary and common. Rather one must acknowledge the necessity of death and 'not grieve without rule for what has happened according to rule' (*FR* 49).

Secondly, it is argued that this life is wretched, miserable, and vain, and so death comes as a release. For holy men it is the case that while they suffer, they also merit and please God, yet even the patient Job wanted to die (*FR* 34). Job, Jeremiah, and Solomon all cursed the day of their birth. Dying is good but it would be better still if one had never been born in the first place (*FR* 30–4). If this is true of holy men, who live good lives, how much more is it true of sinners, who add to their sins every day? 'What ought we to do who are not able to profit others, and who feel that [life], like money borrowed at

---

[6] *FR* 1–49. The second half of the book (*FR* 50–122) gives arguments for belief in the resurrection, from reason, from the universal analogy of nature, and from the evidence of the Scriptures. It contains many points of interest but it is not directly concerned with the question of the goodness or badness of bodily death, and is not therefore of interest to the present discussion.

interest, grows more heavily weighted every day with an increasing mass of sins?' (*FR* 34). Death is then not an evil but is the refuge from all evils and miseries (*FR* 22).

During his discussion of death Ambrose introduces three kinds of death.[7]

According to the Scriptures death is threefold.

1. One death is when we die to sin, but live to God (cf. Romans 6: 11). Blessed then is that death which, escaping from sin and devoted to God, separates us from what is mortal and consecrates us to him who is immortal.

2. Another death is the departure from this life, as the patriarch Abraham died, and the patriarch David, and were buried with their fathers; when the soul is set free from the bonds of the body.

3. The third death is that of which it is said: 'Leave the dead to bury their own dead' (Matthew 8: 22). In that death not only the flesh but also the soul dies, for 'the soul that sinneth, it shall die' (Ezekiel 18: 4). For it dies to the Lord, through the weakness not of nature but of guilt. (*FR* 36)

This passage repeats a discussion from Ambrose's *De paradiso* (*c.*375 CE), a commentary on Genesis 2: 8–3: 18, which at this point was influenced by Origen's commentary on Romans.[8] Origen says that there are many meanings of 'death' in the Scriptures. *Mors in Scripturis unum quidem nomen est, sed multa significat.* He then lists five meanings: death as separation of body from soul; death as the wages of sin; death as another name for the devil; as a name for hell; and death to sin (by which we live to God). In terms of goodness or badness, these five meanings can be grouped into three categories, the first sort of death is not bad or good but midway (*media*), the last is praiseworthy (*laudabilis*), and the rest are bad (*mala*).

---

[7] The doctrine of three deaths recurs in Ambrose's writings. For the sake of comparison each time they occur they shall be numbered as they appear here (1) death to sin, (2) physical death, (3) death of the soul by mortal sin.

[8] The Greek fragments of this commentary do not cover this section, for which therefore we are reliant on Rufinus whose Latin translation is reproduced in *PL* 14. cf. also Origen's *Dialogue with Heraclides* 25–6.

The influence of Origen on Ambrose's *De paradiso* is shown most clearly in the interest Ambrose has in good and bad kinds of death. In his *De fide resurrectionis*, immediately after outlining the three meanings of death in the Scriptures, Ambrose says, 'So, then, death is not only not an *evil* but is even a *good* thing' (*FR* 39). The concern with death as *bona, mala,* and *media,* will continue to be a major interest for Ambrose when he writes his most significant work on the subject, *De bono mortis.*

Whilst Ambrose was influenced by Origen, he used this kernel to develop his own thoughts on the matter. He calls the three deaths (1) 'spiritual death' *mors spiritualis,* (2) 'natural death' *mors naturalis,* and (3) 'death of punishment' *mors poenalis* (*FR* 37). The death of the body is called natural, and not 'of punishment'. Ambrose is explicit that he thinks that bodily death is not a punishment for sin. While, in common with the earlier Latin tradition (e.g. Tertullian), he regard's death as something imposed on human nature by God as a result of the fall, Ambrose thinks God imposed death, not as a punishment, but as a remedy. It is a *limit* to the punishments involved in the present human condition. This marks a development from his *De paradiso* in which he held that death was imposed by God, yet did not say whether or not it was a punishment: he did not even comment on the line 'You are dust and to dust you shall return' (Genesis 3: 19). In *De fide resurrectionis* he is clear that death is given, not as a punishment but as a remedy.

That which is called natural is not also penal, for the Lord did not inflict death as a penalty, but as a remedy. And to Adam when he sinned, one thing was appointed as a penalty, another as a remedy, when it was said: 'In the sweat of thy face shalt thou eat thy bread, until thou return to the earth from which thou wast taken.' (*FR* 37 quoting Genesis 3: 19)

Ambrose regards death as a sort of mercy, a limit placed on this life now that it is no longer pleasing to us. Before the fall everlasting life would have been a joy, but no one would want more of the present sort of life (a view interestingly similar to that of the contemporary philosopher Bernard Williams (1973)): 'It was fitting that an end should be set to the evils, and that death should restore what life had lost. For immortality, unless grace breathed upon it, would rather be a burden than an advantage. (*FR* 47)

In this way Ambrose unites his two main themes, death is the common human lot, a limit of human nature, and it is also a release. It is natural and good. It was not originally a part of human nature but became so, so that it could be a release from the punishments of this life (*FR* 47). Death would be desirable as an escape from misery, even if death brought extinction, but in fact it is better than this. For the soul lives on, free from the bonds of the body, and the resurrection promises a life of bliss for the just:

If on its own account life is to be escaped from, that there may be an avoidance of troubles and rest from miseries, how much more is that rest to be sought for, which shall be followed by the eternal pleasure of the resurrection to come?[9]

DEATH AS *BONUM*

The sermon *De fide resurrectionis* was preached in 379 CE. Ambrose came back to the subject in the late 380s CE, in his commentary on Luke (7: 35), and, more prominently, in a work devoted to the subject of 'death as a good thing' (*De bono mortis*, henceforth *BM*). In this he took up the same points but developed them further. The work starts by asking whether death can be considered an evil.[10] The first answer given is that death can only be considered an evil if it does harm to the soul: 'should death do injury to the soul, it can be considered an evil, but should it do the soul no harm, it cannot' (*BM* 1. 1).

It seems that life is to be regarded as a good thing. In the Scriptures life is thought of as the reward for the good, death as the punishment for the wicked (in the book of Deuteronomy, for example). However, if life is a good, death would seem to be an evil. Before answering this point, Ambrose finds it necessary to distinguish different kinds of death, and so, straightaway, introduces his doctrine of three deaths: 'death due to sin'; 'mystical death' (in baptism); and 'the death by

---

[9] *FR* 123. In the last section on the work (*FR* 123–35) Ambrose returns from considering the resurrection to his original theme of the goodness or badness of death now in the light of the truth of the resurrection.

[10] A question that also echoes Plotinus (*Enneads* I. 6. 7) whose influence is very pronounced in this work, cf. Moorhead (1999: 169–81), Cavadini (1999: 233–7).

which we complete our life-span', that is, 'the separation of soul and body'. The first, he says, is bad (*mala*), the second is good (*bona*), while the third seems to stand midway (*media*), 'for it seems good to the just and fearful to most men' (*BM* 2. 3).

Immediately after suggesting that, in itself, death seems to stand midway, he retracts the suggestion. 'Although it gives release to all, it gives pleasure to few. But that is not the fault of death but of our own weakness' (*BM* 2. 3). He comes back to this point later in his discussion. 'Why do we blame death, which merely pays the wages of life or else destroys life's pain and torment?' (*BM* 4. 13). Bodily death, the final passing of this life, is always, in itself, a good thing, even if the wicked, because of the sort of life they lead, find that death brings punishment along with it. This is not an evil intrinsic to death but is rather the fault of the offences committed in *life*!

This life is vain, wretched, unsatisfying, full of snares and enticements to sin (*BM* 2. 4–6). For the sinner this life just sees sins added to sins (*BM* 2. 7). Death is a good because it is a release from the miseries of life, a safe harbour from the storms of temptation, and an end to sin. Death is better than life, but like a good servant one must not desert one's post until dismissed by one's master. Ambrose quotes with approval the words of Simeon, 'Now let thy servant depart in peace according to thy word' (Luke 2: 29), but the argument is in fact taken from Plato (*Phaedo* 62b). Suicide is wrong, not because it involves contempt for the good of this life, for this life is not so good, but because it involves disobedience and refusal to stay and serve until the time of service is complete and one is able to enjoy blessed repose (*BM* 2. 5).

FREEING THE SOUL FROM THE BODY

Ambrose does not pick up the first of the major themes of *De fide resurrectionis*, that of the naturalness and *inevitability* of death, rather, he develops a point made in passing in the earlier work: the separation of the soul from the body. Ambrose considers that life will always bring its share of miseries, but what if this is not the case? Even if this life is sweet, still the body confines the soul, as though it were in prison.

But suppose that someone remains unharmed, free from grief, in uninterrupted enjoyment of the pleasures of the whole course of a man's life, what comfort can the soul attain to, enclosed by the bonds of a body of such a kind, and restrained by the narrow limits of the limbs? If our flesh shrinks from prison, if it abhors everything which denies it the power of moving about; when it seems, indeed, to be always going forth, with its little powers of hearing or seeing what is beyond itself, how much more does our soul desire to escape from that prison-house of the body, which, being free with movement like the air, goes whither we know not, and comes whence we know not. (*FR* 20)

The central question for Ambrose is whether the soul will be happier, or whether it will be more wretched, without its body. On this question he has no doubt. The body is a prison for the soul, a theme he takes from Plato (*Phaedo* 62b, 67b, 82b, and elsewhere). The soul is happier and better off without the body (*BM* 3. 8). It can praise God properly only when free from the bonds of the body (*BM* 3. 8). The senses of the body are deceptive and often mislead us. 'When is our soul not deceived, when does it attain to the throne of truth, save when it separates itself from the body, and is not deceived or lead astray by it?' (*BM* 3. 10) It is the body that introduces temptations to sin. 'So if the body is clay, it surely soils us and does not wash us, for it contaminates the soul with the contamination of intemperance' (*BM* 3. 12). Therefore, when the soul is freed from the bonds and prison of the body, it is better able to exercise its activity.

But since the life of the soul remains after death, there remains a good which is not lost by death but increased. The soul is not held back by any obstacle placed by death but is more active, because it is active in its own sphere without any association with the body, which is more of a burden than a benefit to it (*majori oneri quam usui est*). (*BM* 4. 13)

If this life is good, it cannot be so because of the union of body and soul, rather the goodness of this life is found in virtue—but by virtue the soul anticipates the happy state it will enjoy in death, when it is finally separated from the body! Life 'obtains the good that is in death' (*BM* 4. 14) because it is in death that the soul is freed from all the 'contagions of the body' (*BM* 3. 9). Here Ambrose remains committed to the Platonic piety for which virtue consists in fleeing from what is bodily and seeking what is 'above'. Vice and temptation are easily identified with 'the flesh'—with disordered bodily passions. 'For the wise man, when he seeks after the divine, frees his soul from the body and forgoes its company' (*BM* 3. 10). Thus, virtue is the very mirror of death and consists in practising for death. Likewise, death is the fulfilment of life, the final realization of the soul free from the body. Life is good only in as much as it is an image of death, but death is a good in itself.

> But if life is a good—and it is the image of the soul separating itself from the body—and it raises itself and draws away from dwelling with the body— indeed death also is a good, for it releases and frees the soul from this union with the flesh. (*BM* 4. 14)

Thus death is not only a good relative to the wretched existence, the sin and suffering with which we live. Rather death is a good in itself, it is 'in every sense a good' (*omnifariam igitur mors bonum est*; *BM* 4. 15) because it separates elements that are in conflict and allows the soul to exercise its powers unfettered. From the very beginning of the book, Ambrose considers the good of the soul, and uses this as his measure. If death does no harm to the soul then death cannot be considered an evil (*BM* 1. 1), yet, death is also good for the body as it is rest for the body as well as release for the soul: 'And what is the effect of this dissolution? The body is released and is at rest, while the soul turns to its place of repose and is free, and if it is devout, is going to be with Christ' (*BM* 3. 8 cf. *BM* 8. 31).

In *De bono mortis* there is relatively little discussion of the resurrection of the body, nor is there a discussion of Adam before the fall. The stress falls on the benefit for the soul of being free from the bond (*nexus*), the fetters (*vincula*), the prison (*carcer*), the burden (*onus*), the deceit (*fraus*), the snare (*rete*) and obscurities (*nebulae*), the contagions (*contagiones*), the indulgence (*indulgentia*) and the contamination (*inquinamentum*) of the body. 'The soul gives life to the body, but the flesh pours death into the soul' (*anima vitam corpori tradit, caro autem mortem animae transfundit*; *BM* 7. 26).

Nevertheless, Ambrose does make mention of resurrection, and does not consider having a body an *absolute* impediment to happiness. This is because, like light that shines on the ground but is not confused with the ground, the soul of the saint is in a body but is not confounded (*nec tamen confunditur; BM* 7. 26) with the body. It is possible for the soul to rule the body as a master rules a slave without becoming subject to the body and thereby becoming tainted by it. This possibility, which is realized by the saints in this life, was realized but then lost by Adam and will be realized securely by all who attain the resurrection of the blessed. Thus Ambrose does not exclude the resurrection of the body, and, while he mentions it only rarely in *De bono mortis* (in contrast to *De fide resurrectionis*), he clearly holds it firmly as Christian teaching, and sees no incompatibility between that dogma and his understanding of death.

AMBROSE'S ACHIEVEMENT

It was Ambrose's great achievement to unite Christian and Platonic piety and metaphysics into a single vision of the meaning of human death. Dying to sin, called 'spiritual death' or 'mystical death' (because it is enacted mystically in baptism) is a way of participating in the death of Christ. Ambrose identifies this Christian spiritual attitude with the Platonic piety of separating the soul from the fetters of the body. Christian and Platonist have it in common that virtue can be thought of as a sort of dying, a real anticipation of death, in which is our salvation. Ambrose brings these two reasons together. Death is in itself a good, as it releases the soul from the body and brings the soul home to Christ. In this vision few texts are as central as the letter of Paul to the Philippians 1: 21–3:[11]

For to me to live is Christ and to die is gain. If it is to be life in the flesh, that means fruitful labour for me. Yet which I shall choose I cannot tell. I am hard pressed between the two. My desire is to depart and to be with Christ, for that is far better, but to remain in the flesh is more necessary on your account.

[11] Philippians 1: 21–2 is quoted in *BM* 2. 3; 2. 7; 3. 8; 4. 13; 8. 33.

Somewhat surprisingly neither in *De bono mortis* nor in *De fide resurrectionis* does he quote 2 Corinthians 5: 8, 'We would rather be away from the body and at home with the Lord', even though it would seem to suit his purpose admirably. Nevertheless, Ambrose makes extensive use of Paul's account of dying to sin with Christ in baptism (Romans 6: 1–11). This text is also interpreted in terms of the supposed good of leaving the body.

While this synthesis of Ambrose remains an impressive attempt to unite at root Christian and philosophical piety, it obscures real tensions between biblical and Platonic accounts of death. Death as 'the end of sin but not of nature', which is saved in the resurrection (*BM* 4. 15; 9. 38), is conflated with death as 'the release of the soul from the fetters of the body' (*BM* 2. 5; 4. 13; 8. 33). Yet these two concepts of death are quite different and are not wholly congruent. The problem for Ambrose is this: if the body is 'more of a burden than a benefit' to the soul (*BM* 4. 13), why did God unite the soul to a body in the first place? And why will the soul get its body back in the resurrection? Ambrose is clear that he considers the soul to be the person while the body is an instrument used by the person. 'The one is what we are, the other belongs to us' (*aliud quod sumus, aliud quod nostrum est*; *BM* 7. 27). This gives him good reason why it is disordered for the soul to subject itself to the passions of the body, but it gives no hint about what the body is actually good for. Likewise the doctrine of the bodily resurrection, which Ambrose acknowledges, seems at best irrelevant, at worst problematic for the freedom of the soul.

Ambrose's theological approach to death and dying was shared by many of his Christian contemporaries. His significance for the theology of death lies not in his originality but in the remarkable clarity with which he articulated what was a fairly common view. It is arguably because of this clarity that the weaknesses of this approach could then be teased out and criticized, as they were decisively by Ambrose's most gifted contemporary, Augustine of Hippo. Augustine seems at first to have shared Ambrose's outlook on death, but as he matured as a theologian he came increasingly to criticize it and to develop his own alternative vision. The following chapters set out Augustine's approach and compare it with that of Ambrose, both from a theoretical point of view and with respect to the practical implications. These implications include issues as diverse as virginity, martyrdom, suicide, fear of death, and care for the souls of those who have died.

3

Not Good for Anyone: Death in the Thought of Augustine of Hippo

BACKGROUND TO THE THOUGHT OF AUGUSTINE OF HIPPO

In many respects Augustine shares a common background with Ambrose.[1] Both born in the mid-fourth century in the Latin West into seemingly devout families, neither was baptized as an infant, and both intended to pursue a secular career. Unlike Ambrose, Augustine came under the sway of the fashionable esoteric sect we know as the Manichees (*Confessiones* III. 10 ff.). There he embraced a dualistic doctrine that stigmatized matter as the work of an evil demiurge. As with Marius Victorinus, his ability at rhetoric took him from provincial North Africa to Rome where he found patronage and was elevated to a position teaching rhetoric in Milan. By the time Augustine arrived in Milan he had become disillusioned with the Manichees. Their system did not seem to square with what was known about astronomy and their greatest teachers were unable to answer his questions (*Confessiones* V. 10–13). His quest for wisdom drew him now to the writings of Neoplatonists (*Confessiones* VII. 13–16) in which he found a doctrine more exalted and more credible than the myths of the Manichees. At the same time, he met Christian Platonists such as Simplicianus (*Confessiones* VIII. 3) and found,

---

[1] For Augustine's biography a revised edition of Brown's groundbreaking work (2000) has to compete with the magisterial and more theologically nuanced work of Lancel (2002). See also Fitzgerald (1999), J. J. O'Donnell (1999), Rist (1994).

in the sermons of Ambrose, a solution to some of his difficulties in reading the Old Testament. The philosophy of 'the Platonists' and the learned allegorical exegesis of Ambrose were formative in Augustine's conversion to Catholic Christianity. Common background, similar stories, and direct influence brought these two great men together, at least intellectually. After baptism Augustine suffered a similar fate to Ambrose, enforced ordination as bishop to place his intellectual gifts at the pastoral service of the Church. Though by no means identical (Cavadini 1999: 243 n. 49), there was a very close harmony of thought between the early Augustine and his older contemporary. However, Ambrose died only two years after Augustine was ordained as a bishop and, whereas Ambrose's thought seems to have undergone no great evolution (Moorhead 1999: 6 n. 7), Augustine's thought developed significantly in the face of various pastoral challenges.

A problem that concerned him very personally was the spread of the Manichaean 'heresy'. Having once followed that path himself, Augustine was keen to present the Christian faith in a way that would inoculate Christians against the fundamental error of the Manichees. This led him to a careful reappraisal of some common Christian themes, in particular, the distinction between the spirit and the flesh. A further pastoral difficulty faced by Augustine as a bishop in Latin North Africa was 'the party of Donatus'. Early in the fourth century a dispute had arisen as to whether the bishop of Carthage, apparently ordained by a *traditor*,[2] could be considered validly ordained and thus the legitimate successor to the apostles. A rival was elected and his successor, Donatus, led a great number of North African Christians into effective schism from the rest of the Latin West. Augustine was shepherd to a flock which understood itself as faithfully 'Catholic' in that it maintained communion with the wider Catholic Church. However, many North African Christians regarded Augustine's church as corrupt, tainted by complicity in an act of public apostasy.

Donatism as a movement was strongly traditional and deeply concerned with the purity of the church. Donatist Christians saw themselves in direct line with Cyprian, the great martyr bishop of

---

[2] A bishop who had betrayed the faith by publicly handing over the book of the Gospels to be burnt during the Diocletian persecution 303–5 CE.

Carthage. To Augustine, they had fundamentally misunderstood the mixed, dynamic, pilgrim, and above all *universal* character of the Church. It was this dispute that set the context for a later and still more important controversy, that of Pelagianism.[3] Pelagius was a British ascetic who, like Jerome and others of the period, was a reformer, highly critical of the laxity and worldly compromise that seemed to have come with the Constantinian settlement. He was critical also of excuses that might be given for failing to live faithfully according to the Gospel and the commandments, and he saw in Augustine's later writing a dangerous tendency to place righteousness out of reach of the human power of free will. Augustine saw in Pelagius a purist who suffered from an attitude analogous to the ecclesial perfectionism of the Donatists. While controversy with Manichaeans, Donatists, and Pelagians was sharpening his awareness of various theological issues, Augustine was also constantly rereading, preaching, and commenting on the Scriptures. Also, from 400 CE or so, Augustine became acquainted with the diatribe of Porphyry *Against the Christians*. From the beginnings of his Christian journey Augustine had been critical of the vanity and pride of certain philosophers (as seen in *Contra Academicos* (*c.*386 CE), an attack on the scepticism of the New Academy). The encounter with this work of Porphyry at this time helped catalyse what was a growing awareness of the shortcomings of even Neoplatonic philosophy (Rist 1994: 16). This complex combination of influences brought about a shift in his thought to a position distinct from, and in some important ways antithetical to, the sort of Platonist Christianity he had once shared with Ambrose.

THREE DEATHS

Augustine considered the subject of human death on many occasions, but his fullest and most mature treatment is given in 'The City

---

[3] For a sympathetic account of the self-understanding of the Donatists see Brown (2000: ch. 19) and for what has become a classic account of the motivation of Pelagius and his immediate followers Brown (1968 and 2000: ch. 29), but see also Lancel (2002: 275–305, 325–46).

of God', *De civitate Dei* (henceforth *CD*) books XIII and XIV. In 415 CE five books of this work were completed (according to Augustine's Letter 169, to Evodius). Around two years later, ten were already in circulation (cf. Orosio *Praefatione ad historiarum*). By 420 CE fourteen were finished (evident from Augustine's *Contra adversarium legis et prophetarum* I. XIV. 18). The whole work was complete by 427 CE. So books XIII and XIV were probably written sometime between 417 and 420 CE, at the height of the Pelagian controversy.[4] It is known that, around this time, Augustine was reading Ambrose on death: he quotes *FR* 6 in *De peccato originali* 47 in 418 CE; he quotes *BM* 9. 49 in *Contra duas epistolas Pelagianorum* IV. 9 in 420 CE (cf. Cavadini 1999: 232 n. 2).

In the first paragraph of book XIII Augustine gives as his starting point that death is a punishment for sin.

The condition of human beings was such that if they continued in perfect obedience they would be granted the immortality of the angels and an eternity of bliss without the interruption of death, whereas if disobedient they would be justly condemned to the punishment of death. (*CD* XIII. 1)

It is a point he was fond of making. Death as a punishment is special to human beings (*Enchiridion* 25 (*c*.421–3 CE)). Angels are by nature incapable of death, or at least of bodily death. The beasts are mortal by nature. Only human beings are such that, though they are mortal they might have been immortal. Their mortality is not necessary but is a punishment brought about by the fall of the first human beings.

Augustine here follows a very well established scriptural and dogmatic scheme. Yet he had also his own reasons for his particular stress on death as punishment: Pelagius had stressed the gifts of human nature and of free will in such a way that he seemed to circumvent any primeval catastrophe. Pelagius was suspicious of Christians who would give original sin as an excuse for their lack of moral effort. God does not command the impossible, therefore what God commands must still be within the capacity of the human will. Pelagius and his

---

[4] Pelagius and Caelestius were condemned by Pope Innocent I in 417 CE, a judgment reiterated by Pope Zosimus in 418 and confirmed by the Council of Carthage of 418.

followers therefore tended to reject any account of the fall that seemed to them fundamentally to vitiate human free will.

This Pelagian concern to limit the extent of the consequences of the fall led some to assert that Adam was naturally mortal and would have died even if he had remained obedient.[5] If the nature which was inherited from Adam had not been changed fundamentally for the worse, and human nature is now mortal, then Adam must have been mortal too. References to death as the wages of sin must refer either to sudden death as with the flood, or to judicial execution, or to spiritual death and the punishment of hellfire. Against this view, Augustine asserted many times in his anti-Pelagian writings that human bodily death came as a result of Adam's fall (*De peccatorum meritis et remissione, et De baptismo parvulorum* (411 CE); *De gratia Christi, et de peccato originali* (418 CE) and elsewhere). In book XIII of *De civitate Dei*, written around the same time, Augustine is quite emphatic on this as a point of orthodox Catholic doctrine:

Hence all Christians who truly hold the Catholic faith[6] are agreed that even the death of the body was not inflicted on us by a law of our nature, since God did not create any death for man in his nature, but it was imposed as a just punishment for sin. For it was when God was taking vengeance on sin that he said to the man, in whom we all existed at that time, 'you are earth and into earth you will go.' (*CD* XIII. 15)

Immediately after laying down the principle that human bodily death is a punishment for sin, Augustine goes on to set out his own doctrine of three deaths. Bodily death is not the only kind of death. Sin may also be spoken of as a sort of death, the death of the soul. 'For though the human soul is rightly described as immortal, it has nevertheless a kind of death of its own' (*CD* XIII. 2). The soul is of its nature immortal, in that it does not cease to exist as a result of

---

[5] It was a charge made against Caelestius, a disciple of Pelagius, that he asserted that 'Adam was created mortal and would have died whether he had sinned or not sinned' and 'Adam's sin affected only himself and not the human race', *De gestis Pelagii* 23 (417 CE); cf. Bonner (1963: 319).

[6] Bettenson (1984: 524 n. 25) supposes that Augustine has the Manichaeans in mind at this point, but it seems more likely that Augustine is reacting again Caelestius, as this is probably written in 417 CE when Caelestius is condemned and Augustine writes *De gestis Pelagii*.

natural decay. Yet the soul also lives by a life it receives from God, and with respect to this life it could truly be said to die. It was an oft-repeated saying of Augustine that, 'the soul is the life of the body; God is the life of the soul' (Sermon 65; *CD* XIII. 2, 7, 12 and elsewhere). The soul, therefore, is only immortal 'according to a certain manner of its own' (Sermon 65). Only God is absolutely immortal and unchangeable, being in complete possession of his own life. The soul dies if it loses the life it receives from God, but this does not mean that the body dies when the soul loses this spiritual life. 'For the soul is so excellent a thing that it has power even though dead to give life to the body' (Sermon 65). The soul both gives and receives life. Without the life it receives from God it can still think and subsist and give life to the body but it cannot find rest, peace, or happiness. With respect to the activity that would truly fulfil it, it is a dead thing (see also Augustine's *De Trinitate* IV. 5–6, 15–17 (*c.*410–19 CE)).

There is, then, a death of the body when it is abandoned by the soul, and a death of the soul when it is abandoned by God—though God does not abandon the soul unless the soul abandons God (*CD* XIII. 15). Yet as well as the death of body and soul taken singly there is another death which is called in Scripture 'the second death' (Revelation 2: 11; 20: 10–14; 21: 8). According to Augustine, this is what Jesus refers to when he says, 'fear him who has the power to destroy both body and soul in Gehenna' (*CD* XIII. 2 citing Matthew 10: 28). This is the final end of the wicked: body and soul are so combined that they cannot be separated; the soul is eternally punished by being deprived of the life given by God; the body is eternally subject to torment without ever being consumed by it. All these three—(1) the death of the body, (2) the death of the soul by mortal sin, and (3) the death of both in hellfire—are properly called death.

Which death is meant when it says in Scripture that death was the consequence of Adam's sin? Augustine unhesitatingly asserts that all these deaths are included in 'total death' (*CD* XIII. 12). Adam, by forsaking God, cut himself off from the source which could have preserved him forever from bodily death, and thus was abandoned to bodily death. Immediately Adam sinned he lost the life God gave to his soul and was reduced to a worse bodily condition, though the death itself did not occur until later.

But when the soul itself forsook the body, worn out with the passage of time and exhausted with the weight of years, another death came into man's experience, the death about which God had spoken when still pronouncing punishment on his sin saying, 'you are earth and into earth you will go'. (*CD* XIII. 15)

The worst death is the eternal death of hellfire. The death of the soul is more terrible than the death of the body, for it merits the death of hellfire, but it is avoidable. Even if the soul is dead in mortal sin, while one is in the present life, it may be raised up again by the grace of repentance. Augustine took the stories of Jesus miraculously raising people from the dead as revealing his ability to raise up the soul by repentance. The three characters in the Gospels who were raised by Jesus were taken by Augustine to represent three different types of sinner. Even the most confirmed sinner, who like Lazarus had been in the tomb four days and was beginning to smell, was not beyond the regenerative grace of Christ (Sermon 98; *In Joannis evangelium tractatus* 49 (*c*.407–17 CE)). The death of the soul is, in itself, worse than the death of the body, yet the death of the soul is reversible whereas the death of the body ends this life irreversibly, and according to one's state at death, the person shall be judged. Mortal sin may give way to repentance. Bodily death may give way to a glorious life in the resurrection. Yet, even though they may later be redeemed, the death of the soul and the death of the body are still, in themselves, evils imposed as a punishment for sin.

DEATH AS *MALUM*

It is obvious that 'the second death', that is hellfire, is not good for anyone. But the first death (the death of the body) (*CD* XIII. 2) would seem to be an evil for those whom it prefaces hellfire, but a positive good for those for whom it is the preface to eternal happiness: 'It can therefore be said of the first death that it is good for the good, bad for the bad; but the second death does not happen to any of the good, and without doubt it is not good for anyone' (*CD* XIII. 2).

Yet, like Ambrose, Augustine is unsatisfied with the idea that death has no essential positive or negative value—being simply good for the good and bad for the bad. He is interested not only in the fate of souls after death, good or bad, but is concerned to know what should be said about death in itself. Can bodily death be thought of as, in itself, a neutral reality, or even as a positive reality? 'Is death, which separates soul and body, really a good thing for the good? If so how can it be maintained that death itself is a penalty for sin?' (*CD* XIII. 3). Notice Augustine's starting point: death is a punishment, a result of the fall; it could only have come about through sin. The other components of total death—the death of the soul and the second death of hellfire—are clearly evils, bad in themselves, so also with bodily death: it is part of the punishment for the fall.

On the other hand, Augustine must say of the holy martyrs that death is good for them, for death is the means by which they pass into eternal life. It seems that the martyrs make of death a good use. How, then, can it be said that death is always a bad thing? It seems that death must be good, or at least capable of taking on a positive value. Augustine will not allow that death is ever a good thing or even a neutral thing. His own solution to this problem is subtle. Death is an evil. It is the separation of body and soul, which were created by God to be one whole person. Yet, even though death is always a bad thing in itself, those who die rather than sinning are able to bring good out of evil. Augustine uses the analogy of the evil use to which the wicked put the law. 'Thus it is that the evil make bad use of the law, though it is a good thing, and the good die a good death, although death itself is an evil' (*CD* XIII. 5). Death in itself always remains an evil, even when good is brought out of it. 'For this reason, the death of the body, the separation of the soul from the body, is not good for anyone' (*nulli bona est*; *CD* XIII. 6).

The union of body and soul is natural, original, and good and its dissociation is always, in itself, a bad thing, even if God should bring good out of it. The good that comes from death is not due to any quality that death itself possesses but due to the power of God (*CD* XIII. 7). Augustine thus moves from stressing that death is a punishment (and therefore a bad thing for the one who suffers it), to stressing that the state of union of body and soul is natural, original, and good.[7] The soul was created to ensoul a body and the body to embody a soul. The soul is, by nature, joined to a body. The separation of soul from body is unnatural, destructive, contrary to its natural appetite. Elsewhere Augustine states explicitly that, as the soul was created to be embodied, it has a natural and ineradicable appetite to exist in a body: 'it has such a will by nature, that is, the nature with which it is created is such that it wishes a body' (*De Genesi ad litteram* VII. 27 (393 CE)).

It follows that any hope for human immortality must *of necessity* take the form of belief in some future resurrection of the body. For the appetite the soul has for a body is natural to it and remains with it. Hence the soul in heaven has to receive its body anew if it is to enter fully into beatitude.

This may be because of some mysterious reason or simply because of the fact that it possesses a kind of natural appetite for managing the body. By reason of this appetite it is somehow hindered from going on with all its force to the highest heaven, so long as it is not joined with the body, for it is in managing the body that this appetite is satisfied. (*De Genesi ad litteram* XII. 35)

PLATONISM

In putting forward his account of death Augustine was aware that he differed fundamentally from the sort of Platonic approach taken by Ambrose and to which he himself had once been attracted. Augustine's conversion had been greatly helped by his reading of Platonic philosophy. 'For all the corrections which his Christianity made necessary, it remained for him what he had recognised in it from the first, a *vera philosophia*' (Burnaby 1938: 28). Thus it was with care and some reluctance that Augustine criticized the Platonists, yet his hand was forced, for these thinkers rejected the notion that bodily death was a punishment for sin.

---

[7] Augustine makes explicit that it is a Manichaean error to see in the union of soul and body a union of good with bad, and hence in the dissolution of death a separation of good and bad, 'But as to the statement which you annex to this, that death is a separation between good and evil, do you not see that, if the soul be good and the body be evil, he who joined them together, is not good?' (Letter 79).

Now the philosophers against whose attacks we are defending the city of God, that is to say, God's Church, think that they show their wisdom in laughing at our assertion that the separation of the soul from the body is to be reckoned among the soul's punishments. (*CD* XIII. 16)

This is not a minor point of difference but is a central plank of Platonic metaphysics (one might say, of Platonic piety), in which the very aim and goal of the soul is to free itself from the body. Augustine in part accepts their premise that 'the *corruptible* body weighs down upon the soul' (*CD* XIII. 16 quoting Wisdom 9: 15), yet he thinks that what is needed is not bodilessness but rather a subtle glorified body. Against those Platonists who allege that the soul could never be happy with a body, and that the body could not become immortal, Augustine appeals to Plato's account of the origin of the *gods*.[8] Plato does not make clear what elements they are composed of (though it would seem to be the higher elements), but the very fact of composition and of temporality shows that they are not intrinsically immortal: 'Now since you had a beginning, you yourselves cannot be immortal and indissoluble' (*CD* XIII. 16 quoting *Timaeus* 41 (inexactly) from Cicero's Latin translation). Yet, even though they are composite and had a beginning, still they can enjoy blissful immortality—because they are bound by the will of God:

You will certainly not be dissolved, nor will any doom of death destroy you or be more powerful than my design, which is a stronger bond for your perpetuity than those bonds by which you were joined together at the time when you were brought to birth. (*CD* XIII. 16)

If the gods are immortal and blissful, though composite and in possession of bodies of some sort, it seems that incorporeity cannot strictly be necessary for either happiness or immortality. Augustine is astute in noticing the reason Plato gives for the immortality of the gods: it is not that they have bodies of particularly strong constitution or of special material, or that they are bodiless, but that *the will of God* is a stronger bond than any other. 'The works of which I am parent and maker cannot suffer dissolution against my will' (*CD* XIII. 16). If *this* is the reason why the gods are immortal,

---

[8] Dyson (1998) refers here to Plotinus but TeSelle (1970: 252–6) gives reason to suggest that Augustine has Porphyry in mind.

then there can be nothing said against the possibility that human beings might also become immortal, if that is within the design of the omnipotent God. Plato does not himself posit a final and enduring resurrection from the dead for human beings, but given what he says about the gods, the possibility of a final resurrection cannot be dismissed as contradictory or as un-Platonic. It is of no consequence that the gods may have stronger, lighter, or more subtle bodies by nature, for Plato is clear that it is not the intrinsic strength of these bonds that gives the gods their immortality. The bond that guarantees immortality of the gods is the same bond that Augustine believes guarantees the immortality of the resurrected body, that is, the bond of the will of God against which nothing can prevail.

Augustine treats Platonic objections to his view of bodily death at several points in the *De civitate Dei*. He returns to the subject in book XIV. He considers the charge that the flesh is the cause of evil desire. If the body is the cause of evil desire, then the union of soul and body is evidently not a good state but a bad state that one should wish to escape from.[9] Yet, if the body is supposed to be the source of all sinful desire, how could souls have fallen into bodies in the first place? This first evil desire at least cannot have derived from union with an earthly body! Furthermore Virgil, following Plato, argues that, even after they have been purified, separated souls still hanker after the life in the body, leading to an endless succession of falls and purifications.

> Father can we believe the soul's return
> to dwell beneath the sky again to assume
> the body's lethargy? Oh! What dread lust
> for life under the Sun holds them in misery!
>
> (*CD* XIV. 5, quoting *Aeneid* 6. 719)

These souls are without bodies and yet they are subject to 'dread lust', therefore union with the body cannot be the only occasion of

---

[9] Significantly Augustine now regards this Platonic doctrine as analogous, though not of course as crude, to the error of the Manichees. Thus reflection on the root problem with the Manichees has forced him to abandon a central tenet of respectable Platonic-Christian piety (*CD* XIV. 5).

excessive desire. In this way Augustine touches upon a contradiction at the very heart of the Platonic myth. The body is supposed to be the *cause* of evil desire and yet the fall of the soul into a body is the consequence of evil desire *prior to* union with a body.

The unsatisfactory unending cycle of purification and fall implied here was modified by Porphyry. He held that it was possible for a soul to escape completely from this cycle of falls and purifications. Augustine considers this view later in the City of God (*CD* XXII. 25–8). Again he refutes the charge that the soul needs to be free of a body in order to be happy. This cannot be necessary, or else it would be equally so for the gods, who would then have to become mortal so they could escape from their bodies! However, in general terms, Augustine is sympathetic with Porphyry's stance, because of his insistence that the soul must come finally to some stable beatitude (O'Meara 1997: 91). Indeed, Augustine thought that if one took Porphyry and Plato together it would be possible to get something close to the Christian doctrine of the resurrection in beatitude of the glorified body (*CD* XXII. 27). Porphyry was right that there must be some stable grasp of beatitude for the purified soul, but Plato was right that the soul inevitably desires a body. A solution to this conundrum is provided by a resurrection to life which is bodily but which is not burdensome. Augustine was no doubt over-optimistic in thinking that one could *derive* Christian doctrine from the tensions within the Platonic tradition. However, his arguments together comprise an effective rebuttal of Platonic *objections* to Christian doctrine. Though Platonic doctrine is clearly superior to the absurdities of Manichaeanism, it nonetheless proved inadequate by the measure of Christian doctrine.[10]

---

[10] It should be noted that, while Augustine came to be critical of certain aspects of Platonic philosophy, most notably its attitudes towards the body, he retained other insights gained from these philosophers. An important example is Augustine's account of the place of evil within the good order of the universe. This account facilitated Augustine's conversion from the sect of the Manichees, who taught that evil was principle equal and opposite to the good. Augustine's understanding of evil as a privation of the good, set out at length in *Confessiones* VII (*c.*397–400 CE) and reiterated in *CD* XI. 22 (*c.*417–20 CE), *Enchiridion* 4 (*c.*421–3 CE) and elsewhere, he took from *The Enneads* of Plotinus 5. 8. 8.

THE FALL FROM EDEN AND THE PLATONIC
FALL MYTH

Augustine became more and more aware of tensions between Platonic and Christian piety; hence he was especially critical of attempts to conflate the Platonic fall myth with the Christian doctrines of creation and fall. In book XI of *De civitate Dei* he takes time to criticize Origen's account of the fall of souls into bodies.[11] Origen had suggested that the physical constitution of the world could be the result of a primeval fall; some souls fell so as to become angels, some demons, some human beings. The angels move the sun and the stars, which were created to be their bodies. Against this view, Augustine points to the providential ordering of material creation. If material creation had been the result of a fall it would be ad hoc. If the sun is merely a prison for a soul, then it easily could have happened that many suns had to be made, or none! Yet the order of creation depends on the world having a harmonious and integrated structure (e.g. creatures on earth depend upon the warmth of the sun). Augustine is not concerned at this point to dispute Origen's notion that sun and stars are moved by intellectual creatures. He does not affirm or deny this point. What he does seek to affirm is that all creatures (including material creatures) were made according to the provident ordering of God.

Origen's account of the fall of souls into bodies was an attempt to conflate the Platonic fall myth with the Eden story but he is not unique in wishing to unite these stories. Though the doctrine of the pre-existence of souls, and of their fall into bodies, was generally rejected by the fourth century, there were other more muted attempts to harmonize the two myths. Gregory of Nyssa stops short of identifying the 'coats of skins', given to Adam and Eve after the expulsion from paradise, as bodies of flesh. Yet he identifies these coats with much that is currently involved in our bodily nature:

---

[11] Origen *De principiis*. It has been argued that Origen's own views were more subtle than this, and, in particular, that Origen did not deny the bodily resurrection or hold to the pre-existence of separated souls (Edwards 1992). In this case Origen's views should probably be seen as more closely analogous to those of his fourth-century followers Ambrose and Gregory. However, Augustine clearly believed that Origen had put forward a doctrine of the fall of separated souls into a variety of bodies.

If a man wearing a ragged tunic should be denuded of his garment, he would no longer see on himself the ugliness of what he discarded. Likewise, when we have put off that dead and ugly garment which was made for us from irrational skins (when I hear 'skins' I interpret it as the form of the irrational nature which we have put on from our association with passion), we throw off every part of our irrational skin along with the removal of the garment. These are the things which we have received from the irrational skin: sexual intercourse, conception, childbearing, dirt, lactation, nourishment, evacuation, gradual growth to maturity, the prime of life, old age, disease and death. (*De anima et resurrectione* in Roth 1993: 114)

Though Gregory was not free to assert that the soul was without a body before the fall, for such a view was no longer acceptable, his account of the fall includes much of what we might think of as 'bodily existence' as being a consequence of the fall. In particular, he denies that there was marriage or carnal intercourse in Eden, for as in the resurrection we will be like the angels (Matthew 22: 30; Mark 12: 25; Luke 20: 35–6), so in Eden we were like the angels, neither marrying nor giving in marriage. 'If, then, the life of those restored is closely related to that of the angels, it is clear that the life before the transgression was a kind of angelic life' (*De hominis opificio* XVII. 2).

According to Gregory, even the division of the sexes was made so that when human beings fell, and could no longer multiply in an angelic fashion, they might have an alternative means of increasing and multiplying:

For this reason, I say, he formed for our nature that contrivance for increase which befits those who have fallen into sin, implanting in mankind instead of the angelic majesty of nature, that animal and irrational mode by which they now succeed one another. (*De hominis opificio* XVII. 4)

Thus the division of the sexes was only made in anticipation of the fall, and marriage and procreation only began after the fall. Had Adam not fallen, there would have been no marriage, but because God knew that he would fall, he provided a means by which a fallen creature could procreate—by carnal intercourse, like the brutes. 'Marriage then is the last stage of our separation from the life that was led in paradise; marriage therefore is the first thing to be left' (*De virginitate* 12).

At every point Gregory stops short of 'Origenist' error, yet his project is fundamentally the same as that of Origen. He wishes to harmonize the Platonic and the Eden myths. There are three elements that enable this correlation to be established:

1. Such fundamental aspects of human life as nourishment, growth and procreation are the result of the fall.
2. The metaphor of *divesting* oneself of the 'coats of skins' given after the fall is a fundamental analogy for the Christian doctrine of salvation.
3. The resurrected state is nothing else than a *return* to the original angelic state.

By means of these three assertions the Eden myth can make contact with the Platonic, and Christian piety with philosophical piety. Gregory of Nyssa was strongly influenced by reading Origen and is perhaps the Church Father of the fourth century most concerned to harmonize Platonic and Christian doctrine. Nevertheless, the three elements outlined above each enjoyed a wide acceptance among Christian believers. Ambrose was also inclined to use the language of 'divesting' oneself of fleshly vices. He also says that in Eden Adam and Eve would not have eaten 'earthly and corruptible food', for 'their life was like that of the angels' (*De paradiso* 9.42). Gregory is illuminating as an example of Christian Platonism contemporary with Ambrose and with the young Augustine. He presents a concerted and consistent attempt to harmonize the Platonic fall myth (of souls into bodies) and the biblical fall myth (of Adam and Eve) in a late fourth-century context.

Against this background, and despite a strong respect for the Platonic philosophy that had played a part in his conversion, Augustine is remarkable in utterly denying the compatibility of these two myths. His concern with the Christian doctrine of bodily death caused him to see that the Platonic and Eden stories are not so much alternatives as *direct opposites*. Consider again Augustine's remark, concerning the philosophers who mock the Christian doctrine, that death is a punishment for sin.

[They] think they show their wisdom in laughing at our assertion that the separation of soul from body is to be reckoned among the soul's punishments. Their reason for this is that in their view, the perfect bliss of the soul comes only when it has been completely stripped of the body and returns to God, simple and alone, and, as one may say, naked. (*CD* XIII. 16)

The Eden myth portrays the *separation* of soul and body as the result of a fall (as a punishment for sin); the Platonic myth portrays the *union* of soul and body as the result of a fall (as a punishment for sin). The Eden story holds that the union of soul and body is natural, original, and good, and that final hope must take the form of a *reunion*; the Platonic story holds that the separation of soul from body is natural, original, and good and that final hope must take the form of a *disentanglement*.

These myths are in direct contradiction and this is shown most forcefully when one asks whether the separation of the soul from the body is a good thing or a bad thing. Understanding the basis of this contradiction leads Augustine to a subtle and quite distinctive account of Eden. The state of Adam before the fall seems paradoxical: Adam was able to become mortal (by sinning) but was also able to be immortal (by refraining from sin). Thus, before the fall, Adam was in one way mortal, in another way immortal (*De Genesi ad litteram* VI. 25). This also shows Adam before the fall to have been in a different state from that which the saints will enjoy in the resurrection. In the resurrection the body will be so glorified that it will no longer be mortal. There are, therefore, three possible human states: the state of Adam (able not to die), the present state of human beings (not able not to die), and the state of the saints in glory (not able to die): *posse non mori, non posse non mori, non posse mori.*

In strongly distinguishing Eden from the situation of the resurrected body, Augustine was rejecting the third of the elements that had seemed to link the Platonic and the Eden myths. By doing this he was able to escape a residual Platonism present in many of the other Church Fathers.[12] He resisted any attempt to spiritualize the existence of Adam and Eve in the garden. He appealed to the apostle Paul who, in the first letter to the Corinthians, contrasted Adam with the

---

[12] Augustine in his early works had also been inclined to present the resurrection as a restoration of our paradisal state: *De musica* VI. 13 (*c.*387–9 CE) and *De vera religione* XII. 25 (*c.*389–91 CE); but he later corrects this view as being inadequate: *Retractationes* I. 11. 3; I. 13. 4 (427 CE); see Garvey 1939: 232, Rist 1994: 98–9.

resurrected Christ (1 Corinthians 15: 42–50). There, Paul asserts that Adam possessed an ensouled body, whereas the resurrected Christ possessed a spiritual body. Augustine regularly appeals to this passage of Paul in his interpretation of Genesis (*CD* XIII. 23 ff., *De Genesi ad litteram* VI. 20 ff.). By 'ensouled body' Augustine takes Paul to mean a body enlivened by a human soul (*anima*). By 'spiritual body' Augustine takes Paul to mean the same body but enlivened by the life-giving Spirit of God so that it becomes immortal.[13] If Adam had had a spiritual body, then he would not have been able to die, for his body would not have been mortal. If Adam had had a body like those of human beings at present, then he would not have been able *not* to die, as human beings in their present state are not able not to die.

Augustine beats a middle path between these Platonic and Pelagian alternatives (as represented by Gregory of Nyssa and Caelestius respectively). The picture he gives of Eden envisions a bodily state that is more like the present mortal body than it is like the resurrected body. Adam and Eve ate normally for nourishment. This kept them strong and healthy but did not prevent disease or old age affecting them. So they were given another sort of fruit, the fruit of the tree of life, to protect them from the ravages of old age and other sources of corruption.

Thus the purpose of other foods was to prevent the ensouled bodies from experiencing any distress through hunger or thirst, whereas the reason for their tasting of the tree of life was to prevent death that might come on them unawares from any source, or that death that would come in extreme old age after their lives had run full course. (*CD* XIII. 20)

It is clear from this that the sort of immortality granted to Adam before the fall was more potential than actual, that is, it was ongoing

---

[13] The Latin translation that Augustine worked with was closer to the Greek than most contemporary English translations have managed. The Revised Standard Version has 'it is sown a physical body, it is raised a spiritual body', while the New King James has 'It is sown a natural body, it is raised a spiritual body'. The phrase Paul uses is not physical body (σῶμα φυσικόν) but as a psychical or ensouled body (σῶμα ψυχικόν). This is preserved in the Latin translation *corpus animale* (*anima* being the Latin for 'soul'). It is sown a body animated by ψυχή or *anima*, it is raised a body animated by πνεῦμα or *spiritus*.

but was not essential to him. 'This immortality was given to him from the tree of life not from nature. When he sinned he was separated from this tree with the result that he was able to die' (*De Genesi ad litteram* VI. 25). Adam's body was the 'ensouled body' of a mortal animal very like that of human beings at present, but, as a reward of a holy life, his body could have been glorified (that is, made spiritual) and then he would have become truly immortal. His body was 'ensouled before but could have become a spiritual body when God so willed after a holy life' (*De Genesi ad litteram* VI. 23). Yet still, Adam's body was in a privileged condition, for he was not under the necessity of death. Augustine points out that human beings are now under necessity of death even if they live a holy life, but this was not true of Adam. 'This makes it clear what Adam lost by sin...so that...this body of ours is also ensouled as was Adam's but although it is the same class as his it is much inferior' (*De Genesi ad litteram* VI. 26).

It was the opinion of some (e.g. Caelestius) that Adam would have died even had he not sinned. 'Thus the death of the body would seem to have happened not as a result of sin but naturally as is the case with lower animals' (*De Genesi ad litteram* VI. 22). Augustine makes a distinction. The bodies of Adam and Eve were ensouled, yet they were kept in a privileged state through a special gift of God, what the scholastics would later call a *preternatural* gift. This gift they received sacramentally by eating of the fruit of the tree of life: 'It could be said that other foods served as nourishment, but that from the tree of life was a kind of sacrament' (*CD* XIII. 20). The human body was and remains an ensouled body, but through the fall the condition of the body has changed: it has lost its privileged state.

In marked contrast to Gregory, Augustine is clear that the sexual differentiation of Adam and Eve was from the first ordered towards procreation. Thus in the garden, had they not sinned, Adam and Eve would still have procreated by carnal intercourse (*CD* XIV. 23–6). Yet it would have been 'the bed undefiled', that is, free from the tumultuous ardour of passion. The placing of marriage, and even of ordinary bodily nourishment, in the garden of Eden, would have been shocking not only to Gregory of Nyssa, but to much contemporary piety (Brown 1989: 399 n. 48). The account of death Augustine gives in books XIII and XIV of *De civitate Dei* represents an attempt to give a consistent Christian analysis of death. It is systematically anti-Platonic in a way that stands out from his Christian contemporaries (O'Meara 1997: 86–93). He accepts that sin and disorder come from the fall and even that our bodies are in a worse condition due to the fall, being liable to disease and death. However, the body itself and the natural powers of nourishment, procreation, and the disposition to civil society are all good and original and, had the occasion arisen, could have been exercised in the garden. Augustine's approach to death is thus in sharp contrast to that provided by Christian Platonists such as Gregory or Ambrose. A detailed examination of the effect of this contrast on a range of practical issues will be set out in the following chapter.

4

An Illuminating Comparison: Augustine and Ambrose on the Theology of Death

The argument of Augustine in *De civitate Dei* is strikingly similar to that of Ambrose in *De bono mortis*. Both mention three different sorts of death, of which two are unambiguously either good or bad, whereas bodily death seems to be midway: a good thing for the good and a bad thing for the bad. However, neither Ambrose nor Augustine is content to understand bodily death as something neutral in itself. For Ambrose, death must be a good thing, for, as this mortal life is a punishment for sin, so death is the remedy. For Augustine, death must be a bad thing because it itself is a punishment for sin. This leads Augustine to re-evaluate the importance of human bodily existence. This in turn affects how he reads the letters of Paul, which is markedly different from the exegesis of Ambrose. Their contrasting attitudes have practical effects on how they regard virginity, marriage, and mortification. The approach of Augustine to death also sharpens the way in which he defines suicide and distinguishes suicide from martyrdom. Furthermore, it leads to a noticeable shift in his treatment of fear of death, grief, and the care of the dead (that is, prayers for those who have died). In many ways Augustine represents a real advance in the Christian understanding of death. However, in omitting 'dying to sin' from his systematic account, he impeded the development of a comprehensive theology of death. 'Dying to sin' would continue to be important in spiritual or ascetical writings but would not be integrated properly into systematic dogmatic theology by the later Latin tradition.

STRIKING PARALLELS

Both Augustine and Ambrose mention three different sorts of death, of which two are unambiguously either good or bad. Both go on to say of bodily death that it seems, prima facie, to be a good thing for the good and a bad thing for the bad:

AMBROSE. The third death stands midway [between good and bad] for it seems good for the just and fearful to most men. (*BM* 2. 3)

AUGUSTINE. It can therefore be said of the first death that it is good for the good, bad for the bad. (*CD* XIII. 2)

Neither, however, is happy with this position. For Ambrose, death must be a good thing, for, as this mortal life is a punishment for sin, so death is the remedy. For Augustine, death must be a bad thing because it itself is a punishment for sin:

AMBROSE. If life is a punishment (*supplicio*), death is the remedy (*remedio*). (*BM* 4. 14)

AUGUSTINE. Death itself is the penalty for sin (*poena peccati*). (*CD* XIII. 3)

Both seek to evaluate death in itself, and both turn to a definition of death as the separation of body and soul. Yet whereas Ambrose regards such a separation as a good thing, Augustine sees this separation as a bad thing:

AMBROSE. What is the effect of this dissolution except that the body is released and at rest (*resolvatur et quiescat*), while the soul turns to its place of repose and is free (*in requiem suam, et sit libera*)? (*BM* 3. 8)

AUGUSTINE. This violent sundering of two elements, which are conjoined and interwoven in a living being, is bound to be a harsh and unnatural experience (*asperum sensum et contra naturam*). (*CD* XIII. 6)

The result is that both construe death, not as indifferent in itself, but as having an intrinsic evaluative character of its own. However, whereas for Ambrose death is, in itself, unambiguously good, for Augustine it is, in itself, unambiguously bad:

AMBROSE. Therefore death is in every way a good (*omnifariam igitur mors bonum est*) ... because it separates elements in conflict. (*BM* 4. 15)

AUGUSTINE. For this reason the death of the body, the separation of the soul from the body, is not good for anyone (*nulli bona est*). (*CD* XIII. 6)

Each goes on to attribute the seemingly indifferent character of death to that fact that it is the *occasion* for goods or evils that do not belong to it essentially. For Ambrose, whereas death as such is a good thing, it is the moment when sinners receive their just deserts. For Augustine, whereas death as such is a bad thing, it is the moment when God by his power rewards the just. Ambrose asserts that the punishment that awaits the sinner after death is not due to death but due to the sins committed in life. Augustine responds that the reward that awaits the faithful after death is not due to death but due to the power of God that rescues us from everlasting death. In both cases they decide what should be considered to be the essential character of death, and then explain the appearance of opposite characteristics by reference to a good or an evil that comes *with* death but that is not *caused by* death:

AMBROSE. Why do we blame death, which merely pays the wages of life or else destroys life's pain and torment? Therefore death either enjoys a good, which is its own repose (*suae quietis*), or suffers under an evil not its own (*malo alieno*). (*BM* 4. 13)

AUGUSTINE. Death ought not to be regarded as a good thing because it has been turned to such a great advantage. For this happened not in virtue of any quality of its own (*non vi sua*), but by the help of God. (*CD* XIII. 7)

Such close comparison reveals the debt Augustine owes to Ambrose. In finally opposing the conclusions of Ambrose, Augustine was not rejecting an opinion that he regarded as shallow or facile. The view put forward by Ambrose represented that held by many Christians and was well supported by the most profound pagan philosophers of the age. The strength of Augustine's own view was owed, in no small measure, to making use of Ambrose's argument while rejecting his major premise—that the separation of the body from the soul is good for the soul. It was not only respect for his mentor that prevented Augustine from explicitly naming and opposing Ambrose in book XIII of *De civitate Dei*; it was also due to a realization of how much his own view relied on Ambrose's position, even while he was rejecting its ultimate conclusion.

Augustine and Ambrose shared not only one particular argument but a common intellectual culture. Each was persuaded of their opinions not by philosophy alone, but by a rigorous reading and rereading of the Scriptures, and especially of the letters of Paul. An assessment of the relative merits of their respective conclusions must, therefore, rest substantially on the cogency of their scriptural exegesis.

PAUL THROUGH THE EYES OF AMBROSE AND AUGUSTINE

The key to Ambrose's reading of Paul is his move to identify the philosophical dichotomy of body and soul (*corpus/anima,* σωμα/ψυχη) with the moral dichotomy of flesh and spirit (*caro/ spiritus,* σαρξ/πνευμα). Such an identification would seem natural within a milieu influenced by Platonism, for it conforms to Platonic ethical categories: for both pagan and Christian Platonists, while the body is good in itself, the union of the soul to the body is regarded as the root cause of moral failure. The paradigm of wickedness is the subordination of the intellect to the passions of the body. Because the body is the occasion of moral evil, the pursuit of the right and the good is construed as the attempt to disentangle oneself from the desires of the body. For this reason Ambrose understood Paul to be characterizing the body, in a Platonic fashion, as one's natural enemy: 'Let us not trust ourselves to this body, let us not join our soul with it. Join your soul with a friend not with an enemy. Your enemy is your body, which "wars against your mind".'[1] The struggle of the inclinations of sin and grace as depicted by Paul in the seventh chapter of his letter to the Romans was thus taken to be a devaluing of the body: 'Therefore [the apostle] rightly devalued and dishonoured this body, and called it "the body of death"' (*BM* 3. 11 quoting Romans 7: 24).

Augustine's controversial engagement with the Manichees and his struggles against the perfectionism of the Pelagians had convinced him that any denigration of the body, even that most respectable Platonic variety, was, incompatible with the Gospel.

[1] *BM* 7: 26 quoting Romans 7: 23: compare with Augustine 'my flesh shall be my *friend* through all eternity' (Sermons 155. 14).

The Platonists, to be sure, do not show quite the folly of the Manicheans. They do not go so far as to execrate earthly bodies as the natural substance of evil, since all the elements which comprise the structure of this visible and tangible world, and their qualities, are attributed by the Platonists to God the artificer. All the same they hold that souls are so influenced by 'earthly limbs and dying members' that they derive from them morbid desires and fears, joy and sadness. (*CD* XIV. 5)

Augustine, therefore, resisted any interpretation of Paul's σαρξ/ πνευμα language which would trace the root of evil desire to the fact of having a body. The use of the phrase 'works of the flesh' does not mean that the body is the source of evil, as though one would be better off without a body. Augustine points out that the 'works of the flesh' (Galatians 5: 19–21) include many sins which are clearly spiritual in character—devotion to idols, sorcery, enmity, quarrelsomeness, jealousy, animosity, party intrigue, envy. Indeed animosity is clearly a sin of the *animus* (mind/spirit) as carnality is a sin of the *caro* (flesh) (*CD* XIV. 2–3).

If 'the flesh' cannot be understood in a Platonic sense, one must look instead to the Scriptures to fix its meaning. Here 'flesh' is often used in a 'part for whole' (*a parte totum*) figure of speech to refer to human beings (*CD* XIV. 2). According to this interpretation, rule of the flesh would mean the same as 'traditions of men', that is, rule of human ways, or more generally rule of self considered apart from rule of God. Such use of 'flesh' to mean (vainly) human can be found in the Old Testament, for example, Isaiah 40: 6: 'All flesh is grass', though Augustine confines his examples to the New Testament. In this way it is possible to understand the terms 'flesh' and 'spirit' in a Jewish/Christian context without having to accept the view that the body is the source of human evil.

On this fundamental point Augustine gives a more convincing exegesis than Ambrose, for Paul develops a very *positive* theology of the body to support both an account of the dwelling of God within the Christian believer and an account of the unity of Christians within the Church. The theme of the resurrection of the body as described in chapter 15 of the first letter to the Corinthians is but one aspect of a theme of the body of Christ developed throughout that letter. Other letters too reveal a fundamentally positive use of the term σωμα in Paul's writing. Ambrose's elision of Pauline and Platonic categories is to be resisted. However, there are difficulties with Paul's thought in this area. The use of the term flesh (σαρξ) as synonymous with perverse or selfish inclination does lend itself to a negative theology of the body. It finds no clear parallel in the Hebrew Scriptures and sits in some tension with other aspects of Paul's theology. Augustine's attempt to render Paul consistent, by abstracting from Paul's σαρξ language any connotations which might imply a negative characterization of the body, is not wholly convincing. Augustine gives a better overall reading, but the language Paul uses in this area remains in some ways problematic.

In any case, Christian doctrine could not accept the body as the primary source of evil; for Satan, whose rebellion against God is an archetype of sin, is a purely spiritual creature. It is true that certain sins can only be committed by a bodily being (such as gluttony or unchastity) but the more serious sins are spiritual in character. Augustine considers not only the Devil's sin but also Adam's sin to have been spiritual in nature. Although Adam possessed a true human body, his first and archetypal sins were pride and disobedience—spiritual sins (*CD* XIV. 13). Disordered physical desire, like physical death, was not the cause but was a *consequence* of the fall. Disordered and excessive desires are not simply the consequence of having a body, for at first Adam's passions would have been well tempered. Disordered desire is a consequence, not of having a body, but of spiritual pride!

A similar problem can be found with Ambrose's reading of Philippians 1: 21: 'My desire is to depart and to be with Christ, for that is far better, but to remain in the flesh is more necessary on your account.' Paul here certainly expresses a desire not to remain in the flesh, that is, in the body, but to depart and to be with Christ. It is not clear that Paul has in mind a disembodied state,[2] but even if this is

---

[2] There are many theologians from Cullman (1958) to Wright (2003) who have argued that Paul could not have had in mind a disembodied state, as this idea would be alien to his Hebrew understanding of the human person. However Barr (1992) brings together an impressive amount of evidence for a popular belief even among Hebrews of in a spiritual element or 'soul' that leaves the body at death and that can sometimes return. Of the many scriptural passages that seem to imply this, he states, 'In view of the enormous amount of evidence of such ideas of "soul" in ancient peoples, I cannot see why this reading of the text must be ruled out' (1992: 40). A good theological discussion of the issue is given by Ratzinger (1977: 104–61).

granted, there is no reason to suppose that Paul regards being disembodied as itself desirable. What Paul desires is to 'be with Christ' which is something that awaits him beyond death. Elsewhere Paul writes that he would not want to be 'unclothed' or 'found naked' (2 Corinthians 5: 3–4) which, in context, seems to express repugnance regarding the disembodied state. Ambrose conflates Paul's desire to find rest in final communion with Christ with a quite alien desire to flee from the body. Augustine, again, is on better ground in arguing that we should desire to be with Christ in spite of, not because of, the concomitant separation from the body (*CD* XIII. 8).

Ambrose based his positive account of death in part on those passages from Paul concerning the need to die to sin by baptism (Romans 6: 3–4, 6.11; Galatians 2: 19–20; Colossians 2: 12; 3: 3–5; 2 Timothy 2: 11). Dying to sin was taken as a model for Christian dying in general, and so, for the Christian evaluation of physical death. By baptism, the believer unites himself or herself to the death of Christ. Christ's death is the cause of salvation and so participation with this death becomes something to be desired. Dying with Christ means renouncing the old way of life and accepting the new life that comes from Christ. Ambrose developed what was an important theme in Paul's consideration of the life of grace, but again he conflated Pauline and Platonic categories. Dying to sin, which in Paul's understanding concerned detachment from sinful practices, was understood by Ambrose as detachment from the *body*. The Gospel, like pagan philosophy, was understood as a process of dying; the difference being that the philosophers merely desired death while the Christian saints accomplish death. The union of Christian and Platonic piety here is as powerful as it is misleading. Dying to sin does not concern bodily desires more than spiritual (one should say—diabolical) desires. It concerns a conversion of heart which must involve at least the willingness to sacrifice everything, even life itself, but which does not involve any denigration of life or the body.

In his later writings Augustine seems to have avoided the theme of dying with Christ. There is no reference to Romans 6: 3–4a or Romans 6: 11 in the whole of *De civitate Dei*—even though an entire two books are devoted to the consideration of death. The presentation of the Christian life as 'dying to sin' or 'dying with Christ' is almost wholly absent. This omission allows Augustine to present all the analogous meanings of death as negative, but at the cost of neglecting an important scriptural theme. While Ambrose misinterprets the language of 'dying with Christ', he gives this language the prominence it deserves. By failing to develop an alternative account of 'dying to sin' Augustine effectively cedes this area of Scripture to Christian Platonists such as Ambrose. This is a disservice to the apostle, and a partial, and therefore misleading, presentation of Paul's message. Nevertheless, it is to Augustine, rather than to Ambrose, that one should look for the resources to develop a richer, more comprehensive, and more consistent presentation of Paul's theology.

It is clear that Augustine's anti-Platonic account of death has implications for many theological and practical questions. Below we will examine Augustine's discussion of suicide and martyrdom and his attitudes to the fear of death, to grief, and to the care of the dead. However, before we focus on these more obviously death-related subjects it is worth considering other areas of Augustine's thought. Strange as it may seem, an examination of his approach to the cult of virginity will demonstrate how Augustine's reflections on the meaning of death had wide-ranging effects upon his theology.

VIRGINITY AND MORTIFICATION

The late fourth century saw a flurry of works in praise of virginity. From the diverse strands of apostolic piety and ascetic practice a definite pattern of life had emerged. Women took vows of virginity, sometimes publicly, received the veil, sometimes even lived in common.[3] Men may be celibate and seek true virginity of heart, but when there is mention of the consecration of virgins it is always women who are understood.

Praise of virginity suited well the Platonic piety of flight from the body that we find in Ambrose or in Gregory of Nyssa. It is particularly striking in Gregory's *De virginitate* that virginity is seen

---

[3] This development seems new to Ambrose in the Latin West: *De virginibus* 1. XI. 57–60.

fundamentally as a disposition of the soul by which she[4] is enabled to gaze on heavenly, that is intellectual and immaterial, objects.

To look with a free devoted gaze upon heavenly delights the soul will turn herself from earth; she will not even partake of the recognised indulgences of the secular life; she will transfer all her powers of affection from material objects to the intellectual objects of immaterial beauty. Virginity of the body is devised to further such a disposition of soul; it aims at creating in her a complete forgetfulness of natural emotions; it would prevent the necessity of ever descending to the call of fleshly needs.[5]

The same attitude is found in Ambrose in the context of theological reflection on death. He exhorts the man who desires wisdom to disengage his soul from all dealings with the body: 'the wise man, when he seeks after the divine, frees his soul from the body and forgoes its company' (*BM* 3. 10). The presentation of spiritual death as 'freeing the soul from the contagions of the body' (*BM* 3. 9), strikes a chord with virginity literature. However, his own work on virginity is different from Gregory's in several respects. Ambrose writes not on virginity but on virgins, *De virginibus*. He writes, reluctantly and by invitation, to his sister, a virgin, on the meaning the life of consecrated virginity. His concern is not only with virginity as an inner virtue, but also with the role played by virgins in the Church: what they are for; what they represent. Ambrose seems to be somewhat in awe of the way of life represented by consecrated virginity: he professes himself ill equipped for the task of instructing those who are living such virtue. 'For it is not for me to teach, nor for you to learn what you ought to guard against, for the practice of perfect virtue does not require teaching, but instructs others' (*De virginibus* 1. IX. 54).

His primary examples are the virgin-martyr Agnes, the Virgin Mary, and an unnamed virgin-martyr from Antioch. This last was martyred together with a soldier who saved her from being condemned to harlotry by swapping clothes with her! The story of their meeting and their martyrdom has all the appearance of a common

---

[4] In a language where common nouns have gender it is difficult to make a distinction between 'she' and 'it' hence they are usually translation with the impersonal pronoun. However, in this context it seems likely that the gender of the soul deliberately echoes the archetypal sex of the virgin.

[5] *De virginitate* V following Wilson and Moore except introducing the feminine pronoun for typological reasons.

romance. These two are characters (*personae*): 'let the characters be also considered, a soldier and a virgin' (*De virginibus* 2. IV. 30). They have a role and a place in society. Men are not called virgins because trade or citizenship defines their status, whereas a woman's status is defined by marriage and family, as daughter, mother, or wife. The consecrated virgin cannot be defined as wife or mother and may even be a virgin against the wishes of parents (*De virginibus* 1. XII. 62–6). Virginity is not only a virtue, much less a simple fact of nature, it is a public status, but one demanding a certain state of virtue. For Ambrose, virgins are a powerful sign of the presence of God in the Church. In some ways they fulfil the role of martyrs who bear witness to the real power of grace, through faith in Christ, to overcome the world. As the time of persecution, and so of martyrdom, becomes more of a memory, it is left to virginity to be a potent sign of the presence of something supernatural in the Church.

Ambrose tends to think of virginity as something that can be accomplished successfully, at least by Christians—as complete and perfect virtue. It is important for him, therefore, to deny that pagans really accomplish virginity (*De virginibus* 1. IV. 14). He is willing to admit that pagan philosophers can *desire* the separation of soul from body in perfect virtue, but this is *accomplished*, not by pagan philosophers but by Christians. ' "I die daily" (1 Corinthians 15: 31), says the Apostle. Better certainly is this saying than theirs who said that meditation on death was true philosophy, for they praised the study, he exercised the practice of death' (*FR* 35).

There are some among the pagans who at least approve of virginity, but they are inconstant in holding it. Some cults make a temporary vow of virginity (which by its temporariness appears to Ambrose as a travesty), others espouse virginity only to fall by threat, or worse by lust. The archetype of the virgin for Ambrose is the virgin-martyr. This is for two reasons: first because virginity is more apparent when it is maintained unto death in the face of threats, and secondly because virginity is analogous to martyrdom. It is an abandonment of the world and the flesh in favour of perfect virtue, which Ambrose regards as the image of death. This is the meaning of Ambrose's cryptic aphorism, 'virginity is not praiseworthy because it is found in martyrs, but because it itself makes martyrs' (*De virginibus* 1. III. 10).

The state of consecrated virginity is, for Ambrose, the image of perfect virtue, and hence the perfection of spiritual death. It is a way of life that has its source in heaven and is revealed most clearly in the Virgin Mary. It is exemplified in the Church as a way of life unlike that of pagans, or even, in general, of Jews. It is the 'practice of the life of heaven' (*De virginibus* 1. III. 13) which was 'implanted in human bodies' through the incarnation of the Son of God in the womb of the virgin. Virginity, then, represents the achievement, through the grace of Christ, of that spiritual death, that inner separation of soul from the snares of the body, which some pagans desired but none accomplished.

Augustine certainly read Ambrose's *De virginibus* (as is evident from Augustine's *De doctrina Christiana* IV. 48, 50) but seems little influenced by it. There are several notable differences between Ambrose's work and Augustine's own contribution to the genre, *De sancta virginitate*. Most obviously, the *De sancta virginitate* is a companion to an earlier work, *De bono conugali*, in which Augustine outlines the natural good of marriage. Ambrose, indeed, is careful to say that marriage is not to be denigrated: 'I am not indeed discouraging marriage, but am enlarging upon the benefits of virginity' (*De virginibus* 1. IV. 24). Nevertheless, he provides no treatise giving a defence of the good of marriage nor does he dwell on marriage in his work on virgins. Augustine, on the other hand, is interested in the natural good of marital friendship, 'the first natural bond of human society' (*De sancta virginitate* 1. 1). This is reflected in his consideration of marital love and procreation as a possibility in the Garden of Eden (*CD* XIV. 23–6). Much as contemporary Christians have often heavily criticized Augustine for failing to appreciate married love sufficiently, he is by far the most positive of the late fourth-century Fathers in his understanding of marriage (Harrison 2000: 159–62; Brown 1989: 402). Similarly, he is much the most reticent in the muted character of his praise of virginity. It was from Augustine that the classic Christian account of the goods of marriage—offspring, fidelity, and the bond of the sacrament—entered the tradition. The limits of his view of the purposes of sexual intercourse within marriage (Lamberigts 2000; Cahill 1996: 179 ff.; Rist 1994: app. 3), and the emergence of Puritan forms of Augustinianism within both Catholic and Reformed traditions in the seventeenth century, should not be allowed to obscure the remarkable character of his contribution. He is the foremost orthodox patristic defender of the good of marriage.

It was only after his work on marriage that, bending to popular expectations, he wrote a book on virginity. 'After I had written *On the good of marriage*, it was expected that I should write *On holy virginity*; and I did not delay to do so' (*Retractationes* II. 23). What comes across most forcefully in the work itself is the danger that the state of virginity holds as an opportunity for pride. Augustine does not dispute that virginity is a better and a nobler state than marriage. He upholds the tradition that 'whosoever gives in marriage does well, whosoever gives not in marriage does better' (*De sancta virginitate* 18 quoting 1 Corinthians 7: 38). The virgin is not distracted by the cares of the world but can devote herself more wholeheartedly to the Lord. Yet it is precisely because the state of virginity is noble that it holds danger for the Christian.

Augustine's concern with grace, and thus with humility,[6] implies a different paradigm of virtue from that given by Ambrose. As he would set out clearly in *De civitate Dei* XIV, the sins of the flesh do not stem from the flesh, but from the mind. The archetypal sin of Satan, and of Adam, was pride. True virtue does not consist in separation of soul from body but in humble fidelity to Christ. Augustine stresses that *all* Christians are required to imitate Jesus in the way of the beatitudes, in being 'meek and lowly of heart' (*De sancta virginitate* 28 citing Matthew 5: 3–10; 11: 29). This is required for married Christians as much as for virgins: 'But surely even married persons may go in those steps, although not setting their foot perfectly in the same print (*forma*), yet walking in the same paths' (*De sancta virginitate* 28).

Augustine is much more sceptical than Ambrose about how many actually achieve the perfection of virtue in the virgin state. Here again, Augustine shows that suspicion of perfectionism that was engendered by the Donatist dispute and that would come to the fore again in the Pelagian controversy. The perfection of virtue is seen in the martyrs—here Augustine and Ambrose agree—yet a married woman may be more perfect, and more ready to die than a virgin.

---

[6] Present already here in *De sancta virginitate, c.*401 CE, long before the Pelagian crisis had emerged.

Until her resolve is tested by martyrdom, it is not clear how perfect anyone has become: 'Whence, I say, does she know but that she herself be not as yet Thecla, while that other be already Crispina'[7]

Augustine does not deny the good of virginity; he upholds it. Yet the stress falls elsewhere. The paradigm of sin is no longer with the sins of the flesh. The virgins are not yet seen as perfect even if they persevere in chastity and simplicity of life. Virtue is found in humility, in accepting the grace of God by which alone salvation comes. Vice is found in pride, envy, and malice before it is found in gluttony, self-indulgence, or unchastity; therefore, whereas Ambrose praises virgins Augustine admonishes them, lest what they had gained by continence they lose by pride:

We lately put forth a book 'of the good of marriage' in which also we admonished and admonish the virgins of Christ, not, on account of that greater gift which they have received, to despise, in comparison of themselves, the fathers and mothers of the people of God. (*De sancta virginitate* 1)

Thus differences in the account given of death, and whether it be a good thing or a bad thing, have implications elsewhere, not least in the theology of marriage and virginity. The Platonic paradigm of virtue as the soul separating itself from bodily passions (anticipating the separation that comes with death) is thoroughly rejected by Augustine. He replaces it with an account in which humility and love are paramount and provide the measure for the passions and for every honest walk of life: '[Christians] find fear and desire, pain and gladness in conformity with the holy Scriptures and sound doctrine; and because their love is right, all these feelings are right in them' (*CD* XIV. 9).

SUICIDE AND MARTYRDOM

It seems to follow from the claim that 'death ought not to be regarded as a good thing' (*CD* XIII.7) that it ought never to be chosen. It is contrary to one's natural appetite, indeed to one's proper and natural state, to seek one's own death. Death is an evil. It is a punishment for

---

[7] *De sancta virginitate* 48: Thecla was a virgin martyr, whereas the martyr Crispina was a married woman.

sin. Augustine is very strict concerning the circumstances in which one may take life, even one's own life. One may only take life when God commands it, or when justly commanded by the state, acting as the instrument for divine justice. One may never seek to kill oneself, though one may willingly submit to death at another's hand if there is no moral alternative. Augustine's paradigm of the martyr is the Christian who submits to death rather than committing sin. 'It was then said, "If you break the commandment you will certainly die." Now it is said, "If you shrink from death, you will break the commandment."' (*CD* XIII. 4).

The martyr does not *seek* death but chooses to witness to Christ even though this means he or she will suffer death.[8] Augustine does not make the point here, but the death of the martyr is the result of a decision to kill, which is always wickedness on the part of another. The evil of death is directly chosen by the wicked persecutor. The holy martyrs do not choose death but choose not to sin, even though this leads to their being killed. Through their fidelity, by the grace of God, the martyrs merit an eternal reward and a new life. Yet eternal life is given by God, not by death. 'This happens not in virtue of any quality of its [death's] own, but by the help of God' (*CD* XIII. 7).

The clear characterization of bodily death as always a bad thing in itself gives the theological context for Augustine's treatment of suicide. In his discussion of suicide in book I of *De civitate Dei*,[9] Augustine does not explicitly refer to his doctrine that bodily death is always a bad thing in itself. Rather he begins with the precept, 'you shall not kill' (Exodus 20: 13). This precept is not subject to further justification but is put forward as the revealed commandment of God (*CD* I. 20). Yet what is said by way of explanation and qualification is consonant with what Augustine will later say on the theology of human bodily death.[10]

---

[8] Hence Augustine states that, 'even those who, through death, go to that life where one can never die, do not want to die' Sermon 280. 3 quoted by Lancel (2002: 442).

[9] *CD* I. 17–27. This was to be the locus classicus of the later Latin tradition on suicide, see Murray 2000: ii.

[10] Lancel (2002: 442) argues that 'the root, of the very long standing, of Augustine's condemnation of suicide [is] whoever makes an attempt on his own life is attacking being, [and] thus creation.'

According to Augustine, God can justly command someone to be killed and we must obey such a command, acting as instruments of God's justice. Yet, no killing of an innocent party can ever be justified except on God's particular command, nor can any killing whatsoever on an individual initiative. This prohibition includes killing oneself, 'for to kill oneself is to kill a human being' (*CD* I. 20). Thus, 'anyone who kills himself is a murderer' (*CD* I. 17). To aim to kill a human being is to intend to do harm. Such action can be justified if the harm is a just punishment specifically commanded by God, but if it is not done at the command of God it is simply evil-doing. It is evil-doing because bringing about the death of the body is always in itself a destructive act. This is the unspoken premise of Augustine's account, a premise justified by the discussion in book XIII of *De civitate Dei*.

Different theological approaches to death may lie at the root of an interesting disagreement between Augustine and Ambrose. There was a celebrated case of a virgin called Pelagia who threw herself to her death rather than submit to a violation of her chastity. She and others like her were venerated as holy martyrs. Ambrose, perhaps accurately articulating a certain strand of popular piety, does not hesitate to praise her actions. He presents her as saying, 'God is not offended by a remedy against evil and faith permits the act' (*De virginibus* 1. III. 7; cf. Ambrose Letter 37). Yet Augustine disputes this, for what is sin on the part of the rapist, is not (*per se*) a sin on the part of the one violated. There are several differences here between Augustine and Ambrose. Augustine has a less exaggerated view of virginity, but also he may have particular pastoral concerns: (Augustine Letter 111; cf. Moorhead 1999: 69 n. 50) he wishes to console some virgins who have been violated and yet did not take their own lives; he wishes to stress that they did not sin in being raped, rather, they were right not to follow the example of Pelagia. Furthermore, Augustine has another concern: Ambrose, though he criticizes suicide (*FR* 11), fails to distinguish carefully suicide (self-killing) from martyrdom (accepting being killed by another, rather than commit infidelity oneself). Hence Pelagia says, 'faith permits the act', whereas Augustine would say that 'the act' of killing, except on divine authority, is one thing the faith does not permit. Even Samson could not be praised for bringing about his own death, except that he was inspired by God (*CD* I. 21).

Augustine is sensitive enough to the popularity of the cult of Pelagia not to condemn her. After all, God may have secretly commanded her to kill herself (*CD* I. 26)! Yet, he will not allow that her example should be used to encourage someone to kill herself in an effort to avoid temporal troubles, affliction, or temptation. For none of these are sin, whereas deliberately to kill oneself, except at God's direct command, is a sin. Augustine makes a clear distinction between self-killing and martyrdom, a distinction obscured by popular piety and less clear to other contemporary bishops.

Another important pastoral reason for Augustine to make the distinction between suicide and martyrdom as clear as possible was his struggle, as bishop, to reconcile the Donatist Christians of North Africa. Donatists claimed to represent the true Church which was recognized not by its apostolic descent but by its purity and, above all, by its martyrs. 'For the authenticity of Donatist claims was at best precarious, and martyrs promised to do for Donatism what they had once done for Christianity'[11]—that is, act as a witness to its authenticity. The cult of martyrs was hugely important for Donatism and, of course, they counted as martyrs those who died at the hands of secular authorities aiming to enforce unity upon the Church. More significant for the present discussion, some seem even to have courted martyrdom. It was this that galvanized Augustine into examining exactly 'where martyrdom stopped and reckless self-homicide began' (Murray 2000: ii. 106) and caused him to question not only Donatist 'martyrs' but also the behaviour of accepted figures such as Pelagia.

Ambrose does condemn the madness of taking one's own life (*FR* 11); and regards it as deserting one's post (*BM* 2. 7). Nevertheless, Ambrose's idea that death is always in itself a gain, prevents him from attaining the clarity of Augustine on the difference between suicide and martyrdom. Augustine, on the other hand, achieves a consistent attitude to human bodily death, according to a principle enunciated in book XIII of *De civitate Dei*, 'the death of the body, the separation of the soul from the body, is not good for anyone' (*CD* XIII. 6).

---

[11] Murray 2000: ii. 105. On the particular importance of martyrdom to the Donatists Murray (2000: ii. 105 n. 33) cites Frend (1985: 319), 'Martyrdom and devotion to the word of God as contained in the Bible were at the heart of Donatism.'

FEAR OF DEATH, GRIEF, AND CARE
FOR THE DEAD

For Ambrose death is in every sense a good thing. It is the end of a miserable life and an end of sinning. In the present circumstances of life, death is not a curse but a blessing. It should not, therefore, be a source of grief or fear.

And therefore we deem that death is not to be mourned over; firstly, because it is common and due to all; next, because it frees us from the miseries of this life and, lastly, because when in the likeness of sleep we are at rest from the toils of this world, a more lively vigour is shed upon us. (*FR* 3)

And all this can be said without the hope of the resurrection! If the hope promised in Christ is added to the equation then death is even more than an escape from the ills of this life. It is a transition to a life of perfect happiness.

If on its own account life is to be escaped from, that there may be an avoidance of troubles and rest from miseries, how much more is that rest to be sought for, which shall be followed by the eternal pleasure of the resurrection to come? (*FR* 123)

It is true that sinners may fear the judgment that lies in death, but this fearful prospect can be rendered hopeful by repenting of sins and accepting the grace of Christ. Apart from the fear of judgment there is no sting in death and so, for a Christian, 'there is, then, nothing for us to fear in death' (*FR* 49). In saying this Ambrose is wholly in line with the dominant Christian tradition, which exhorted Christians to put aside altogether any fear of death and embrace death as a homecoming. In times of persecution the martyrs were presented as rejoicing that they had the opportunity to die for the sake of Christ. This is how Tertullian (if he is indeed the author) describes the great Carthaginian martyrs Perpetua and Felicity on the occasion of their martyrdom:

The day of their victory shone forth, and they proceeded from the prison into the amphitheatre, as if to an assembly, joyous and of brilliant countenances; if perchance shrinking, it was with joy, and not with fear. (*Passio Perpetuae et Felicitatis* 4. 1)

In the second and third centuries of the Christian era, this attitude of joyful anticipation in the face of death, seen in the case of the martyrs, was commended to all Christians. Cyprian, himself to become a martyr, argues that unwillingness to undergo death is unwillingness to go to Christ.

What room is there here for anxiety and solicitude? Who, in the midst of these things, is trembling and sad, except he who is without hope and faith? For it is for him to fear death who is not willing to go to Christ. It is for him to be unwilling to go to Christ who does not believe that he is about to reign with Christ. (*De mortalitate* 2)

A common thread can be seen running from Tertullian and Cyprian to Ambrose, that fear of death betrays either a failure of reason or a lack of faith or both. If it is seen for what it is, facing death should not even require particular courage. For it should be recognized as a transition to perfect joy and 'who would not hasten to better thing?' (*De mortalitate* 22). It is not death that requires courage but continuing to live in this life that requires courage and endurance. Christians should endure in order to serve their brothers and sisters, submitting their wills to God as to when they will be summoned. However, when their time comes they should rejoice like Simeon that their wait is ending and their consummation is near (*BM* 2. 5, *De mortalitate* 3).

There are many passages in Augustine's writing that echo the traditional Christian belief that 'by his resurrection Christ has taken away the fear of death' (Sermon 147. 3). The example of the martyrs and of Christ himself shows that, by the grace of God, it is possible not only to overcome fear of death, but even the fear of a terrible death: 'It was not death alone that they did not fear; but even crucifixion, a death than which none was thought more accursed. It the Lord endured, that His disciples might not only not fear death, but not even that kind of death.'[12]

Nevertheless, while Augustine happily proclaims a victory over death and over the fear of death as demonstrated by the resurrection

---

[12] *Enarrationes in Psalmos* 141. 9 using the numbering of the Psalms from the Hebrew (as does the translation in the *Library of the Nicene and Post-Nicene Fathers*, series 1, vol. 8). This differs somewhat from the Septuagint numbering which Augustine followed.

of Christ and by the example of the martyrs, he feels it necessary to qualify this traditional Christian teaching in certain important respects. Augustine accepts that, among Christians, and even among the martyrs, there can be a natural and reasonable fear of death that does not amount to a failure of faith. He is drawn to this view by a number of reasons.

- In the first place, as argued above, Augustine comes to see the separation of body and soul in death as itself a punishment, the destruction of a union that is natural, original, and good. A certain fear of death is therefore proper and natural.
- In the second place, in his mature thought, Augustine becomes increasingly suspicious of the perfectionism of Pelagian forms of Christianity and of their claim that Christians could perfectly overcome human frailty.
- In the third place, while death was originally imposed as a punishment for sin, its imposition upon those whose sins are forgiven cannot be a punishment, so it must remain for some other reason. Augustine thus comes to see the struggle with death as something salutary.

Let us consider these in order. In his commentary on Psalm 69 Augustine makes explicit the link between the natural union of body and soul and the naturalness of fear of death. Whereas the martyrs wish to cleave to Christ, they do not wish to suffer death, and would avoid it if they could. Death is in itself repellent to the will because by it body and soul, which belong together, are torn apart. Augustine appeals to the words of Paul concerning the resurrection, not to diminish the significance of death, but to point out that salvation ultimately must consist in the reuniting of body and soul, so that there separation by death contradicts not only the original state but also the final destiny of human nature.

For though we desire to cleave to Christ, yet we are unwilling to die: and therefore willingly or rather patiently we suffer, because no other passage is given us, through which we may cleave to Christ. For if we could in any other way arrive at Christ, that is, at life everlasting, who would be willing to die? For while explaining our nature, that is, a sort of association of soul and body, and in these two parts a kind of intimacy of gluing and fastening together, the Apostle saith, that 'we have a House not made with hands, everlasting in the Heavens': that is, immortality prepared for us, wherewith we are to be clothed at the end, when we shall have risen from the dead; and he saith, 'Wherein we are not willing to be stripped, but to be clothed upon, that the mortal may be swallowed up of life.' (*Enarrationes in Psalmos* 69: 3 quoting 2 Corinthians 5: 1–4)

It is for this reason that, though the final state is blessed, 'the very passage is somewhat bitter' (*Enarrationes in Psalmos* 69: 3), referring not just to the tortures that may accompany death but to the very fact of death as a separation of body and soul. Hence even the martyrs retain a proper natural aversion to death. To show this Augustine appeals to the text where Jesus says to Peter that he will be bound and taken where he would not go (John 21: 18). Even after being strengthened by witnessing the risen Christ and by the power of his grace, still there is in him some unwillingness to die.

He was willingly carried away; unwillingly he came to it, but willingly he conquered it, and left this feeling of infirmity behind that makes every one unwilling to die—a feeling so permanently natural, that even old age itself was unable to set the blessed Peter free from its influence. (*In Joannis evangelium tractatus* 123. 5 (*c.*407–17))

By describing the fear of death as natural Augustine is stating that such a feeling is to be expected and is compatible with the holiness of the saints, providing it does not so distort our actions as to lead to sin. This coheres with his more general claim that the passions of fear and desire are not themselves vicious unless they go beyond reason and the measure of love (*CD* XIV. 9). The martyrs retain a natural fear of death but nevertheless submit to death out of love for Christ.

The second major reason that leads Augustine to reassess the traditional attitude to fear of death is his unwillingness to ascribe human perfection to any except Christ and Christ's mother. This is a consequence of Augustine's controversy with the Pelagians who seemed to minimize the effects of original sin and claimed that everyone has the freedom to obey the commandments perfectly if they so wish. The Pelagians saw themselves as defending human freedom and responsibility and the inherent goodness of creation, but Augustine sees in them the same pride and perfectionism he had seen in the Donatists. In contrast he argues that, even among those who are forgiven and transformed by grace so that they are pleasing to God, there remains a tendency to sin. Christians do well if their life is free of external blame (*sine querella*) but if they think they are completely without sin (*sine peccato*) they deceive themselves (*CD* XIV. 9; *De perfectione justitiae hominis* 11. 24 (415 CE) appealing to 1 John 1: 8).

Augustine conceives the life of grace not as the instant attainment of Christian perfection by baptism but as a process of healing and transformation, through many falls and many acts of repentance.

He has kept God's ways who does not so turn aside as to forsake them, but makes progress by running his course therein; although, weak as he is, he sometimes stumbles or falls, onward, however, he still goes, sinning less and less until he reaches the perfect state in which he will sin no more. (*De perfectione justitiae hominis* 11. 24)

The state after which Christians strive, the perfect state in which he or she will sin no more, is not found in this life but is found only in heaven. In this life there is no end to the struggle with sin and with human imperfection. This life is therefore lived in the shadow of sin and death.

The claim that the martyrs rejoice without any ambivalence in the face of death thus seems to Augustine at best an unhelpful exaggeration at worst the sort of Pelagian error that can lead to pride or despair. Against this supposition Augustine appeals to the example of Peter who was led where he 'would not go' (John 21: 18 quoted in *In Joannis evangelium tractatus* 123. 5; *Enarrationes in Psalmos* 69. 3; 90. 7) and that of Paul who 'would not be stripped' of the body but rather clothed with immortality (2 Corinthians 5: 4 quoted in *Enarrationes in Psalmos* 69. 3; 78. 15; *CD* XX. 17). Scripture thus seems to show that these two great martyrs retained ambivalence in the face of death. According to Augustine, this is because the martyrs, while seeking to imitate Christ, cannot imitate Christ perfectly with regard to his sinlessness or his willingness to suffer and die. For Christ alone death was purely voluntary in that he was under no necessity to die; furthermore his death accomplished salvation in a way that no other death could: 'One might imitate Him in dying, but no one could, in redeeming' (*In Joannis evangelium tractatus* 84. 2). To think that the martyrs are equal to Christ in innocence is likewise dangerous presumption. Hence there must of necessity remain an element of reluctance or unwillingness in facing death.

Thus Augustine's ideas on the fear of death were certainly shaped, in part, by his dispute with the Pelagians (see Dodaro 1989). Nevertheless, it is important also to note the prior reason Augustine has to regard fear of death as a persistent feature of human existence, even for the Christian—and that is because the separation of body and soul is an evil, contrary to the essential unity of human nature. Thus, it is possible for Augustine to attribute a natural fear of death even to Christ.[13]

A third line of reasoning that altered Augustine's thinking on fear of death stems from his reflection on death as a punishment for sin. As mentioned above, Pelagius claimed that Adam would have died even if he had not sinned, for death is due to an essential characteristic of human nature and is not a punishment for sin. The death with which Adam was threatened must refer either to sudden death or to spiritual death and the punishment of hellfire. If sin was the reason for bodily death then why were those whose sins were forgiven in baptism not at the same time freed from the necessity of death? Augustine's answer to this is to say that, God could indeed have exempted Christians from death, but in this case people would become believers simply out of fear of death for the wrong reasons and Christians would not have their faith tried by the fear of death (*De peccatorum meritis et remissione* II. 31–4; *CD* XIII. 4).

It may seem difficult to take this line of argument seriously. Whether or not death is a punishment for sin, it is surely also a fact of our nature. Human beings are animals and like all animals they have a limited span before they must die. The embracing of a Christian life may bring a new spiritual life and hope for a life beyond the grave, but it clearly does not bring freedom from bodily death. Who would expect such a thing? Augustine makes heavy weather to reply to an objection that many would think incredible. So also, Augustine's answer to this seems very weak. He claims that people might become Christians for the wrong reason if baptism brought

---

[13] 'For our consolation the Saviour Himself transfigured also the same feeling in His own person when He said, "Father, if it be possible, let this cup pass from me" ' (*In Joannis evangelium tractatus* 123 quoting Matthew 26: 39).

freedom from bodily death, for then Christians would not have to face a trial of their faith. However, the motives of converts are often mixed, and wishing to escape mortality is not obviously worse as a motive than wishing to escape the fires of hell, or wishing to enjoy a life beyond the grave. Nor would it seem that if the saints escaped death they would have no trials in life of a different kind. Augustine himself comments that some people regard torture as being worse than death.

While it would be easy to dismiss both the seriousness of the objection and the seriousness of the answer, this would be a great mistake. The seriousness of the objection is rooted in Augustine's claim that human beings need not have been under the necessity of death. Adam need never have died and, had he not sinned he would not have died. If the prospective immortality of Adam is not thought of as a possibility that could be realized, then why should the resurrection of Christ or the life of the world to come be taken realistically? In all cases, hope rests with the power of God to give undying life to human beings. Similarly, the forgiveness of sins given in baptism through faith in Christ must be thought of as a real change in the relationship between the sinner and God, for this is at the very root of the Gospel message. If the link between sin and death is made so forcefully, then it needs to be asked why the forgiveness of sins does not translate more immediately into the enjoyment of an immortal life. Augustine has to take this objection seriously or else he could be accused either of not believing that bodily death is the wages of sin, or of not believing that our sins are forgiven through faith and Christian baptism.

Once it becomes clear that Augustine holds that there is an intrinsic or essential link between sin and death, this not only clarifies why the continuation of death after baptism is a real question for him, but also clarifies the character of his reply. Some elements of this reply seem ad hoc, such as the concern that people would embrace the grace of Christ 'just to avoid being released from the body' (*CD* XIII. 4). If many did rush to Christ for that reason, would that necessarily be a bad thing? However, other elements of his reply reflect a deeper and more constant theme in Augustine's theology. God brings good out of evil, turning what was originally a punishment into a means of salvation.

He yet permits [death] to remain for the contest of faith, in order that they may become the means of instructing and exercising those who are advancing in the struggle after holiness. (*De peccatorum meritis et remissione* II. 33)

This 'contest of the faith' is not an accidental feature of some human lives but is a necessary part of the life of grace after sin. The struggle exists because the redemption, accomplished perfectly by Christ, is not yet accomplished perfectly in the lives of believers; and sin, forgiven through Christ, still has to be resisted by believers. The Pelagian dream of human perfectibility is a dangerous illusion, hence the need to confess sins. It is this essential struggle with sin that is described as a conflict with death, and one that is only completed in death.

Although, weak as he is, he sometimes stumbles or falls, onward, however, he still goes, sinning less and less until he reaches the perfect state in which he will sin no more...he who, although he has sin, yet never ceases to persevere in fighting against it until he arrives at the home where there shall remain no more conflict with death. (*De perfectione justitiae hominis* 11. 27)

This mortal life is thus a sort of training. The conflict with death, which was originally imposed upon human beings as a punishment for sin, functions in the saints as a means to holiness. It is, 'an exercise of discipline, in order that our great fear of it [death] may be overcome by us as we advance in holiness' (*De peccatorum meritis et remissione* II. 34). Fear of death and recognition of human weakness helps believers to avoid the pitfall of pride, which was the first sin and remains the most dangerous. According to Augustine, the martyrs overcome fear of death precisely through recognizing their weakness and their need for God's grace. The triumph of the martyrs consists in the fact that, while they remain weak in themselves and experience fear, they nevertheless triumph through God's grace.[14] Augustine is at one with much of the early tradition in seeing martyrdom as an image of the Christian life. Though not every

---

[14] This theme is evident also in the *New Roman Missal* in its preface for martyrs, 'His [her] death reveals your power shinning through our human weakness. You choose the weak and make them strong in bearing witness to you.'

Christian dies by martyrdom, the witness of the martyrs reveals the meaning of the death of every Christian. The conflict with death, and overcoming the natural fear of death, is an essential element of martyrdom and hence an essential element of the Christian life. It can therefore be said that, 'the fact of the faithful overcoming the fear of death is a part of the struggle of faith itself' (*De peccatorum meritis et remissione* II. 31).

What may be said about grief over the death of another closely parallels what has been said about fear over one's own death. The tradition before Augustine emphasized the exhortation that Christians should not grieve over the deaths of those who had gone before them. Probably the most commonly quoted scriptural text concerning grief was the verse from Paul's letter to the Thessalonians: 'do not grieve like those who have no hope' (1 Thessalonians 4: 13). While it is clear that Christians often grieved intensely for those who had died, such feelings tended to be regarded as self-indulgent, concerned with one's own loss rather than the gain of the one who had died.

Ambrose is typical of this tradition. While he expressed profound grief over the premature death of his younger brother to whom he was devoted, he regarded this expression of emotion as due to weakness. 'I indulged my longing to some extent, lest too sharp remedies applied to a burning wound might rather increase than assuage the pain ... [as] it was not out of place to let natural feelings have a little play, since they are somewhat satisfied by tears, soothed by weeping, and numbed by a shock' (*FR* 1). Nevertheless the sermon preached a week after the death of his brother was understood as a corrective demonstrating by rational argument and appeal to faith that 'the departure of our loved ones should not be mourned by us' (*FR* 4). Ambrose did mourn but he did not admit that he should mourn. Grief is an expression of weakness that should be permitted for a time out of compassion but which should not be indulged overmuch, and even when felt, is better not expressed. 'Put aside your grief, if you can; if you cannot, keep it to yourself' (*FR* 7). The lack of moderation in grief is itself 'no small evil'. It can lead to extreme and sometimes immodest behaviour (as with women who tear off their clothes in a customary expression of grief, *FR* 12) and occasionally it can lead to the bereaved person taking his own life and so separating himself permanently from the deceased beloved.[15]

Early in his theological development, Augustine shares many of the same attitudes. His *Confessiones* contains two accounts of grief. The first before he became Christian at the death of a friend he had known since childhood, the second after his baptism at the death of his mother. Both accounts are vivid and detailed. He tells us not only of his tears but also, for example, how familiar things and places became hateful because 'my eyes looked for him everywhere, and he was not there' (*Confessiones* IV. iv. 9). So great was his grief over the death of his friend that he moved from Thagaste to Carthage, 'where should I go to escape from myself? Where is there where I cannot pursue myself? And yet I fled from my home town, for my eyes sought him less in a place where they were not accustomed to see him' (*Confessiones* IV. vii. 12). In looking back, from a Christian perspective on this first grief, Augustine sees in it too great an attachment to worldly things and a lack of faith in God. In the event, his grief over his friend was assuaged by time and by the company of new friends. However, these friendships were neither deep nor immune from the same pattern of loss and grief being repeated. Only the person who loves his friend in God can never lose him (*Confessiones* IV. ix. 14).

The death of his mother proved a much more difficult for Augustine to rationalize in this way. Despite sharing with Monica a profound faith, hope, and love of God, and despite having no doubts about her salvation, he finds his life 'as it were torn in pieces since my life and hers had become a single thing' (*Confessiones* IX. xii. 30). Thus, like Ambrose, Augustine ascribes his feelings of sadness as due to 'softness' (*mollitia*),[16] and he feels it a duty not to weep publicly or to express his grief openly. Furthermore he feels grief at the fact of his grief—at not being able to rejoice in these circumstances.

---

[15] *FR* 11; note here strong condemnation of suicide as deserving the punishment of hell and hence eternal separation from the person over whom the suicide was grieving, assuming that person is in paradise.

[16] *Confessiones* IX. xii. 31 cf. *FR* 7 succumbing to grief as 'soft and effeminate' (*mollem et effeminatum*), see J. J. O'Donnell 1992: iii. 140 commenting on *Confessiones* IX. xii. 29.

Finally, in private unable to contain his tears, he weeps 'about her and for her, about myself and for myself' (*Confessiones* IX. xii. 33). He asks that those who would consider this a sin should not deride him but should weep for him, that is, pray for him. The tone clearly suggests that this is an example of weakness that anyone with charity should regard as pardonable. However, it is noteworthy that, even though Augustine seems to regard this behaviour as forgivable, it still seems to fall short of Christian perfection. It is an indulgence that should be accepted out of mercy, but it is not defended as proper upright or virtuous behaviour. At this point Augustine seems harder on himself even than Ambrose is about his grief over Satyrus. It could be said that Augustine's vivid and sympathetic account of grief itself shows a level of acceptance of grief, but the same should then be said of Ambrose. Ambrose is willing even to talk of 'natural feelings' (*affectum naturae*; *FR* 1) of grief that are consoled by tears, and condemns only 'lack of moderation in grief' (*immoderatio doloris*; *FR* 11), whereas Augustine seems, at least at some points, to regard even the inner feeling of sadness as a sort of weakness.

In another work Augustine is affected not only by doctrinal reflection but also by pastoral experience to take a much more positive view of mourning. In his letter to Sapida (date uncertain) he seeks to console a consecrated virgin over the death of her brother, a deacon in the Church at Carthage. In this work Augustine explicitly defends a degree of mourning and even tears. When Paul exhorted Christians not to weep like those who have no hope, he did not mean to prohibit sorrow altogether, 'but only such sorrow as the heathen manifest who have no hope' (Letter 263. 3). The legitimacy of tears is shown by the example of Martha and Mary who wept over the death of Lazarus, and even more by the example of Christ who himself wept.

The Lord Himself wept for that same Lazarus, whom He was going to bring back from death; wherein doubtless He by His example permitted, though He did not by any precept enjoin, the shedding of tears over the graves even of those regarding whom we believe that they shall rise again to the true life. (Letter 263. 3)

This permission Augustine reinforces with the positive injunction of Ecclesiasticus to 'let tears fall down over the dead, and begin to lament as if thou hadst suffered great harm thyself' (Sirach 38: 16). Augustine adds that Ecclesiasticus also counsels that those who mourn should not remain permanently in grief but should console themselves. The grief of Christians should certainly be moderate and not despairing. This doctrine echoes that of Ambrose. Nevertheless, in this letter, Augustine's defence of moderate grief provides stronger justification for the tears of believers over their dead—the very example of Christ. In his sermons over the death of his brother Ambrose mentions Lazarus a number of times (*FR* 39, 77–80, 101) but does not allude to the tears of Jesus over his friend's death, nor even to those of Martha and Mary. There is clearly a difference between the treatment of Christian grief by Ambrose and by Augustine in the *Confessiones* on the one hand, and that by Augustine in this later letter on the other. This may be due in part to the fact that in the former case Augustine is considering his own grief while in the latter he is seeking to console another in her grief, but it also coheres with the clarity of thought we have seen throughout the mature Augustine in regarding bodily death as, in itself, a bad thing.

Another theme that is more prominent in Augustine than in Ambrose is how the living can benefit the dead, in particular by praying for the dead and offering the 'sacrifice of redemption' for them. This is already evident in the *Confessiones* (400 CE) and is developed later in *De civitate Dei* (417–20 CE) and also in a short work devoted to the question of the care that should be given to the dead: *De cura pro mortuis* (421 CE).

In the *Confessiones*, Augustine relates how, in his last conversations with his mother, she expressed no anxiety about dying far from home. She had previously been concerned with where she should be buried, and had provided for and prepared a plot close to where her husband was buried, in Thagaste. However, as death approached it became of no concern to her whether or not 'she had a tomb in her homeland' (*Confessiones* IX. xiii. 36). She instructed her sons not to be overly concerned with caring for her dead body, 'I have only this request to make of you, that you remember me at the altar of the Lord, wherever you may be' (*Confessiones* IX. xi. 27). Monica's attitude made a strong impression on Augustine, who took it as a sign of great spiritual maturity. The desire to be buried in a particular place, though common, was in reality a 'vain conceit', for nothing is far from God and there is no danger that, when God comes to raise the dead he will be ignorant of where they are buried (*Confessiones* IX. xii. 28)!

Augustine discusses this theme in a more general way in the first book of his great work on the city of God. Here the immediate question before him is whether the martyrs suffer when, after being killed, their bodies are deprived of burial (*CD* I. 12). This had sometimes been the deliberate policy of the persecutors as at Lyons where the bodies of the martyrs had first been exposed to dogs then the remains burnt and the ash scattered on the River Rhone so that nothing should be left for any kind of memorial (*De cura pro mortuis* 8). His answer is clear and unequivocal. The martyrs are in no way harmed by anything that happens to their bodies after they are dead. He invokes in support the words of Christ, 'Do not fear those who kill the body and have nothing that they can do after that' (*CD* I. 12 quoting Luke 12: 4). Attacking a dead body cannot harm the soul of the one who has died 'since there is no feeling in a body that has been killed' (*CD* I. 12). It is rather those who survive who are consoled by burial customs or offended when none can be performed. 'Such things as a decent funeral and a proper burial, with its procession of mourners, are a consolation to the living rather than a help to the departed' (*CD* I. 12).

Augustine's central doctrinal concern, though he does not make it explicit here, is to deny that anything that happens to the dead body could prevent the martyr from receiving his or her reward from the hand of God (this is more explicit in *De cura pro mortuis* 3 but seems to be the underlying concern already in *CD* I. 12–13). Hence the emphasis is placed first on denying the necessity of burial. Nevertheless, this having been said, Augustine is keen to defend the traditional piety of burying the dead. If the belongings of a departed loved one, such as clothes or a ring, are valued in proportion as the person is loved, how much more important is it to show devotion to the body of the dead person which was not a mere adornment but 'belongs to his very nature as a man' (*CD* I. 13). In the Scriptures there are many examples of concern for proper burial and funeral rights and Tobit is specifically commended for giving burial to the dead (Tobit 1: 17). Jesus also commends the pious woman who prepared his body for burial (Matthew 26: 12). Augustine argues that this is approved by

God so as to promote faith in the resurrection of the body. His concern here to defend this traditional piety towards the dead body represents a shift away from the attitude expressed in the *Confessiones* where he expressed his admiration for Monica's indifference concerning the burial of her body. In the same context he uses overtly Platonic language to describe her death: 'this religious and devout soul was released from the body (*corpore soluta est*)' (*Confessiones* IX. xii. 28, cf. *Phaedo* 62b).

Augustine returned to these questions in the work dedicated to the care that is due to the dead (*De cura pro mortuis*). There he reproduced in full the relevant passage from *De civitate Dei* and reiterated his belief that the burial of the dead in no way affects the state of the departed. Christians should not accept the pagan myth according to which, if the body is not properly buried then the soul is not transported across the Styx to its final resting place. The place of burial has significance for the living but not for the dead. Nevertheless, there is a way that the dead can be helped and that is by the prayers of the living, and in particular by the offering of the sacrifice of the altar and by the commending of the dead to the martyrs. Augustine reconciles this with Paul's teaching that we shall be judged according to what we have 'done in the body' (2 Corinthians 5: 10) by arguing that only those who have lived a sufficiently good life are in a position to be helped. Those who have neglected to repent of serious sins while they are alive are beyond help after their deaths. Nevertheless even the most exemplary of the saints (and Augustine clearly regarded his mother as a holy woman) are not perfect in this life and can be helped by the prayers of those who remain. If being buried near the shrine of a martyr helps to inspire the prayers of the living, then it can be of benefit for the dead. However, it is not the burial itself but the prayers of the living that benefit the dead—and these prayers can take place even if burial is prevented for some reason.

As with Augustine's thought on fear of death, his attitude to grief and the care of the dead changes discernibly between his earlier and later works. This is due to a complex of factors including both a greater emphasis on the goodness of the body (first against the Manichees and later even against the Platonists) and also an increasing tendency to characterize the Christian life as a gradual struggle against sin and death (against the Pelagian claim that perfection could be achieved in this life). While Augustine remains constant in exhorting Christians to have hope in the face of death, he is more willing to give some place to fear of death and grief over the dead and to distinguish the good that God brings out of death from the grievousness of death in itself. Indeed if death were not a trial, what would there be in the sacrifice of the martyrs and of Christ himself, to be admired?

But however great be the grievousness of death, it ought to be overcome by the power of that love which is felt to Him who, being our life, was willing to endure even death in our behalf. For if there were no grievousness, even of the smallest kind, in death, the glory of the martyrs would not be so great. (*In Joannis evangelium tractatus* 123. 5)

THINGS LEFT UNSAID

Ambrose—like his contemporaries Gregory of Nyssa, Basil the Great, and Didymus the Blind (all followers of Origen)—had endeavoured to harmonize Christian doctrine with Platonic philosophy. This is seen most clearly in his view of death, which presents the death of the body as being, in itself, a good thing (*bonum*), on account of freeing the soul from the prison-house of the body. Augustine comes to Christianity via Platonism and is strongly influenced by Ambrose. His early works reflect this attempt to marry Platonic and Christian piety. However, Augustine's continuous reading of the Scriptures, and his controversies with Manichees, Donatists, and Pelagians, reshape his understanding. He becomes more critical of Platonic piety, certain aspects of which he comes to see as essentially different from true Christian piety. Again, this is most evident in his mature treatment of death, which he argues is always a bad thing (*malum*), on account of depriving the soul of its natural union with the body.

Augustine's describing of the 'law of the flesh' and the 'law of the spirit' in a way which does not denigrate the body, his caution concerning the cult of virginity, and his clarity on the subject of suicide all seem to stem from this single overarching vision. The death of the body is a bad thing *per se*. The separation of the soul from the body is not a good thing in itself and, therefore, cannot provide a proper model for virtue. From the apparently unpromising starting point of regarding death as a punishment for the fall (*CD* XIII. 1), Augustine achieves a vision of death, sin, and virtue which allows him properly to value the natural goods of the body.

However, although Ambrose's theological analysis of death is taken up and criticized by Augustine, not all the elements of the former vision are saved in the latter. Of the three sorts of death outlined by Ambrose, Augustine mentions only two, the death of the body and the death of the soul by mortal sin. Augustine also discusses another kind of death, the 'second death' of eternal punishment, but he does not mention the death of baptism, dying to sin, or 'mystical' dying which plays such a prominent role in Ambrose's thought.

In an earlier work, written in 396 CE while Ambrose was still alive, Augustine had referred to the good sort of death that is dying to sin:

Just as there is a death of the soul, a forsaking of one's former life and habits, which comes about through repentance, so the death of the body is also a releasing of the principle that previously animated it. (*De doctrina Christiana* I. 19)

There is more than a suggestion here that death may be a good thing in itself. It is the soul that does *not* die in this world that is drawn by bodily death into a more serious (*gravior*) death in the world to come (*De doctrina Christiana* I. 20). At this point there is no sign of a fundamental parting of the ways between Augustine and Ambrose on death: death is understood primarily as a good and necessary separation. Twenty years later there is no suggestion at all that death may be a good thing in itself. In none of his later major works does Augustine treat of this good of spiritual death. By omitting 'dying to sin' from his account, Augustine can understand every kind of death as a bad thing and as resulting from the fall. Mortal sin, bodily death, and the second death of hell are all aspects of 'total death' (*CD* XIII. 12). Death is an analogical concept, used slightly differently in these three cases, but all share certain common features—all are understood as punishment, as lack or deprivation, and as a separation from the good of life: death is in every sense a bad thing.

The price Augustine pays for this systematic clarity is to leave unsaid anything concerning dying to sin or dying with Christ in baptism. What is the centre of Ambrose's understanding of human death—the identification of dying to sin with separation from the body—has no chance to get a foothold in Augustine's vision, for dying to sin is simply not treated, at least not in his systematic account of death. This lacuna allows Augustine to identify every kind of death as a bad thing *per se*, but it is not a happy oversight. The themes of dying to sin, of taking up one's cross, and of dying in baptism comprise a significant element of New Testament teaching. In the context of ascetical theology or in preparation for death the Christian seeks understanding of what it is to die well by dying with Christ. Ambrose gives a powerful and thoroughly argued account of this teaching, integrated with that good death that philosophers' commended, striving to separate ourselves from all that is contaminated by the body.

It is not enough for Augustine, or someone following Augustine's account, to gloss over this aspect of death: in the absence of a more comprehensive Augustinian account, Christians will turn to that given by Ambrose and other writers in the same vein, despite Augustine's theologically penetrating critique.[17] This, in turn, threatens theology with a bifurcation between a dogmatic account of death which is unable to speak of dying well and a 'spirituality of dying' which remains uncritically Platonic and, to that extent, unchristian. This is undoubtedly to caricature the later Latin tradition, which was, and is, complex, multifarious, and never static, but it contains more than a grain of truth. It was against what at least *appeared* to be such a bifurcation between dogma and piety that several great twentieth-century theologians endeavoured to struggle. The present study will consider one such theologian, Karl Rahner; however, it is impossible to understand the development of later Catholic dogmatic reflection on death without touching upon another significant moment in the tradition. After Augustine, much the

---

[17] An important figure in the transmission of the Ambrosian vision of the good of death is Bernard of Clairvaux. While Bernard uses Augustine's analysis of the death of the soul by mortal sin (*Sermones divers.* 116; cf. Burch 1940: 8), his famous lament for his brother (*Sermones Cantica* 26) echoes Ambrose's lament for his brother. He is significant in the tradition for his famous dictum that the contemplative, by putting away thoughts of material things, 'should die the death of the angels' (*Sermones Cantica* 52 cf. Burch 1940: 77). This phrase aptly encapsulates Ambrose's doctrine of the good of death.

most prominent theologian in the Catholic tradition is also the most significant for the theology of death, which exercised his mind for quite different reasons. The theologian in question is the thirteenth-century friar Thomas Aquinas, who wholeheartedly embraced Augustine's mature vision, but who did so in a highly creative manner and within a quite different intellectual world. His aim was nothing less than to synthesize the genius of Augustine with that of Aristotle.

5

In One Way Natural, in Another Unnatural: Death in the Thought of Thomas Aquinas

BACKGROUND TO THE THOUGHT OF THOMAS AQUINAS

Ambrose and Augustine lived in the last days of the ancient Latin civilization, prior to the collapse of the Western Roman Empire before the barbarian incursions that brought with them a general decline in civil structures and a subsequent decline in the culture of learning that those structures had supported. Thomas d'Aquino was born in 1226 CE, eight centuries later, into a newly emerging world of expanding towns, commerce, and new academic institutions (Weisheipl 1983; Torrell 1996; Tugwell 1988: 201–351). The cathedral and monastic schools of the eleventh and twelfth centuries had given birth to a number of universities and with them a self-confident scholastic culture (Aertsen 1993). Thomas was from a minor aristocratic family in the south of the Italian peninsula and was sent to be educated at the monastery of Monte Cassino. The monastery, however, was occupied by the Holy Roman Emperor, the excommunicate Frederick II, as part of his fierce campaign against the Pope. Thomas was thus sent, at the age of 13, to complete his education at the University of Naples. Being under imperial control, the arts faculty was influenced by a sort of Aristotelianism that had become fashionable in the imperial court.

This was a new and a potentially threatening intellectual development in thirteenth-century Europe: many works of Aristotle were becoming available for the first time through contacts with Islam, and the reception of these works was heavily influenced by the Arabic commentators, particularly Avicenna and Averroes (Davidson 1992). Throughout the century two questions dominated controversy over the Christian acceptability of Aristotelian thought. The first was how to deal with Aristotle's claim that one could demonstrate by rational argument that the world had always existed (*De Caelo* 1. 11. 280b). This seemed to run counter to the scriptural doctrine that the world was created 'in the beginning' (Genesis 1: 1). The second major problem was how to understand Aristotle's doctrine of the soul and, in particular, whether Aristotle taught that there was only one intellect which was somehow shared by all human beings (the influential interpretation of Averroes). The doctrine of a single mind in all human beings seemed to undermine free will and individual responsibility and, more importantly, to contradict the doctrine of divine judgment in death and the subsequent reward or punishment of individuals after death.

While at Naples, Thomas met the Order of Friars Preachers (the Dominicans). This order was less than thirty years old, and had that freshness and vitality common to emergent religious movements (Tugwell 1982: 1–47; Lawrence 1994: ch. 4). The friars held all things in common, like other religious orders, but unlike other orders they begged for their living and they were primarily devoted to the work of preaching. The vision of their founder, Dominic, coincided with that of the great pastoral council Lateran IV (1215 CE) and shared much in common with the vision of Francis of Assisi who founded the Friars Minor in 1209. The preaching of the Dominicans was directed to the care of souls (*cura animarum*) and also, in particular, was much involved with preaching against the Cathar heresy widespread in the Languedoc region of southern France (Vicaire 1964: 49–52). The Cathars or Albigensians (so called because of their association with the area around Albi) seemed to their contemporaries to repeat the doctrines of the long-extinguished sect of the Manichees. Thomas entered the order in the early 1240s and became a pupil of Albert 'the Great' of Cologne (Tugwell 1988: 3–129) who was already heavily involved in facilitating the Christian reception of Aristotle's works. During his life Thomas continued to argue for the compatibility of Aristotelian understandings of the world with those of the Christian tradition. He made use of Aristotelian categories in his understanding of God, though to be correct one should say: in his understanding about what could not be understood about God (Davies 1992: ch. 3). He used them in his defence of the coherence of mysteries such as the Trinity and the presence of the body and blood of Christ in the Blessed Sacrament. He also used Aristotle in developing the concepts of disposition (*habitus*) and virtue (*virtus*) into a systematic account of the place of grace in the moral life. He wrote commentaries on many works of Aristotle including *De anima, Ethica Nicomachea, Physica,* and *Metaphyisica* (Owens 1974, 1993).

Thomas Aquinas was an accomplished philosopher and his thought may be understood simply in this fashion, as a penetrating account of the human person based on rational reflection. Indeed, the twentieth-century revival in appreciation for his thought in English-speaking countries has come primarily from philosophers rather than from theologians. However, Thomas was a preaching friar who held a chair in theology, rather than in the arts faculty. His philosophical vision was constantly informed by theological concerns. The teaching of the Averroists posed a threat to Christian teaching about death and individual responsibility. The teaching of the Cathars posed a threat to Christian teaching on the goodness of the body and the created order. From the first, the preaching mission of the *Ordo Fratrum Praedicatorum* was especially devoted to extolling the intrinsic goodness of material creation and the efficacy of the sacraments in the face of Catharism. The tag 'grace does not destroy nature but rather presupposes and perfects it',[1] expressed a vision common to all the early friars. Thomas himself was particularly noted for his devotion to the person of Christ as God made flesh, especially in the mystery of the Eucharist. This is related in the earliest biographies, which were written by fellow Dominicans

---

[1] *Quaestiones disputatae De veritate* 14. 10 ad 9; *ST* Ia 1. 8 ad 2; *ST* Ia 2. 2 ad 1 and elsewhere.

when many were still alive who remembered him (Bernard Gui 15, 26, 39; William Tocco 29, in K. Foster 1959: 78 n. 88; Prümmer and Laurent 1911–37.). His magnum opus, the *Summa Theologiae*, concerns the effect of grace on the powers, emotions, dispositions, and moral actions of the human creature. Thus Thomas's philosophical arguments concerning the nature of body and soul take their place within a theological scheme of the gift of creation and the redemption of sins through the power of the incarnation and the sacraments.

Among many areas of engagement between Catholic faith and Aristotelian reason, key to Thomas's attitude to death, indeed key to his theological approach more generally, is the nature of the soul and its relation to the body. In common with other medieval thinkers, Thomas understands the question of the goodness or badness of human death as a question of how human *nature* is affected by death. What effect does death have on the human being, understood as a natural unity of body and soul? What does bodily death mean for the body and what does it mean for the soul? Does the soul survive death? In what sense is death natural to human beings? These questions require a thorough account of the nature of the soul and of its relationship with the body in the case of a living human being, and, only on this basis, an enquiry into the separation of body and soul at death. The nature of soul with respect to body is a subject Thomas tackles many times: in his commentary on the *Sentences* of Peter Lombard; in the *Summa Contra Gentiles*; in the *Quodlibet* questions asked of him in public disputation; in his commentary on Aristotle's *De anima*; and also in two substantial works devoted to the subject: his *Quaestiones disputatae De anima* and his *De unitate intellectus contra Averroistas*. It is set out with particular clarity in the section of the *Summa Theologiae* that concerns the human being that provides the main framework for the following discussion.[2]

---

[2] The *Summa Theologiae* was intended as an introduction to theology for the training of Dominicans (Boyle 1982). It is divided into three parts: the first part (*prima pars*, Ia) concerns God, creation and human nature; the second part, which is divided into two (*prima secundae* IaIIae, *secunda secundae* IIaIIae), concerns the moral and spiritual life by which human beings find happiness in communion with God. The third part (*tertia pars* IIIa) concerns Christ and the sacraments by which the

SOUL AND BODY

Thomas starts his enquiry into the nature of the human being by asking whether the soul is a body of some kind (*ST* Ia 75. 1).[3] What he means by 'soul' is whatever it is that living things have and that non-living things lack. To have a soul (*anima*) is to be alive, *animate*. His first question is significant. Before Thomas can examine the relation of soul and body he first has to ask what kind of thing a 'soul' is. He starts with the question 'is the soul a body?' because of his conviction that human beings are best adapted to understand bodies, material objects that can be seen and touched. Thomas suggests that the human mind expands its understanding only slowly and painfully beyond such objects. If, as Thomas will argue, the soul is a 'something' which is not a material object, then the best way to understand the soul will be in comparison with and in relation to material objects.[4]

Thomas answers his question in this way: the soul is the source or 'principle' of the activities of a living thing (*vitalis operationis principium*) but it cannot just be any source of action or the eye, for example, would be a soul, for the animal sees through the action of the eye. If the source of life and movement were an organ (say the heart, the liver, or the brain) then, even so, the organ would not be life-giving simply in virtue of the fact that it was a body, for otherwise every body would be life-giving! Even on the assumption that there is a principal organ in the living body, the first principle of life would be, not any bodily organ *qua* body, but something about the organ,

spiritual life is represented and sustained. The final section of the third part, which would have considered the last things, was never completed. Each part of the *Summa* consists of a large number of questions, each of which in turn is divided into several articles. The *prima pars* contains 119 questions. After considering God in his unity, and as Trinity, there are questions on creation in general, on angels, and on the scriptural account of the six days of creation. This provides the context for 28 questions concerning human nature (*ST* Ia 75–102).

[3] Thomas gave the section *ST* Ia 75–102 the heading *De homine, qui ex spirituali et corporali substantia componitur*. The most important questions of this section are the first two: question 75 concerning the soul in itself; and question 76 concerning the soul in relation to the body.

[4] Thomas uses the same method with respect to God (*ST* Ia 3. 1) that he starts with: is God a body?

some property or 'actuality' (*actus*) of the organ in virtue of which it was alive and life-giving. The soul, therefore, is a not a physical moving part inside the organism (like an internal engine) but is the fundamental first principle which explains why the movements of this body are activities of a living being.

The question then arises: if the soul is not a physical part inside the body but is a property or actuality of the body as a living whole, is the soul something that exists in its own right? In other words, can the soul act or exist independently of the body, or is the soul something that exists only as a quality of a living body? The article that deals with this question (*ST* Ia 75. 2) is foundational for Thomas's account of the human soul. In order to argue, much later, that the soul can survive death, he must first argue that the soul is something that exists in its own right (*subsistens*). If the soul were only a quality of a living body and not something that really existed of itself, then obviously it could not survive the death of the body.

Thomas argues that thinking is not itself the activity of any bodily organ, because knowledge, as such, can be knowledge of *any* material object and so the intellect, through which one understands, cannot be composed of just one kind of material object. Knowing seems to be analogous to sensing, yet, in order to see different colours, the eye itself must be colourless, otherwise the only colour it could see would be its own colour. If the tongue itself was bitter, it could not taste sweet things—as happens when someone has a fever. If the soul contained any particular material, it would impede its knowing any other material thing. So, in order to know all material things, the rational soul must be no material thing. This argument is taken directly from Aristotle (*De anima* 3. 4. 429a), as is clear from Thomas's commentary on the passage (*Sententia super De anima* III. 7, 677–83). The human soul has an activity that is proper to it alone, and it is not limited to activities proper to the composite of soul-and-body. Thus the human soul is not only a quality of a body but is a something that exists in its own right.

Despite its endorsement by Aristotle, the key argument here is very weak. It relies on the analogy between sensing and intellectual knowing, but both Aristotle and Thomas are aware that this analogy is imperfect. Thinking is different from feeling in various ways, not least in that thought is communicable. Whereas two human beings can have the same kind of feeling, it seems that they cannot have the very same feeling: you cannot experience my pain as I experience it (Kenny 1969: 273–96). However, human beings can share and communicate the very same thought (the thought that the universe is between 10 and 20 billion years old, for example). Rather than basing his argument on a questionable analogy between perception and thought, it would have been better for Thomas to focus precisely on the difference between perception and thought, as he does in other places (*ST* Ia 84. 1). A thought is not limited to the particular circumstances of its origin. It is communicable or immaterial. Therefore, if thinking is engagement in thought which is communicable in this way, then there is at least one human activity that transcends the limits of the body (for a modern version of this argument see Braine 1993).

When it comes to other animals, Thomas asserts that they have sense but not intellect; therefore they have no activity that is not, essentially, an activity of some bodily organ; therefore the souls of other animals do not exist in their own right; and therefore they do not survive the death of the body (*ST* Ia 75. 3). However, unlike his teacher Albert, Thomas is not a keen observational scientist, and his knowledge of other animals mainly comes through Aristotle or Albert. While he attributes to animals an emotional life (*ST* IaIIae 40. 3, 46. 4) and an ability to calculate conclusions (*vis aestimativa*, *ST* Ia 78. 4), it seems that he underestimates the evidence for intellect among non-human animals. At least one contemporary Thomist (MacIntyre 2001: 21–61) allows that there is a body of evidence to suggest that some other animals (dolphins in particular) engage in thought. The interpretation of this is controversial but it seems rash to exclude the possibility of reason among other animals absolutely.

Nevertheless, it does not seem to be an essential element of Christian teaching that human beings are the only creatures to possess a spiritual life. After all, the presence of angels in classical Christian cosmology shows that there are intelligent species other than human beings who are included in the scheme of salvation and damnation (D. A. Jones 1992). Also, if the whole of creation is implicated in salvation (Romans 8: 19–23) this must include all animal creation in some fashion (Atkins 1999, 2000). Thankfully, it is possible to set aside Thomas's opinions on the question of the nature and salvation of non-human animals, for even if he is mistaken on this point it does not affect his central argument. That Thomas shows ignorance of the activities of other animals does not affect the validity of his argument with respect to the animal he knows best. His central point is that there is at least one animal that exhibits an activity of an immaterial kind, the animal *Homo sapiens*.

One possible objection to Thomas's position would be to say that, if the soul existed in its own right, it would be 'this thing' (*hoc aliquid*) whereas, in fact, it is the living human being as a whole, the composite of soul and body, that is 'this thing'. In his reply to this objection Thomas asserts that 'this thing' may be said in two senses (*ST* Ia 75. 2 ad 1; *Quaestiones disputatae De anima* 1 cf. Kretzmann 1993: 134 ff.). In the first sense it is said of any existing thing, and in this sense the soul is 'this thing', but in another sense 'this thing' is only what has a complete nature and is not merely a part. In this second sense the soul is *not* 'this thing'. This assertion represents an important qualification to the main argument: at the same time as arguing that the soul exists in its own right, Thomas also wishes to defend the essential unity of soul and body. Thus for Thomas, the soul considered in itself, even though it is an existing thing, is an *incomplete* thing.

The implications of this incompleteness are taken up more fully when Thomas asks whether the soul is the human being (*utrum anima sit homo*) (*ST* Ia 75. 4). According to Thomas the answer is 'no'. The soul is not a human being but is only part of a human being. It might be supposed that, if a soul is an independently existing being, then it must be a human person, for to be a person is simply to be 'an individual substance of a rational nature' (the classical definition given by Boethius, *De duabus naturis* c.2). Against this supposition, Thomas argues that as a hand or a foot is not an 'individual substance' so neither is the human soul an 'individual substance', for they are merely parts and do not possess the complete nature of the species. Hence the soul does not fall under the classical definition of a person (*ST* Ia 75. 4 ad 2). Thomas also gives a second argument: there are activities of the soul (sensation and imagination), which can be performed only by the soul and body together. Thus, it is only the composite that can perform the full range of natural human action and, therefore, only the composite which is the human person, properly speaking.⁵ Thomas's view may thus be expressed in terms of two parallel arguments: the soul has natural activities which are independent of the body, therefore it exists in its own right; the soul has natural activities which are dependent on the body, therefore it is not a complete substance.

From the fact that the soul is not a body (*ST* Ia 75. 1) it follows that the soul has no matter, for to have matter is to be a body.⁶ From this, and the fact that it exists in its own right (*ST* Ia 75. 2), the crux of the argument, it follows that the soul is, by nature, indestructible (*incorruptibilis ST* Ia 75. 6; cf. McCabe 1969; Gilson 1957: 187–8). Material things are susceptible to decay or destruction because the stuff of which they are made can take on a new form and turn into something else, for example flesh rotting or wood turning to ash. If the soul exists in its own right, independently of the stuff of the body then, even if the body rots away, the soul will continue to exist in some manner. This leads to a further question: if the soul is indestructible by nature, what happens to it at death when the human being, the composite of body and soul, decomposes? This is an issue at the heart of Thomas's approach to human death and to which he returned many times, for it gave him considerable difficulty. In due course it will be considered in detail, but it is better first to consider the remainder of these two questions of the *Summa Theologiae*, so as to understand the balance of Thomas's systematic thought on the soul. This will give a basis from which to consider the fate of the human soul at death and thus Thomas's attitude to death taken more generally.

The aim of question 75 as a whole is to demonstrate that the soul is something that exists in its own right, that has no matter, and that is

---

⁵ Thomas places a lot of weight on this argument and goes so far as to say that it was Plato's mistake of supposing that sensation was proper to the soul which led Plato to say that a human being was a soul *using* a body (*ST* Ia 75. 4).

⁶ *ST* Ia 75. 5 Throughout his analysis, Thomas invokes the Aristotelian categories of form and matter. In this context 'matter' is not defined as extended substance (as it would be by René Descartes), nor is it understood as a coalescence of solid indivisible atoms (as it was by Democritus and would be by the later atomists). Rather, matter is that out of which a material being comes to be, and the principle of potential for it to become something else. According to this understanding, matter is not a specific kind of stuff but is always relative to some form; cf. Physics 1. 7. 190a.

therefore indestructible. The last article of this question changes the focus somewhat: if the soul is immaterial and indestructible, is it the same sort of thing as an angel—wholly spiritual and with no essential relation to matter? (Thomas treats the nature of angels in detail in an earlier section of the *Summa*: *ST* Ia 50–64.) Thomas replies that the soul is, by nature, a different sort of thing from an angel. Each different angel is of a different kind (*species*) because angels are differentiated only by form and not by matter. Human beings, on the other hand, share the same species and nature as one another and are distinguished by matter, we might say, by their particular material and particular historical story. Angels are not distinguished from one another by who their parents are and where they were born and where they are now. Whether or not one believes in angels, the comparison of human beings with angels serves to make an important point: that, in contrast to angelic existence, human existence is essential bodily and historical. It is not the soul in abstraction from the body but this particular soul and its body that is a member of the human species. The last article of question 75 thus shifts attention away from the soul in itself and towards the nature of its union with the body, a subject treated in detail in question 76.

Within question 76 the first article (*ST* Ia 76. 1) is the key to all the others. Here Thomas argues that the intellectual soul is joined to the body as the first principle of the life of the human being. It therefore encompasses *all* the vital activities of the living being, both intellectual activities and bodily activities. As the principle of the life of the body cannot be a body (*ST* Ia 75. 1), so it must be the *form* of the body. The language of form and matter is taken from Aristotle's physics (*Physica* 2. 1–3). At a first approximation 'form' refers to shape and 'matter' refers to the stuff that is shaped. However, shape in this sense is not surface appearance but goes to the inherent shape or essence of what a thing is. When an animals dies, the stuff that it is made of separates out into its constituent chemicals. The stuff remains, but the particular animal has passed away. What makes this living being a plant or an animal of this particular species is not the stuff of which it is made but the shape it has at a fundamental level (which includes, we might say, its biochemistry and its genotype). The essence of a living thing is thus more to do with its form (so long as this word is used in a thoroughgoing sense) than with its matter.

Thomas calls the form which makes a particular thing the thing it is (a cabbage, a rabbit, or a human being) the 'substantial form'. Thus Thomas arrives at the formula: 'the intellectual soul is united to the body as its substantial form'.[7] The whole of Thomas's teaching on the soul may be summarized by saying that the human soul is both a real existing thing, and the form (in a thoroughgoing sense) of a living human being.

To assert this position Thomas has to overcome the objections of those of his contemporaries who followed Averroes, an Arabic commentator on Aristotle. Averroes wrote detailed commentaries on Aristotle and in the thirteenth century his interpretations became influential among certain philosophers in the arts faculties of Paris and elsewhere. These Latin Averroists argued that human beings did not think for themselves. Rather, all human thinking was the activity of a single intellect which thought in and through individual human beings. Hence, while Averroists agreed that thinking was an immaterial activity, they did not believe that individual human souls were indestructible by nature. Averroism was popular among medieval philosophers because it seemed to give a clear and coherent way to understand Aristotle. However, the interpretation of Aristotle provided by Averroes was not easily reconciled with Christian teaching on the responsibility and destiny of individual human beings.

Thomas Aquinas felt it necessary to expend a great deal of energy in combating this position, both as a credible reading of Aristotle and as a credible account of reality.[8] He argued that, if the intellect is not the principle of life of *this* body, then there is no way to explain how

---

[7] *anima intellectiva unitur corpori ut forma substantialis* (*ST* Ia 76. 6) cf. *ST* Ia 76. 1.

[8] Among contemporary academic philosophers even the defenders of Thomas concede that his account of the soul is strained as an interpretation of Aristotle (J. T. Martin 1993; Treloar 1990; Reyna 1972). The argument between Thomas and Averroes concerns issues that make sense only in a much later intellectual context, downstream of other commentators and motivated by other questions. At best, Thomas must be understood as having developed Aristotle's ideas to produce something new that was nevertheless true to the spirit of Aristotle. The overriding concern for Thomas was not simply to establish an anthropology that would accord with his theological beliefs (*pace* Reyna) but also to defend the essential unity of the human person. At this point even Aristotle faltered, for his account of intellect left it unclear how the soul, and indeed, how the rational animal, was one being. Thomas's great insight was to realize that the principle of human intellectual life must be one with the substantial principle of being and life.

these thoughts are the thoughts of *this* human being. If an external intellect were to grasp the intelligibility of images (*phantasmata*) in my imagination, this would not mean that I was thinking, but that someone else was thinking about me. Images and perceptions are not themselves the understandings of the mind but are things *understood* by the mind, just as the colours on the wall are not acts of seeing but things seen. More fundamentally, the doctrine of Averroes seems to contradict universal human experience that 'each one is conscious that it is he himself who understands'.[9] The Averroist position has some initial plausibility because, as mentioned above, it is the case that the same identical thought can be thought by different people.[10] However, the Averroist account cannot explain how there are different *thinkers*, not just different occasions of the identical thought. Nor can it explain how one person's actual knowledge is greater that someone else's.

Granted that Thomas's account of the *unity* of the soul (at once intellectual, sensitive, and vegetative) of a human individual is superior to that of the Averroists, it remains for him to account for the *multiplication* of human souls in different individuals. According the categories developed by Aristotle, material beings of the same kind are different because the same essential form shapes different pieces of material stuff. Rabbits have the same form, they are members of the same species, but this rabbit is composed of this stuff while that rabbit is composed of that stuff. On the other hand, purely immaterial beings such as angels cannot be differentiated by matter. It is for this reason that Thomas holds that it is impossible to have two angels of the same species, 'just as, apart from matter, it would be impossible for there to be several whitenesses or several humanities' (*ST* Ia 50. 4).

How, then, can a form which exists in its own right, the human soul, nevertheless be multiplied within the same human species? Thomas answers that, whereas human souls are not made of matter nor are they limited only to material activity, they are, nevertheless,

---

[9] *experitur enim unusquisque seipsum esse qui intelligit* (*ST* Ia 76. 1).
[10] A view opposed by many empiricists but rediscovered by modern analytical philosophers following Frege.

the forms of particular material beings, and for this reason souls are multiplied according to the number of material bodies.

What happens, however, when the soul is separated from the body at death? Does the soul coalesce with all the other separated souls, no longer differentiated by being the forms of different bodies? Or is the soul extinguished? Or does the individual soul somehow survive despite being separated from the body? Thomas answers that the unity of something follows its existence. He has shown that the intellectual soul is indestructible and retains its existence after death (*ST* Ia 75. 6), therefore each soul must retain its unity after death. This conforms to the general truth that number follows being: 'we must judge of the multiplicity of a thing as we judge of its being' (*idem est iudicium de multiplicatione rei, et de esse ipsius; ST* Ia 76. 2 ad 2).

There are a number of human souls of the same species because there are a number of human bodies and the soul is, *of its essence,* the form of a body. It is not by accident or as a punishment for sins of a past life that soul and body are joined, but it is intrinsic to the nature of the soul that it is the principle of life of this particular body. Nevertheless, while souls are multiplied *according to* bodies, this does not mean that the soul is individuated *by* the body.[11] As the soul can act through itself without the body, its 'act of being', what makes it the thing it is, is proportioned to the body, but is not dependent on

---

[11] More fundamentally, one might question the sense in which matter is ever, of itself, the *cause* of individuation. (R. A. O'Donnell 1959; C. Martin 1988: 65–9; Owens 1988, 1994; Potts 1995; Dewan 1999). Clearly material forms are multiplied in matter and this is possible because of materiality. Yet the material aspect is always 'that from which' and the potential aspect of a thing that *actually* exists through a particular substantial form, for 'form is the principle of existence' (*ST* Ia 76. 2 and elsewhere). Material things are individuals only inasmuch as they exist through some actual form. Neither is material identity constituted by the identity of each and every material part, for in a living body the matter is constantly changing but is informed by the same form (*Summa Contra Gentiles* IV. 81; Veatch 1974; Charlton 1972; Anscombe 1983*d*, 1961). What makes this thing *this* thing is its individual substantial form, even though it is also true that some such forms can exist only as the actuality of matter. 'Even in regard to existence in matter, then, and in regard to the undefined dimensions that individuate, the form of the material thing is the cause of the individuation. It causes the individuation not insofar as it is simply a form, but insofar as it is a form meant by its own nature to actuate a particular portion of matter' (Owens 1994: 185).

the body for its existence. Thomas is explicit on this point in the *Summa Contra Gentiles*:

It has been shown that the human soul is a form independent of matter as to its being. Wherefore it follows that souls are indeed multiplied according as bodies are multiplied, and yet the multiplication of bodies is not the cause of the multiplication of souls.[12]

Thomas also expresses this by saying that the human soul differs essentially from an angel in that it is able to be united to a human body (*unibilis corpori humano Quaestiones disputatae De anima* 3) as its substantial form. The soul cannot to united to just any body but this soul is able to be united as the form of this particular body. Moreover, the human soul continues to exist as an individual after its separation from the body in death because it is not the kind of form that is limited to matter: it has its own proper action *independent* of matter. Human souls are thus metaphysically peculiar in that they are, essentially, the forms of certain bodies, but also, they are capable of action independent of the body, and therefore they exist in their own right. Hence they are multiplied according to bodies (as are the souls of all animals) but also they can exist separately from the body (as angels do).

These two questions (*ST* Ia 75, 76), taken together, present the heart of Thomas's teaching on the soul. It is instructive to note the authorities cited in the *sed contra* for each article.[13] In question 75, on the nature of the soul in itself, four out of seven citations are from Augustine, two are from Dionysius, and none is from Aristotle. In question 76 only one out of eight is from Augustine, none is from Dionysius, whereas five are from Aristotle. This is because the former

[12] *Summa Contra Gentiles* II. 81. 'But the human soul differs from other forms in this, that its being does not depend on the body; neither does its being individuated depend on its body' (*Quaestiones disputatae De anima* 3; cf. *De unitate intellectus contra Averroistas* 104; *Quaestiones disputatae De spiritualibus creaturi* 9 ad 3). Thus Geach (1961: 99; 1969: 23) seems mistaken in ascribing to Thomas the view that what individuates a separated soul is its continuing relationship to *this* parcel of matter to which it could be reunited.

[13] 'But, on the other hand...' This gives not the considered final answer but simply a prima facie reason for holding to the position. Generally, though not always, the *sed contra* represents Thomas's own view. Generally, though not always, it will be an appeal to some authority.

question is concerned centrally with defending the existence in its own right of the individual soul, a project welcomed by Christian Neoplatonists,[14] whereas the latter question concerns the soul as the 'form of the body', a distinctively Aristotelian conception of the soul. Though Thomas is only one of many thirteenth-century thinkers to attempt to assimilate Aristotelian psychology within a Christian world view, he is remarkable for his clarity and for his critical stance towards the main Arabic commentators on Aristotle. Many theologians took enthusiastically to the synthesis of Avicenna, who had mixed his Aristotelianism with a heavy dose of Neoplatonism. Avicenna considered that the essence of the soul could be understood quite apart from its relationship to the body. This led Albert the Great to say that one should not say that the intellectual soul is the 'form' of a material body, but that it is the first act or perfection of a material body.[15] Bonaventure held that the soul, in order to subsist, must contain matter of some kind ('spiritual matter') and that the body must possess a substantial form of materiality that it did not receive from the intellectual soul.[16] The Franciscan school after him postulated a plurality of forms or souls in the human being.[17] On the other hand, there were philosophers in the arts faculty who approached the text of Aristotle primarily through the commentary of Averroes. They considered Avicenna to have confused the clear teaching of Aristotle and they devoted themselves to expounding Aristotle in the most precise and most radical way possible. The most notable of these Latin Averroists was Siger of Brabant (Dales 1995: 132 ff.; Zedler 1968: 1–11).

Thomas could be thought of as a middle term between a Christian Platonist who thinks of the human being as a union of two distinct

---

[14] Though Augustine was critical of many aspects of Platonism, he favoured no alternative philosophical school and, in a thirteenth-century context, appears in some ways Neoplatonic. 'After reading Augustine's polemic against the Platonic and Origenist anthropology in the *City of God* it is strange to reflect how he is often spoken of as the arch-Platonizer of Christian thought' (Suttor 1970: 258).

[15] Albertus Magnus, *Summa de Creaturis* II. 4. 1. 6 (Dales 1995: 89–98; Park 1980; Pegis 1934: 77–120).

[16] Bonaventure, *Commentaria in IV libros Sentiarum* II. 17. 1. 2 (Dales 1995: 99–107; Pegis 1934: 26–76).

[17] R. Cross 1999: 74; Weisheipl 1983: 285–92; Dales 1995: 106, 192–202; cf. *ST* Ia 76. 3, 76. 4.

substances (the soul and the body); and a radical Aristotelian who thinks that there is only one intellect that is active in different material human beings. Yet, it would be a great mistake to see the position of Thomas as an ad hoc compromise between alternatives which have mutual exclusive rationales. There is, rather, a single and coherent rationale in the account of the soul given by Thomas. His move is to assert that the human soul is at the same time something that exists in its own right which can act without a body and the substantial form of the human body. The idea is essentially simple, but its implications are complex and the influence of Avicenna (on the one hand) and Averroes (on the other) prevented any of his contemporaries from attaining the same clarity as Thomas attained on this point.

Immediately after his death there was an attempt by conservative elements to condemn Thomas's position that the soul was the only substantial form in a human being (Dales 1995). Thomas's view was eventually vindicated against the charge of heterodoxy, and the tag that the rational soul is, of itself, the form of the human body was defined as Catholic dogma at the Council of Vienna in 1311 (Tanner 1990: 361). Nevertheless, this account of the soul was far from being the universally understood and accepted Catholic doctrine of the high Middle Ages, nor was it the dominant view in the Renaissance and early modern period (Treloar 1990; Kennedy 1988). In its essentials, this debate is still ongoing: contemporary Anglophone philosophy of mind consists of a few advocates of more or less sophisticated forms of mind–body dualism struggling against the dominance of more or less sophisticated forms of materialism. What Thomas Aquinas offers is an account of the rational animal that is neither dualistic nor materialist. In recent years, dissatisfaction with dualistic and materialist accounts of the person, and interest in the human person as a language-using animal,[18] have created a context within which Thomas's

---

[18] Significant in this shift was the influence of Ryle (1949) and the later Wittgenstein (1953), though one might also mention such diverse contemporary philosophers as Midgely (1980) and Wiggins (1980) who have stressed that human beings are animals of a particular sort, yet without falling into reductionist materialism.

non-reductive conception of the unity of the human person can receive a sympathetic hearing.[19] The basis for Thomas's account of human nature is his use of the Aristotelian categories of form and matter to understand the relation of soul and body. Nevertheless, for Thomas Aquinas, unlike Aristotle (who is frustrating silent on this point), no account of the soul could be considered comprehensive which did not include consideration of the state of the soul after death. It is not only modern philosophers such as Heidegger who have held that an adequate understanding of human nature must include some grasp of the meaning of human death; this was already true in the thirteenth century. Many times during his career Thomas returned to the topic of human death. He sought to understand death through discussion of the state of the separated soul (*anima separata*), that is, the state of the human soul which has been separated from the body by death.

THE SEPARATED SOUL

The most important article of the *Summa* for Thomas's treatment of the state of the soul after death (*ST* Ia 84. 7) is also a very significant article in its own right.[20] It poses the apparently rather technical question: can the intellect act without actualizing the imagination in some way?[21] Thomas is clear in his answer: in this present state of life (*secundum praesentis vitae statum*) the intellect cannot understand anything without turning to *phantasmata*, that is, to objects of the imagination. He gives two empirical grounds to support this assertion. First, the influence which injury or lethargy have on the intellect is obvious, yet the intellect is not, of itself, the power of a bodily organ (*ST* Ia 75. 2). Therefore, if the intellect can be impeded by material factors, this must be because it needs to make use of some

---

[19] Geach 1969; Kenny 1984, 1989; Braine 1993; Klima 1997; Haldane 1998.

[20] *ST* Ia 84. 7 is perhaps the most significant article of the *Summa Theologiae* on the nature of the soul outside questions *ST* Ia 75 and *ST* Ia 76, which have formed the basis of the previous section of this chapter.

[21] *Utrum intellectus possit actu intelligere per species intelligibiles quas penes se habet, non convertendo se ad phantasmata* (*ST* Ia 84. 7).

other power (i.e. the imagination) which itself *is* the operation of some bodily organ. Secondly, we actually experience that in order to understand we need to use images and examples.

Thomas goes on to explain why the intellect requires the imagination. The human mind is most apt to understand material objects. Yet, in order to understand individual material beings one must grasp not only their forms, but also the fact of their present individual materiality. This second act cannot be done by intellect alone but only by the imagination grasping the individual by sense (for material objects are not distinguished solely on the basis of form but as 'this-here'). Thomas thinks that angels can grasp singulars, even without the use of sense, but that this sort of angelic intellectual grasp is beyond the power of the human intellect, which works by abstraction from sensible things. The human intellect works by the use of the senses; hence, human beings can only have an indirect and imperfect knowledge of purely immaterial beings such as angels. A deeper question now seems unavoidable: if the human mind depends on the human imagination, which itself is an act of a bodily organ (the brain), how can the intellect act when it is in a disembodied state? The problem is not confined to the acquisition of new knowledge. It seems that, without recourse to the imagination, the soul would be unable actually to consider even the knowledge it already possesses. Further, if, as Thomas holds, something can only be said to exist if it can act in some way, is it still tenable to argue that human souls can exist at all in the separated state?

Thomas faces this problem head on with a question devoted to the scope of the intellectual activity in the separated soul (*ST* Ia 89). He develops the position that, when separated, the soul has a different mode of acting (*modus operandi*) (*ST* Ia 89. 1, cf. *Summa Contra Gentiles* II. 81) which follows from its different state. When in the body, it acts according to its union with the body, and when separated, it understands in a separated way, as do other separated intellects; that is to say, it has an understanding like that of the angels. Thomas had set out this position in some earlier works, however, by the time he was writing the *Summa Theologiae* he was much less comfortable with this answer than he had once been. In the *Summa Contra Gentiles* Thomas had written that the separated soul would enjoy a *more* perfect knowledge than it possessed while it was informing a living body. 'Wherefore when it shall be wholly separated from the body, it will be perfectly likened to separated substances as to the manner of understanding and will receive their influence abundantly' (*Summa Contra Gentiles* II. 81).

But this makes it seem as though the body where a hindrance to the soul! Such a view would be conducive to a Neoplatonist such as Ambrose, but it runs counter to Thomas's whole project.[22] Thomas needs to defend the possibility of knowledge in a separated soul, while insisting that it is better off when it is embodied. Thomas's view developed on this issue between writing the *Summa Contra Gentiles* and writing the *Summa Theologiae* (Pegis 1974). The later discussion (*ST* Ia 89. 1) is dominated by the concept of nature, a term wholly absent from his earlier consideration of the issue (*Summa Contra Gentiles* II. 81). He starts by saying that, if the mode of action, involving the imagination, were accidental to the nature of the soul 'as the Platonists said', then the difficulty would vanish. For, when the soul was separated from the body, it would return to its natural state and natural mode of operation. Yet this is unreasonable because then the soul would be better off without the body. The body is adapted for the sake of the soul, as in general matter is for the sake of form, and not vice versa. Yet the body would not exist for the sake of the soul if the soul were better off without it!

In that case, however, the union of soul and body would not be for the soul's good, for evidently it would understand worse in the body than out of it; but for the good of the body, which would be unreasonable, since matter exists on account of form, and not form for the sake of matter. (*ST* Ia 89. 1)

On the other hand, Thomas cannot admit that imagination is *absolutely* required for the working of the human intellect, or else the soul could not exist separated from the body. His solution is to say that the human intellect does have another possible mode of action when separated from the body but it can act in this way only very imperfectly because it is not its *natural* manner of action.[23] The

---

[22] The defence of the significance of the body was fundamental, not only to Thomas's Aristotelianism but, more radically, to his evangelical mission to overcome the Catharist distortion of the Gospel.

[23] Some later theologians reversed this move and again claimed that separated souls had a clearer understanding *because* of their separation from the body (Kennedy 1988).

soul is, by nature, the form of a particular body. Thus, if it continues to exist without the body, it is, as it were, out of its proper place, forced away from what its fitting, natural, and congenial.

Now the soul has one mode of being when in the body and another when apart from it, its nature remaining always the same, but this does not mean that its union with the body is an accidental thing. For, on the contrary, such union belongs to its very nature, just as the nature of a light object is not changed, when it is in its proper place, which is natural to it, and outside its proper place which is [beyond] its nature (*ei praeter naturam*). (*ST* Ia 89. 1)

How can it be that souls have a better understanding through the body than when separated if understanding is essentially an immaterial act? Thomas answers that there are different grades of intellect from the highest to the lowest angel. The highest angels understand more things through fewer but more powerful concepts (*species*). The lower angels have a grasp of fewer things and in a less profound way and require more concepts to do so. On this gradation human intellect is the lowest and so, if it were to depend only on the understanding it could have in the separated state, the knowledge it could have would not be complete but only confused and general (*non perfectam sed confusam in communi*; *ST* Ia 89. 1). Thus it is for the soul's good that it is, by nature, the form of a material body by which it can get a better grasp of intellectual things through abstraction from the senses than it could in a pure way. Thomas uses the analogy of less intelligent people who can understand better with the help of many examples rather than with a few simple powerful concepts that are more difficult to grasp.

The answer to the question, 'how can the separated soul understand without phantasms?' is the same throughout Thomas's writings: the soul has a different mode of acting that goes with its different mode of existing. Yet what is new in his later writings is the stress upon the nature of the soul. The understanding it can have without the body is confused and imperfect due to its uncongenial state. Though it is possible for the soul to act when separated from the body, such a mode of action lies beyond what is natural to it (*ei praeter naturam*). It goes against the grain, so to speak.

Thomas goes on to consider what things the soul could know in its separated state. It would have a knowledge of its own nature and this at least would be clearer than its knowledge of the soul while on earth. It would also be able to consider things it had learnt in its mortal life on earth, but without the benefit of the imagination. It would, by nature, receive intellectual understandings as the angels do, from God, but these it would understand only in a weak way. It would have no ability to acquire knowledge from the senses or acquire new knowledge of what was happening on earth. It would have no better knowledge of God than it possessed while on earth. By nature it would have a pretty miserable existence (Rousseau 1979; Geach 1961: 100; Davies 1992: 216–17). If the soul has less perfect grasp of singulars (*ST* Ia 89. 4) and has no access to the imagination, then this will restrict rationality and the intellectual virtues. Many of the characteristic human virtues concern the ordering of singulars (most notably prudence) and those virtues which ordered the passions (courage and temperateness) could not be present at all, except virtually. Finally, the diminution of natural reason would mean a diminution even of the soul's natural knowledge of God, for there is no direct knowledge of God by nature, in this life or the next. Thomas describes the state of the soul in death as a strange and unhappy half-life: an existence without sensation, imagination, warmth, or colour, without any access to what is happening on earth, without the ability to think and reason in the accustomed and natural way, but only, like a fish out of water, by means of naked abstract thought. Elsewhere, Thomas considers the blessedness of the soul which is granted the vision of God, a topic which will be considered below, but he carefully distinguishes this supernatural and gratuitous gift of God from what can be said of the separated soul on the basis of nature. The place of the beatific vision as the fruition of the life of grace is not to be confused with an understanding of what death is by nature for the human being. Of itself, death is the destruction of the human being as a living whole and is the displacement of the soul into an unnatural and diminished state.

IS DEATH NATURAL?

Human beings are animals, though animals of a particular sort with a rational soul which exists in its own right. Therefore, before considering death in human animals, it is useful first to take the case of animals without intellect which, therefore, have a soul that cannot exist apart from the body. In all material beings, death comes because a disorder in the body overcomes the life principle (*ST* IaIIae 72. 5, 73. 2, 74. 4). This may happen because of disease or injury, but it may also happen through the exhaustion of the powers of the soul in old age. This is not because death could be the proper object of some action of the animal. Death is to be understood as a *loss* of life, and privation does not have a cause *per se*. Further, as Albert the Great observed, nothing is destructive of itself ('*nihil corrumptivum sui*'; *Quaestiones de Animalibus* XVI. 4). There is no death 'instinct' nor is dying as such an action of the animal. Dying is always something suffered by an animal, not something done. The 'natural death' of an animal comes as the natural powers reach their limit and are unable to sustain the activities that maintain bodily integrity, especially, according to Albert, the maintenance of body heat (*Quaestiones de Animalibus* XVI. 5).

This may be illustrated by imagining what happens when a glacier is in retreat and is withdrawing up a mountain valley. In such a case the ice does not move up the hill, for that would be against its natural downward motion (due to gravity). What actually happens is rather that the snowfall replenishing the glacier (at the top) is no longer able to equal the loss due to melting (at the bottom). So the glacier is moving down but it is melting more quickly than it is moving. The glacier is not being replenished quickly enough to sustain its existence, hence it retreats until it reaches its source and then finally disappears altogether. In an analogous way, the animal's powers continue to aim to replenish the animal's reserves and to sustain the animal in being, but the losses due to being acted upon from outside become more than the animal can replace, until finally its fundamental order is compromised and its vital principle of order is destroyed.

Every power of a physical body is weakened by continuous action, for as a body acts it is also acted upon by external forces. Therefore the transforming power is strong at first so as to be able to transform not only enough for the renewal of what is lost, but also for growth. Later on it can only transform enough for the renewal of what is lost, and then growth ceases. At last it cannot even do this and then it begins to decline. Finally when this power fails altogether the animal dies.   (*ST* Ia 119. 1 ad 4)

In the *Summa Contra Gentiles* Thomas denies that brute animals have any desire for perpetual being, except as relates to the species. This is part of an argument for the indestructibility of the human soul based on the human desire for perpetual being.[24] In the *Summa Theologiae* this view is qualified. It may be that an animal cannot grasp perpetual being as such (for that would require an act of the intellect), but an animal can perpetually desire to be, even though it cannot desire to be perpetually. Each part is ordered first towards its own perfection as a part, and then through this, to the whole (*ST* Ia 65. 2). The individual animal is ordered towards its species, and that species towards the perfection of the universe as a whole, but as a part, as a particular nature, it also desires to remain in being as long as it can. Thus, the death of the particular individual animal can be seen to be opposed to the proper object of its natural powers (which strive to keep the animal in being), though it is natural that these powers have a finite limit and are eventually overcome by other natural causes. Thomas expresses this in terms of particular and universal nature: death is contrary to the particular nature of the animal but is in accordance with universal nature.[25]

Each thing's particular nature has its own proper active and conservative power; according to this all corruption and defect is against nature, as is said in *De caelo* (1. 6. 288b) because this power tends to the being and conservation of that which is. On the other hand, universal nature . . . tends to the good and conservation of the universe, which requires alternate generation and corruption in things. According to this, corruption and defect are natural.[26]

For an animal whose soul cannot exist independently of matter, death is in one way against nature and in another way it is natural. It is against the nature of the particular form that strives to remain in

---

[24] 'In brute animals there is not found any appetite to perpetual being . . . For, since the sensitive soul does not apprehend except here and now, it cannot possibly apprehend perpetual existence'(*Summa Contra Gentiles* II. 82).

[25] 'Death and the other defects of nature are the effects of universal nature; and yet the particular nature rebels against them as far as it can' (*ST* IaIIae 42.2 ad 3).

[26] *ST* IaIIae 85. 6, translating *intendo* as 'tends' throughout.

being, but it is in accordance with the order of nature. For nature acts to conserve not the individual, but rather the species through the generation and passing away of many individuals. The good of an individual animal is given by the species and is for the species, and this is shown by the fact that animals act in the same way in similar circumstances according to the instincts of their nature. Yet those instincts serve, not only to perpetuate the species indefinitely, but also to perpetuate the individual up to its allotted span. It is therefore natural for any individual animal to fear death and strive against it, even though such a struggle will be one in which it will eventually be overcome.

Human beings, as animals, face death as in one sense natural to them, in another sense against their particular nature. Yet human beings are unlike other animals as regards the intellectual soul which is, of itself, immortal and indestructible, so that immortality is *more natural* to human beings than to other animals. However, as regards matter, human beings are just as liable to decomposition as any other animal, and indeed as any 'mixed' bodies—a category which includes animals, plants, and inanimate material objects.

Thomas states (*ST* IaIIae 85. 6) that, whereas the indestructible soul is adapted to its end, which is everlasting happiness (*beatitudo*), the body is in one way adapted to the soul, and in another way not. In respect of its nature it is so adapted (for the soul is the form of the body and it understands by means of the senses), but as regards its susceptibility to decay it is not so adapted. Thomas gives the example of a craftsman who chooses iron as a useful substance for making a knife, on account of its hardness and flexibility. Yet in choosing this he does not choose that the knife should also be breakable and susceptible to rust, for these are beyond his intention, not willed or adapted to the purpose but tolerated. So the body is well adapted for sensation, but its natural susceptibility to decay is not adapted to its final end and is not chosen as such by God. Nevertheless, God was able to supply the defect of nature, which he did in creating human beings in original justice, with the potential for immortality.

The concept of original justice, and the related concept of original sin, brings to light another distinction which must be made with regard to the naturalness of human death. In one way death has a natural cause—the susceptibility of the body to decay due to its mixed nature, but in another way the proper cause of human death is sin—through which human beings lost the super-added gift of immortality. Thomas reiterates several times that human death is the result of the sin of Adam: 'Death comes to all human beings from the sin of the first parent' (*ST* IIIa 14. 4 ad 3 and elsewhere).

This is not to deny that, in some sense, it is natural for the human body to decay. Human bodies are composed of contraries and thus they are, by nature, liable to be destroyed. If, then, human death is in accordance with nature, how can it also be due to sin? Thomas says that there is a double causality at work. Given the current condition of the body, it is naturally destructible, yet this was not the original or intended condition of the body. Rather, human nature has been stripped of a gift that had completed its nature, so that what is deficient would once have been supplied and in that state it could have reached its proper goal of everlasting happiness with God while remaining in the body.

> The cause of death and other corporal defects of human nature is twofold: the first is remote, and results from the material principles of the human body, inasmuch as it is made of contraries. But this cause was held in check by original justice. Hence the proximate cause of death and other defects is sin, because of which original justice has been lost. (*ST* IIIa 14. 3 ad 3)

Thomas devotes a whole article to the question of whether death is a punishment for the sin of the first parents (*ST* IIaIIae 164. 1). There he repeats the argument set out earlier when considering the naturalness of death (*ST* IaIIae 85. 6). Death is against the nature of the soul, which is indestructible, but it is in accordance with the nature of the body, which is composed of contraries. In general the body is adapted to its purpose, as for example the organs of sensation are apt for their purpose, yet the body's susceptibility to decay stems not from the body being adapted to a purpose, but rather from natural necessity. For an organ of sense must be composed of contraries and what is composed of contraries is destructible. Hence, if it were possible, the matter ought to be *both* adapted to sensing and indestructible. Analogously, people would have made knives out of iron without the susceptibility of rusting if they could have (and indeed now that they can, they do). So also God remedied this natural weakness by giving human beings the super-added gift of immortality, so that the human body might in every way be adapted to the purpose of human life. Yet, this original gift was lost because of sin, depriving human beings of what would have completed their nature. Sin, then, is the proximate cause of human mortality.

When God first made the human being he conferred on him the favour of being exempt from the necessity resulting from such matter. However, this favour was withdrawn due to the sin of the first parents. Accordingly death is both natural on account of a condition attaching to matter, and a punishment on account of the loss of the Divine gift preserving the human being from death.[27] (*ST* IIaIIae 164. 1 ad 1)

Thomas gives an account of the character of the gift of original justice at the end of the *prima pars* of the *Summa Theologiae*. Here he follows Augustine very closely (*CD* XIV. 10 and elsewhere), though developing some points through his own interest in natural philosophy. Like Augustine, Thomas is clear that the graced life of Adam would not have been like the state in the resurrection (*ST* Ia 97. 3). In Eden, Adam would have eaten and drunk, slept and worked, married and produced offspring—had he been granted the time to do so—but in the resurrection there will be no need for food and drink and there will be no more generation. Thus, when Thomas asks whether, in Eden, Adam would have suffered from death and destruction (*ST* Ia 97. 1), he is required to distinguish three sorts of indestructibility: first there is the indestructibility of substances who have no matter (angels) or matter which is potential to only one form (heavenly bodies): these substances are indestructible by nature; second there is the indestructibility of that which would be destructible by nature but which is preserved by some inherent principle: this will be the

---

[27] The fact that death is a punishment for original sin does not mean that it falls on everyone equally, for some die young or violently and others in old age and in peace. Thomas says that the bad consequences of the loss of this gift are not all distributed equally or in accordance to just rewards, because many of these effects are accidental to the original loss itself. The loss of original justice and the susceptibility to death is a fair punishment, but the *manner* of someone's death is not related to his or her sinfulness. Yet in another way, Thomas insists, Providence also orders these varying effects, not so that they are equal or proportionate to sin, but so as to give some the opportunity for repentance, or the opportunity to show virtue. Others may even die in such a way as to punish their parents, but not necessarily on account of their own sins (*ST* IIaIIae 164. 1 ad 4).

state of the bodies of the saints after the resurrection; third there is the indestructibility of something which is preserved by some external efficient cause so as to be protected from destruction as long as this cause acts: this last is the potential immortality which Adam had, and which he lost by the fall.

For the human body was indissoluble not by reason of any intrinsic vigour of immortality, but by reason of a supernatural force given by God to the soul, whereby it was enabled to preserve the body from all corruption so long as it remained itself subject to God. (*ST* Ia 97. 1)

Thomas is able to give a detailed account of the sense in which death is natural to the human creature and the sense in which death is unnatural. Because Thomas is concerned with the category of nature (see Pegis 1974), there are some things that he can explain more comprehensively than can Augustine. In his discussion of death Augustine asks the question why baptism, which removes the guilt of sin, does not restore the baptized to a state of immortality (*CD* XIII. 4). He suggests that, if baptism had conferred immortality, people would have wanted to be baptized for the wrong reason. Also, there would not be an opportunity for their faith to be tested. It was argued above (in Chapter 4) that the second of these reasons, the contest of the faith, touches on a deep theme in Christian theology and needs to be taken very seriously. However, the first of these reasons seems ad hoc and does not engage with the fundamental question. If people who prayed were always given what they asked for, some people might pray for the wrong reasons; but, nevertheless, God does *sometimes* answer prayers in a straightforward and obvious way. However, baptized infants are not *sometimes* made immortal—they never are. The concept of nature allows Thomas to give a more satisfying reply to this question. He answers that, as original sin came from a personal sin but then affected human nature, so people are first saved in what regards the person (sin and guilt) and only then, in due order, will they be saved in what regards human nature (the overcoming of suffering and death in the general resurrection). Thus, though physical death is a result of sin, forgiveness does not lead to immortality immediately because the problem has become a problem of *nature* to be dealt with when nature as a whole is redeemed: Christ's resurrection being a sign and an anticipation.

Consequently by baptism [God] immediately takes away from the baptised person the guilt of original sin and the punishment of being deprived of the heavenly vision. But the punishments of this present life, such as death, hunger, thirst, and the like, pertain to the *nature* from the principles of which they arise, inasmuch as it is deprived of original justice. Therefore these defects will not be taken away until the ultimate restoration of nature through the glorious resurrection. (*ST* IIIa 69. 3 ad 3; emphasis added)

Thomas is clear that death was neither part of the original state, nor will it be part of the final state of the human creature. Death is, rather, a consequence of sin. Thomas can even go so far as to say that mortality can be thought of as a property which human nature acquired through sin and which is taken away by Christ (*Summa Contra Gentiles* IV. 81). Thomas's account is admirably clear but seems to presuppose a reading of Genesis that raises difficult questions for contemporary Christians, both from the perspective of scriptural exegesis and from the perspective of evolutionary biology. These issues will be addressed in the next chapter through a discussion of the thought of Karl Rahner, a twentieth-century Catholic theologian strongly influenced by Thomas Aquinas.

Thomas argues that, for all animals, death is contrary to the particular nature of each, but it is natural in regard to the cycle of generation and decay in universal nature. Furthermore, for all animals, death can properly be said to be natural in regard to the body, which is naturally susceptible to decay and destruction. However, in human beings death is contrary to nature in regard to the soul, for the human soul is by nature indestructible. Furthermore, while Thomas argues that the human soul can exist apart from the body, this state of separation is, in an important sense, contrary to its nature. The human being thus rightly recoils from physical death. By the criterion of what is fulfilling to human nature—understood as a unity of body and soul—death is in itself a *bad thing*. On this fundamental point Thomas Aquinas comes to the same conclusion as Augustine. Though they drew on different philosophical resources, both came to see the dangers of a philosophical disintegration of the human being.[28] It is

---

[28] By Neoplatonists in the case of Augustine; by radical Aristotelians such as Averroes (on one side) and Neoplatonists such as Avicenna (on the other) in the case of Thomas.

interesting to note that both Augustine and Thomas were made more aware of these dangers through their struggle against contemporary religious movements which involved a dualistic repudiation of the flesh.[29] Thus theological controversy sharpened their philosophical sensitivity.

As with Ambrose and Augustine, Thomas's theological and philosophical anthropology shaped his practical approach to death and dying. This is expounded below first in relation to bringing death about by homicide and suicide, then in relation to the fear of death, the hope of heaven, and the care for the dead.[30]

HOMICIDE AND SUICIDE

Thomas's most important and influential discussion of homicide is in question 64 of the *secunda secundae* of the *Summa Theologiae*.[31] He starts with a general question as to whether the killing of any animal is wrong (*ST* IIaIIae 64. 1). He replies with the authority of Augustine (*CD* I. 20) and Aristotle (*Politica* 1. 8. 1256b) that animals are ordered by nature for human use. For material things are ordered towards things with sense and things with sense towards things with intellect; there is no sin in using something for what it is for. As a defence of meat-eating this must be admitted to be rather thin. It is in part based on a classification of non-human animals which was not well informed by observation. It is further based on a rather rough schematization and of the place of animals in creation which seems excessively anthropocentric. The Scriptures, in contrast, often refer to animals as being created to give glory to God by their existence and not only so as to be useful for human beings in a crudely pragmatic sense (D. A. Jones 1992). This is an example of an area that Thomas treats

---

[29] By Manichees in the case of Augustine; by Cathars in the case of Thomas.

[30] The importance of context is demonstrated by the whole plan of the *Summa Theologiae* which places moral enquiry (*secunda pars*) between discussion of God, creation, and human nature (*prima pars*) and discussion of Christ, the sacraments, and the last things (*tertia pars*). Such deliberate architecture suggests that Thomas himself desired that prominence be given to the theological/anthropological context before engaging in moral reflection.

[31] Occasioning many commentaries, e.g. Vitoria *De homicidia* (cf. Doyle 1997).

Death Natural or Unnatural? Thomas Aquinas   119

in a cursory fashion because the alternative view was not well represented within his society. It is tangential to his primary concern, which is to investigate the justice or injustice of bringing about human death.

His discussion of killing animals provides Thomas with the basis for discussing the killing of an unjust human being. Thomas asserts that, as other animals are ordered to human beings, so also within society the part is ordered to the whole. As human beings are parts of the community, so the prospective good of the community justifies the harm done to a sinner in punishing him, even by death. At this point Thomas seems to hold it as a universal truth that any part is ordered to the whole as the imperfect is to the perfect. Yet the human person does not stand to the human community simply as a part to a whole. In an important sense, the human person is already a whole whose moral integrity is not to be compromised. In the previous article, Thomas had defended the position that animals are for the use of human beings because they are by nature directed by another (*ST* IIaIIae 64. 1 ad 2). A human being, however, in so far as he or she is naturally free, exists for himself or herself (*naturaliter liber et propter seipsum existens*; *ST* IIaIIae 64. 2 ad 3).

How is it that one could compromise the intrinsic good of the free individual, even for the greater good of the community?[32] Thomas's answer is that, by sin, sinners fall away from their natural dignity (*decidit a dignitate humana*) and fall into the slavish state of beasts and therefore are no longer for themselves but for others. Only for this reason is it lawful, for the sake of the whole, to kill a sinner. If this answer is taken at face value it seems to imply that those who are justly imprisoned are not entitled to be treated with dignity as human beings. This contradicts both the injunction of Jesus in the Gospel to visit prisoners (Matthew 25: 36 with no indication that this is restricted to those unjustly imprisoned). It also seems to contradict Thomas's own teaching on the possibility of conversion even for

---

[32] For Thomas holds that one may not do something that is evil in itself, even for the sake of a great good, again with the weight of Augustine and Aristotle behind him—Augustine *Contra mendacium* 8; Aristotle *Ethica* 2. 6. 1107a; cf. Romans 3: 8.

seemingly incurable offenders.[33] Thomas clearly wishes to defend the idea of just punishment for the sake of the common good, but as it stands his justification seems to prove too much.

In the next two articles Thomas has to work hard to qualify or restrict the apparent implications of the idea that sinners fall from their natural human dignity. This he does by means of the question, 'If a sinner may be killed, does it follow that anyone may kill him?' His answer is that, even though the sinner no longer possesses human dignity, an ordinary citizen may not kill a sinner. This is because, whereas a non-human animal is distinct from human beings by nature, a sinner is not distinct from other human beings by nature (*ST* IIaIIae 64. 3 ad 2). Here again Thomas invokes the category of nature to explain why vendetta killing is contrary to justice. Every human being has dignity by nature. The just condemnation of a human being is a matter of judgment for the good of the whole and this judgment must have the authority of the whole. Hence, a sinner is only legitimately killed when the killing rests on public authority; when it is done by some individual who has been given authority for the care of the community.

The exercising of authority, even by the use of lethal force, is good and useful for the community and ultimately rests on the authority of God from which all authority springs (*ST* IIaIIae 64. 3). Nevertheless, exercising authority is not the responsibility of everyone equally, and, in particular, it is not the responsibility of clerics as it is not suitable to those who must represent the forgiveness of the new law (*ST* IIaIIae 64.4). These two articles (64. 3 and 64. 4) helpfully restrict those who may punish the sinner, but they do not help in delimiting the scope of the punishment itself or the proper treatment of criminals. The claim that criminals have lost all human dignity is not convincing and also seems to open the way to inhumane punishments. A better approach is exemplified in the argument of various modern thinkers (e.g. Finnis 1980: 260–4; Anscombe in Geach and Gormally 2005: 267–71) that punishment is compatible

[33] *ST* IIaIIae 25. 6 ad 2. The apparent contradiction Thomas asserts in describing someone as incurable but later admitting that he might repent was pointed out to me by Dr Margaret Atkins. It reveals the underlying problem of supposing that some criminals fall so far from human dignity as to be beyond charity, while at the same time admitting that they are not beyond the reach of God's grace.

with respecting the human dignity of the criminal. However, this contemporary approach is convincing only to the extent that it specifies which punishments do respect human dignity, and this poses problems in particular for capital punishment (Grisez 1993: 891–4; John Paul II 1995: 56).

The fifth article of this question is the longest and, for the purposes of this study, certainly the most interesting: is suicide ever lawful? (*ST* IIaIIae 64. 5). It would seem to be lawful to kill oneself, given sufficiently grave reasons, as it is generally lawful to endure an evil in order to avoid a greater evil (as when someone undergoes surgery) and seems not to be against *justice* to kill oneself (for it is not unfair to someone else). Against these arguments Thomas brings three counter-arguments: first it is against one's own natural love of self, second it is unfair to the community, and third it usurps the authority of God. These counter-arguments are not multiplied ad hoc but concern the proper understanding of the place of the human creature within society and with creation.

First, as a living being, every human being has a duty of self-preservation. For modern people, given that each person's life is his or her own, suicide is often thought of as an exercise in autonomy. Thomas agrees that the life of a human being is more his or her own than is the life of other animals, for they exist for another but the human being exists for himself or herself (*ST* IIaIIae 64. 1; 64. 2 ad 3; *Summa Contra Gentiles* III. 112). However, as argued above, every being naturally seeks to keep itself in being and resists destruction as far as it can, and hence to will its own death is not natural to any creature (*ST* IaIIae 85. 6). This is more true of human beings than it is of other animals, for human beings have the ability to understand the value of a life well lived, and each human life is worth more than any number of non-rational animals (Matthew 10: 31). If one's life is what is most one's own, this implies not only an ability to dispose of one's life but also a responsibility which is also most one's own, prior to any other responsibilities.

Thomas's understanding of being is influenced strongly by Dionysius and also by Avicenna, the Arabic commentator on Aristotle. The foundations of this view are laid down at the very beginning of the *Summa Theologiae* where Thomas discusses the nature of goodness in general, and, asks whether goodness and being are coextensive.

Thomas argues that every being, inasmuch as it exists, is actual, and this implies that it is in some way perfect since every act implies some perfection or completion, and this in turn implies desirability and hence goodness (*ST* Ia 5. 1–3). Evil, on the other hand, as imperfection, is a lack of due actuality, a privation (*ST* Ia 48). It is thus conceptually necessary that a creature desire its own perfection, and hate (find repugnant, withdraw from) its own imperfection. Even destructive actions are done under the aspect of some desired perfection. Life does not just happen to be a good (as though some might find life attractive and desirable while others find it painful and burdensome, or simply dull). For any creature, desire for its own perfection implies a desire to remain in being, and for animals, this means to remain alive. 'For a living thing to live is to be' (*ST* Ia 18. 3, quoting Aristotle *De anima* 2. 4. 415b).

As God creates every creature, God is the source or creator of all that is good or desirable in the creature. According to Thomas, this is because God is supremely good and the goodness of the creatures bears some (distant) resemblance to the goodness of the creator who made it. This follows from the general rule, which Thomas accepts, that there is always some resemblance between an agent and its effect (*ST* Ia 4. 3). Therefore, when a creature desires its own perfection, what it desires is some reflection of the goodness of God from whom all good things come (*ST* Ia 6. 1). All creatures do not desire in the same way: there is a natural appetite, a sensitive appetite, and an intellectual appetite. When it is said that human beings have a natural desire for being, as have all things, this does not mean that they have the desire in the way that all things have it. Rather, the human creature desires according to a nature that is at once material, sensitive and intellectual. The natural desire for being in the case of human beings is not only a physical instinct from which one might infer a certain moral good, rather it is a rational grasp of the desirability of being in itself. From this it follows that, for human beings, the desire not to exist, while imaginable, is never rationally justified.[34]

---

[34] In another work (*Quaestiones disputatae De potentia* 5. 4. 6) Thomas discusses whether it would not be better for God to annihilate the wicked, rather than damn them in hell. In response he says that it is more fitting that they continue to exist and

According to Thomas, what distinguishes good acts from wicked acts is that they are good in all respects (*ST* IaIIae 18). This involves a correct measure of the goods that are aimed at in action. As the good of bodily life is essential to human nature (as discussed earlier in this chapter), to seek *per se* to destroy one's own life is to act against the most basic of bodily goods. Someone who chooses to kill himself or herself rather than enduring suffering is thus choosing a lower good over a higher one. All bodily goods are rooted in the existence of the body and repugnance of bodily pain cannot rationally be greater than the love of self-preservation that is its cause (*ST* IaIIae 29. 3). The desire for death thus stems not from reason, but from the desperate desire to avoid an evil that seems too heavy to bear. In some cultures suicide is regarded as a noble and courageous act, but if courage is the virtue that helps us live well in the face of present evil, then suicide should be recognized as a failure to bear evil courageously.[35] Suicide may be regarded with compassion but should not be regarded with admiration.

The second consideration that weighs against suicide is that the human being is not only a whole but also is a part of a greater whole that is community. In this sense suicide is not only a failure of courage and of rightful self-love but is also a failure of justice towards others. Suicide is unjust to others in that it deprives the community of one of its members. This is an injury, not simply because of the

---

are punished than that they are punished by being annihilated: sinners are those who have used their wills and abused their natures; therefore, it would not be fitting to punish the nature for the sin of the will, rather better to restore the nature but confound the ill will. Now, if the ill will is being punished, presumably it would resent this, as the ill will *ex hypothesi* fails to acknowledge the justice and order of Divine government. So the souls in hell might well prefer not to exist, but this is a sign of their lack of appreciation of the good of their own created being and also a lack of appreciation of the justice of their punishment. If, then, even the damned cannot reasonably desire not to exist, it is still less the case that someone in this life could reasonably desire not to exist. This is to leave to one side for the moment the prospect of life beyond death, which implies that death does not bring total extinction, in which case the desire for death need not be thought of as the desire for non-existence. Some of the implications of this more theological approach to death will be explored below.

[35] *ST* IIaIIae 64. 5 ad 5. Thomas buttresses his arguments by appeal to the authority of Augustine (*CD* I. 20–23) and Aristotle (*Ethica* 3. 6. 1115a; 5. 11. 1138a).

usefulness of the person in working or producing,[36] but because persons *constitute* the community. If a family is deprived of one of its own by suicide, the sense of betrayal that is commonly experienced reflects not loss in utility or producing power but an abandonment of familial solidarity. The bonds of society may be less obvious than these family ties but they too are unjustly broken by a suicide.

Suicide can also have other harmful effects on society, as when someone attempts suicide out of shame at falling into a particular condition. In such cases, the judgment that, to take a contemporary example, the prospect of life in a wheelchair is worse than death, both draws from and feeds into public perceptions of disability. It directly threatens both the individual self-respect of those who live well with disability and their wider public recognition. It is not only a failure to appreciate the possibilities for one's own life, but also, implicitly, a judgment on all who are in the same situation. It says, in effect, people in this condition are better off dead.

Thirdly, suicide usurps the authority of God who alone has power over life and death. This may seem to be an arbitrary curtailment of human freedom: were human beings not created with self-mastery? However, it is not arbitrary, for it reflects an unchangeable truth concerning creatureliness. Only God can create, for only God can bring something into being out of nothing. God can create any creature at all, but he cannot create a creature that does not depend on him, nor can he give to another the power to create (*ST* Ia 45. 5; *Quaestiones disputatae De potentia* 3. 4; *Summa Contra Gentiles* II. 21); there can be only one first cause, only one ultimate power and end from which and to which all things move. Furthermore, as discussed earlier, death comes to all human beings since Adam as a punishment for the fall (*ST* IIaIIae 164. 1). It is only for God to impose this punishment, for it is bound up with the human nature which is given by God to each person at conception.

According to Thomas, God *could* give a creature the authority to kill the innocent, as happened with Isaac (*ST* IaIIae 94. 5 ad 2), for it

---

[36] This seems to be the implication of saying that 'it is difficult to see what *practical* interest the state could have in the continuance of the life of someone who is already in the process of dying and is racked in pain' (Porter 1995: 116; emphasis added).

is justly within his power to invoke the sentence of death. Yet God could not make a creature who could justly kill *without* having received authority from him. In recent years a number of theologians have gone further and doubted whether God could give this kind of authority to human beings. This is not because of any lack of authority on God's part, but rather because it does not seem proper to human beings to intentionally kill the innocent, even with authorization from above (Grisez 1983: 219). This stance is compatible with an acceptance of the authority of the Scriptures taken as a whole if it can be acknowledged that 'the Bible reflects a considerable moral development, which finds its completion in the New Testament' (Pontifical Biblical Commission 1994: III. d. 3). According to this interpretation, the story of Abraham and Isaac does not imply that God could authorize someone to kill the innocent. If one accepts the claim of Thomas (who here follows Augustine) that God could authorize any killing, then in any individual case one might wonder whether God had secretly commanded someone to commit suicide (*ST* IIaIIae 64. 5 ad 4, cf. *CD* I. 25). However, the claim that God has the power specially to authorize every sort of killing, torture, or punishment so that it could become a good human action seems to undermine any account of the inherent goodness or badness of human actions (such as Thomas in fact defends). If, therefore, we reject the view that God could arbitrarily authorize the killing of the innocent in some cases, then it seems the same must be true of suicide. To intentionally bring one's life to an end is to assume an authority that is simply not proper to the human creature.

Thomas's discussion may seem to have presupposed that death aims at extinction or non-existence when, from a theological perspective, death is not an irremediable loss, for the general resurrection awaits both the righteous and the wicked, who will enjoy or suffer an everlasting sentence. Death is not the ultimate destruction it appears to be, nor does it lead to that non-existence which might be desired as much as feared. How does this alter our understanding of killing? According to Thomas, we should distinguish here what is true of death essentially and what is true incidentally. In itself, death is destruction: a disintegration of the living person; a loss to the human community that it has no power to remedy; and a limit of the earthly life of the human creature. Bringing about or seeking death should be judged according to what death is in itself, not according to what might come afterwards by God's decree; it is wrong to do an evil in one's own power in the hope that God will redeem that evil by *his* power. Among the goods of this world bodily life is the most basic and so may not be disposed of for the sake of avoiding physical hardship.

If it is sometimes right to kill wrongdoers, is it ever right to kill the innocent? Thomas answers that, considered in itself, it is unlawful to kill *any* human being because one should love the created nature God has made. Indeed, even God does not will the death of anyone *per se*, for death is a privation and the consequence of sin, which he permits but does not will (*ST* Ia 19. 9). Yet God wills death under the aspect of the good of punishment (*ST* IIaIIae 164. 1 ad 5). According to Thomas, a human being may also lawfully will death as punishment if he is so authorized by the community, for the injustice of the sinner is corruptive of the common good. As discussed earlier, for Thomas, this claim rests on an account of the way in which criminals are said to lose their human dignity (*ST* IIaIIae 64. 2). This is not satisfactory as it stands for it proves too much and sets no reasonable limits to what may be done in the name of punishment. If capital punishment is to be justified, it seems it must rely on other arguments. Be that as it may, the death of the innocent can never be legitimated as a punishment, for they do not merit punishment. Nor can killing the innocent be justified otherwise in terms of the common good, because the lives of the just are constitutive of the community. They are the chief part of the community (*principalior pars multitudinis*; *ST* IIaIIae 64. 6). On the presumption (criticized above) that God can give human beings authority to kill the innocent, such killing could be justified. It would gain its justification from its end—obedience to God—even though it would seem like an exception to what would normally be done according to the natural law. It would still be natural in a sense, as miracles also are not against nature (*ST* IIaIIae 64. 6 ad 1; *ST* IaIIae 94. 5 ad 2; *Summa Contra Gentiles* III. 100). However, even if this were accepted, it would never be legitimate to kill the innocent on the basis of human authority. If the presumption is rejected, then there are no circumstances whatsoever in which it would be legitimate to directly aim to kill the innocent.

As with suicide, it is helpful to distinguish between essential (*per se*) effects and incidental (*per accidens*) effects. Otherwise it might be argued that in killing the innocent one benefits him or her, for he or she will end in heaven, whereas in killing the sinner one harms him or her, for he or she will go to hell! If we judge the act for what it does essentially and only secondarily by its incidental effects, we see that killing is rightly understood an offence against the person. What is done essentially and directly is that the person is deprived of bodily life, the community is robbed of one of its members, and the soul is reduced to an unnatural state. It is not by any human power or any essential character of this action that God afterwards sees fit to reward the just and punish the unrepentant sinner. In itself, it is far worse to kill an innocent person than to kill a wrongdoer: first as an innocent person is more to be loved; second as he or she deserves the injury less; third as the community is deprived of a greater good; and fourth as God is despised more, for God loves the lives of his saints (*ST* IIaIIae 64. 6 ad 2). Thus, while no one may be killed without proper authority, it is worse to kill the innocent than wrongdoers, for the innocent are especially deserving of protection. Thomas also believes that there is an order to charity and that it is worse to kill those closer to us by natural bonds than to kill a stranger. So, also, it is worse to commit suicide than to commit murder, not because of what may follow, but simply because it betrays a more basic and more deeply rooted love.[37]

Finally Thomas discusses killing in self-defence (*ST* IIaIIae 64. 7). He accepts that such an act may be excused but only if killing is not the aim (or object) of the defender but is *praeter intentionem*, and if the defender is behaving moderately. The basis of the wrongness of killing is the fundamental goodness of the creature, shown in its natural desire for being. Yet this is equally true both for the aggressor and for the defender. The aggressor is wrong to attack someone, and the defender would equally be wrong if he intended to kill the aggressor (unless, as an officer of the community he was authorized

---

[37] *ST* IIaIIae 64. 5 ad 3, *ST* IaIIae 73. 9 ad 2. Fearon (1969: 91 note d) mistakenly judges the relative gravity of suicide and murder by appeal to what might happen after death, which Thomas would regard as incidental to the judgement of the morality of the act. For the order of charity cf. *ST* IIaIIae 26. 4.

so to intend). Nevertheless the defender may use reasonable force to protect his life against assault, even if this results in harm to his assailant. A similar point is made concerning accidental homicide more generally (*ST* IIaIIae 64. 8). Such killing may be wrong, not through deliberate malice, but through lack of due care, or through being involved in unlawful activities (so the person has no excuse, for they should not have been at such a place, at such a time). If, however, someone has taken due care and is acting lawfully, then that person is not guilty if in the course of some reasonable and lawful act he or she kills someone by accident.

Thomas's account of killing forms a coherent whole. It is not a series of ad hoc objections to practices the community has received as taboo. Rather, the act of killing is understood in the context of an account of the nature of body and soul. This includes: the character of the separated state of the soul after death; the sense in which death is contrary to human nature; the good of existence *per se*; and the place of the human being in relation to body, community, and God.

The taking of human life is an act of unique metaphysical seriousness, for only human death is the destruction of a being that has an indestructible soul. For the same reason, the human being cannot be totally subordinated to the whole of which he or she is a part. Unlike other animals, the human person is free and master of himself or herself, informed by education and discovery, rather than by instinct and training—ordered to an individual good and not only the good of the species (*Summa Contra Gentiles* III. 112). Animals are not conserved by nature as individuals, but as species. Angels are conserved, but each one is a species in itself. Only human animals (or other animals which have a share in reason if there are any such) have a soul that is indestructible and 'is in a way all things' (*Summa Contra Gentiles* III. 111 quoting Aristotle *De anima* 3. 8. 431b) and yet is multiplied in individuals who are material and social beings. This is the root of the peculiar metaphysically mixed nature of human beings.

At the same time, human beings exist as social animals and as parts of a spiritual community, therefore the human good is in part social and is directed towards the common good even though the human being cannot be completely subordinated to the whole. This is seen in Thomas's account of the punishment of the wicked and the inviolability of the innocent. The wicked put themselves in opposition to the common good and so their punishment is, of itself, an act of justice. While Thomas's account of punishment is inadequate as it stands, it has the benefit of recognizing that every human being, as such, has an inherent dignity and that punishment of criminals is justified not simply on pragmatic grounds but only in relation to the injustice done by the criminal. In relation to the innocent, there is no injustice that puts them in opposition to the community. Rather, they are constitutive of it and are not to be sacrificed for the sake of the whole. Each one, in a sense, *is* the whole. There is also a strong sense here of the unassailable dignity of each human being by nature, which is central to the purpose of the entire material universe. Yet also society is natural to human beings; it is not a contract that happens to be undertaken by strangers. The human good encompasses a common and social good and human community is naturally ordered to support the emergence of political authority.

MORTAL FEAR

Living well, for mortal creatures, not only requires observation of the principles of justice so as to avoid wrongful killing, but also requires that one possess the right attitude or disposition in the face of death so as to act well when under the threat of mortal danger. Moral reflection on death and dying therefore involves discussion of the emotional life of the human person and especially the emotion of fear and the virtue of courage.

In the course of a general account of the emotions in the *prima secundae* of the *Summa Theologiae* IaIIae 22–48, Thomas devotes five questions (*ST* IaIIae 41–45) to fear (*timor*) and its contrary, daring (*audacia*). The emotions are each defined by their object, which, in the case of fear is *a future evil which requires effort to avoid or to resist.* As an emotion of the assertive (*irascibilis*) appetite, it specifically concerns evils as difficult to avoid, in contrast to dislike (*odium*), which recoils from a readily avoidable future evil, or sorrow (*tristitia*), which suffers a present evil. Sudden things are feared more because they are harder to guard against (*ST* IaIIae 42. 5); however, if one regards some evil as *absolutely* unavoidable, then it cannot be an object of fear at all, for it is no longer thought of as *future*; hence Thomas quotes with approval Aristotle's saying that the convict already on the scaffold has no more fear (*ST* IaIIae 42. 2). The things most feared are those that may be avoided, or at least postponed, with difficulty, but for which, when finally present, there is no remedy (*ST* IaIIae 42. 6). First among these is death, for which there is no natural remedy.

While the *object* of fear is the difficult-to-avoid future evil, the *cause* of fear is twofold: love and weakness. As with all the passions (*ST* IaIIae 25), fear is caused by love, for fear regards an evil, and every evil is relative to some desirable good (*ST* IaIIae 43. 1). In as much as one loves something, one will fear to lose it. Yet one only has cause for fear if the evil is difficult to avoid or to resist. If the evil is easily avoided, or, once present, is easily remedied, then it will not be feared. What gives certain evils power over the agent is some perceived weakness in the agent such that he or she can avoid or resist the approaching evil only with difficulty. In this way weakness or defect is the cause of fear.

Alongside fear, Thomas goes on to discuss its contrary—daring. Whereas fear leads us to withdraw from an evil that is difficult to resist, daring leads us to resist the evil in the hope of overcoming it (*ST* IaIIae 45. 1). Daring is thus the result of hope, the emotion that helps one pursue the difficult good; whereas fear leads to despair, whereby one withdraws from a good that is considered unattainable (*ST* IaIIae 45. 2). As fear is caused by a certain defect, so daring is caused by real or perceived strength in comparison to the approaching evil (*ST* IaIIae 45. 3). Sometimes this perception may be unreliable or may be due to ignorance about the true character of the approaching harm. In these circumstances the spirited resistance will soon evaporate when the true character of the evil becomes apparent. Hence the saying 'Fools rush in where angels fear to tread.' However, daring which is based on an accurate measure of the situation will not be deterred when the evil is present but will become perseverance (*ST* IaIIae 45. 4).

The *emotions* of fear and daring are shaped by the *virtue* of courage, as discussed later in the *Summa Theologiae* (IIaIIae 123–40). According to Thomas's account, no emotion is evil in itself, but emotional reactions may be good or evil depending on their conformity with the objective requirements of reason. The habitual conformity of emotional reactions with the rule of reason is ensured by stable dispositions which shape or condition the emotional life: the virtues. Thomas accepted the received classical list of four principle ('cardinal') virtues, as developed by Plato and as popularized in the Latin West by Cicero (prudence, justice, courage, temperateness), but his account of what constitutes a virtue owes more to the philosophy of Aristotle than to Plato. Thomas did not understand the cardinal virtues in terms of a threefold psychology of spirit, soul, and body, but in terms of a twofold division of principles of human action: intellect and emotion; the intellect divided into understanding and will, and the emotions divided into desire and assertiveness. The virtues of prudence (understanding) and justice (will) are perfective of the intellect, whilst the emotional life is perfected by the virtues of temperateness (desire) and courage (assertiveness).

According to this analysis, courage is concerned with the passions of the assertive appetite, that is, the emotions of fear and daring (*ST* IIaIIae 123. 3). It is a courageous disposition that curbs fear and moderates daring so that difficult obstacles can be faced well. Thomas says that the name courage is used for the general quality of firmness of purpose that must accompany any virtuous act, in which sense it is a general virtue. However, courage is also used more narrowly of that virtue that allows one to act well in the face of the worst dangers. Now the worst of all bodily dangers is death, since death does away with all goods of the body (*ST* IIaIIae 123. 4). Elsewhere Thomas quotes Aristotle on this point, but here he appeals to Augustine (*De moribus ecclesiae* 22). Mortal fear in the face of death requires a special virtue because to love one's own life is natural (*ST* IIaIIae 123. 2 ad 1).

The Aristotelian understanding of the excellence of courage was forged within the context of the citizens of the Greek polis. There the courage of the soldier who faced death in defence of the city gave the archetype of that virtue. For Thomas, the archetype of courage is seen less in the soldier and more in the martyr.[38] While he agrees with

---

[38] This is a shift of connotation already worked out in the patristic age and it is implicit in such characteristic stories as that told by Ambrose involving the martyrdom of a virgin and a soldier *De virginibus* 2. IV. 30.

Aristotle (*Ethica* 3. 6. 1115a) that courage properly concerns death in battle, he extends this to any who face death for the sake of some good. He gives the example of one who attends a friend in spite of the danger of deadly infection, and of another who undertakes a journey for the sake of some godly purpose despite the dangers of shipwreck and robbers.[39] Furthermore, Thomas argues, courage is seen *more* in enduring evil than in fighting against it.[40] In this way, the martyr shows more courage than the soldier, for the one endures a great evil for the sake of a great good, whereas the other strives to avoid having to bear the evil.

Thomas devotes a whole question to the courage of the martyrs (*ST* IIaIIae 124). He first has to distinguish the heroism of martyrdom from the sin of suicide. This is a problem he inherits from Augustine, who also sharply condemns suicide, and who struggles to give an account of how martyrdom differs in kind from suicide (*CD* I. 17–27). Thomas asserts that 'martyrdom consists in the right endurance (*sustinentia*) of sufferings unjustly inflicted' (*ST* IIaIIae 124. 1). Far from seeking death by martyrdom, one ought not to tolerate such an act of injustice unless justice itself requires it; one ought to tolerate the injustice of others only in moderation (*ipse debet moderate tolerae*). However, when required, martyrdom is an act of courage greater even than the courage of the soldier (*ST* IIaIIae 124. 2), and it is a meritorious act, not simply as a demonstration of valour, but because of the love that inspires it (cf. John 15: 13). Love is shown most vividly when it overcomes the most fearful of prospects.[41] The prospect of

---

[39] *ST* IIaIIae 123. 5. The latter was a real threat: Jordan of Saxony, second master of the Order of Friars Preachers was drowned in shipwreck, together with a number of other friars, while on a missionary journey.

[40] *ST* IIaIIae 123. 6. A similar point is made elsewhere in the *Summa Theologiae* where Thomas asks whether the life of a contemplative, who shares the fruit of contemplation with others, is the best kind of life. In one objection he puts forward the suggestion that the military orders provide a more excellent way of life, for they give more opportunity for martyrdom. He replies that the point of military orders is not that one might die for the sake of the faith, but that one might kill the enemy before one has to die (*ST* IIaIIae 188. 6 ad 2). The soldier aims to avoid getting killed if he can! He faces the *danger* of death but the martyr faces a death which is more certain and often more drawn out, and so requires a greater constancy of purpose than needs be shown by the soldier.

[41] Death is the most deep-seated fear for all animals. *ST* IIaIIae 124. 3 cf. Augustine *De diversis quaestionibus octoginta tribus* 36.

death, therefore, is essential to martyrdom because there can be no greater witness than the one who is willing to give up even the life of his or her own body (*ST* IIaIIae 124. 4). Witnessing to divine truth is also an essential component of martyrdom, yet this witness may concern any truth, so long as it is referred to God; hence, for example, John the Baptist is accounted as a martyr for witnessing to the divine law by his preaching against adultery (*ST* IIaIIae 124. 5).

Courage is a mean between the vice of fear (*ST* IIaIIae 125. 1) at one extreme and, at the other, the vices of fearlessness or daring. The vice of fear (*timor*), which is also termed cowardice, should be carefully distinguished from the emotional reaction of fear, which may be quite appropriate. The emotion gives its name to the vice of *excessive* fear that becomes an obstacle to doing the right thing. Fear may excuse from sin to a certain extent (*ST* IIaIIae 125. 4) as it reduces the voluntariness of actions. Nevertheless, fear does not remove the voluntariness of action altogether, and wicked action done out of fear may still be mortal sin (*ST* IIaIIae 125. 3) if it affects not only the emotions but also the will so that it turns away from the good.

Thomas considers two vices opposite to cowardice: fearlessness (*intimiditas*) and daring (*audacia*). Daring is the more obvious vice (*ST* IIaIIae 127), the boldness of a rash spirit which is inclined to resist evil rather than flee even in circumstances when flight would be more profitable whereas unnecessary resistance would cause pointless suffering. The other vice opposed to courage is less obvious, but more interesting. Thomas asserts that it is possible to fail in virtue by failing to fear to the extent that one should. This may be due to a failure to love if one fails sufficiently to fear something because one does not care enough about losing a thing of great value. This is especially relevant to the case of approaching death. Someone might fear death less than he or she ought, because he or she fails to *love* this life in the body as much as it should be loved. As it is natural to love one's own life, it is impossible to get rid of this love altogether. Nevertheless one might fail to love properly or one might value other things, such as public esteem or comfort, above life or health. Another way people might fail in fear is through thinking themselves invulnerable, as people do through pride or even through stupidity like the Celts who fear nothing because they are too stupid (*Celtae propter stultitiam nihil timent*; *ST* IIaIIae 126. 1, cf. Aristotle *Ethica* 3. 7. 1115b) yet this last is excusable if the ignorance be invincible (*ST* IIaIIae 126. 1).

HOPE OF HEAVEN AND CARE FOR THE DEAD

Because death is the greatest of natural evils, without natural remedy, Thomas regards fear as the appropriate emotional response in the face of death, even for a Christian. The good that follows death does not change its essential character as the destruction of the living being. Nevertheless, while death is in itself an affront to human nature, it is also the occasion of judgment and, for those who die in a state of grace, it is the prologue to eternal life. The vision of human death from a natural perspective and that from a supernatural perspective are thus radically at variance. Understood in the light of revelation, this bodily life is not an end in itself, but human beings are wayfarers (*viatores*) yet to reach their homeland. For those who die in Christ, death becomes the occasion of blissful communion with God. And yet, even for these, it is still the unnatural tearing apart of soul and body. It is in this manner that Thomas understands Paul's words in his second letter to the Corinthians:

Here indeed we groan, and long to put on our heavenly dwelling, so that by putting it on we may not be found naked. For while we are still in this tent, we sigh with anxiety; not that we would be unclothed, but that we would be further clothed, so that what is mortal may be swallowed up by life. (2 Corinthians 5: 2–4)

According to Thomas, the desire to be with God is supernatural. It moves one to an end that is beyond what any creature could hope or imagine: the very vision of God. Natural appetites are suited to natural ends but this end could not be the object of any natural appetite.[42] While, in general, grace perfects nature, in the face of death graced and natural desires pull one in different directions. The

---

[42] Therefore the rational creature is not moved to this desire by nature (*a natura*) but only by God himself (*sed ab ipso Deo*) who causes this desire in us (*Super II ad Corinthianos* 5. 2. 160).

natural desire to remain in the body opposes (*retardans*) the graced desire to be with God. For this reason death is hard to contemplate, for while the Christian desires communion with God, he or she rightly fears bodily destruction.[43] This is why Paul says that he would not wish to be 'naked'. However, it is the graced desire, rather than the natural, which wins out (*desiderium gratiae vincit) Super I ad Corinthianos* 5. 2. 162. A similar conflict is detected in Paul's letter to the Philippians: 'I am hard pressed between the two. My desire is to depart and be with Christ, for that is far better. But to remain in the flesh is more necessary on your account' (Philippians 1: 23–4).

The impulse of nature is to resist or flee from death. In his commentary on this passage, Thomas refers back to Paul's letter to the Corinthians, 'not that we would be unclothed, but that we would be further clothed,' (2 Corinthians 5: 4) and also refers to the words of John's Gospel concerning Peter, 'another will carry you where you do not wish to go' (John 21: 18; a passage used to the same effect by Augustine *In Joannis evangelium tractatus* 123. 5). Hence, Thomas writes, 'my desire is to depart, *not absolutely*, but to be with Christ' (*Super ad Philippenses* I. 3. 36; emphasis added). It is far better to be with Christ, but Paul is content to stay in the flesh for the sake of his flock. At this point Thomas entertains a doubt. Is this to place love of neighbour above love of God? No. There are two kinds of love of God, the desiring love that wants to find delight in God—and this is a good thing, and the love of friendship by which honouring and serving God is preferred even over this delight—and this is the perfection of love (*Super ad Philippenses* I. 3. 36). The prospect of bliss after death should be enough to overcome the fear of death, yet the love of friendship by which one desires to serve God, gives one reason to live as long as God so wills, and not to seek an early end to it.

As graced desire for union with God conflicts with the natural desire to remain in the body, so also the divine promise of communion with God beyond death radically alters the account one gives of the state of the 'separated soul'. The souls of the blessed are not left to endure that shadowy half-life which is all that they could attain by virtue of their natural powers, but they are given the vision of God,

---

[43] At this point Thomas appeals to Augustine who wrote that the apostle Peter, in his old age, still retained a natural fear of death *Super II ad Corinthianos* 5. 1. 159, cf. Augustine, *In Joannis evangelium tractatus* 123.

which is, in fact, their final happiness (*ST* Ia 12; *ST* IaIIae 3–5). The souls of the blessed are made perfectly happy, not because of their separation from the body, but because of the vision of God, which is a gift surpassing any natural created power. The souls of the just are happy not because of, but in spite of their separation from their bodies.

In this context Thomas asks, is the body necessary for happiness (*beatitudo*)? (*ST* IaIIae 4. 5). He answers that it is not. For, while the limited happiness possible in this life requires a body for the proper exercise of intellect and virtue, human happiness ultimately consists in the vision of God, and to see God is not an act within the scope of the imagination, or indeed of any created concept. It is only by God making himself immediately the object of the created intellect that such a vision is possible. Thus the vision of God is as far beyond the natural powers of the embodied soul as above the disembodied and, indeed, as far above any angel as it is beyond the human soul. It is not by the natural perfection of the intellectual powers that God is grasped and so their imperfection, and the incongruous state of the human soul when separated from its body, is no obstacle to final human happiness.

Thomas immediately follows this question with another: is the perfection of the body necessary for complete happiness? (*ST* IaIIae 4. 6) To which he answers that it *is* necessary. Since it is natural for the soul to be united to a body, the perfection of the soul must include the perfection of the body. This is not because the soul's happiness is somehow intensified by the presence of its body—as though a lesser saint when he or she is reunited with the body might rise to the same level of happiness a greater saint had without a body. The imperfection lies not with the object of happiness, which is God, but with the subject, which is imperfect in nature. Thus happiness, to be perfect, must include the whole subject, body as well as soul, not so that it increases in intensity, but so that it extends to the soul in its informing of the body, and to the body itself, and not only to the separated soul (Bazan 1991). This is the meaning of the somewhat obscure reply to an objection.

The desire of the separated soul is entirely at rest, as regards what is desired; since, to wit, it has that which satisfies its appetite. But it is not wholly at rest, as regards the desirer, since it does not possess that good in every way that it would wish to possess it. Consequently, after the body has been resumed, happiness increases not in intensity but in extent (*non intensive sed extensive*). (*ST* IaIIae 4. 5 ad 6)

These two articles (*ST* IaIIae 4. 5–6) contain seven references to works of Augustine, five of which are from *De Genesi ad litteram*, one is from *De civitate Dei* and one is from a letter written around 410 CE. For his doctrine of the resurrection Thomas cannot turn to reason alone, so he relies on the Scriptures and the Christian tradition, especially the later works of Augustine. Similarly, in his commentary on the Sentences, when discussing the distinctions concerning the resurrection (*Scriptum super libros Sententiarum* IV. 49–50), he quotes Augustine some fifty-seven times, of which twelve are from *De Genesi ad litteram* and twenty-three are from *De civitate Dei*.

The resurrection is necessary for complete human happiness, but even to talk of complete human happiness is already to have moved into the area of revealed theology. The very possibility of complete human happiness is dependent on a gratuitous act of God; and this is outside the powers and aspirations of any created nature (*ST* Ia 12.4; *ST* IaIIae 5.5). This has implications also for the sense in which the resurrection may be said to be beyond nature and yet seemingly demanded by nature. The soul is by nature indestructible; it is also, by nature, the form of a destructible body. Only the possibility of a future resurrection of the body, brought about by God's power, can resolve this tension. In the *Summa Contra Gentiles*, a work that consistently argues for the credibility of the faith on the basis of arguments from reason, this is presented as an argument for the fittingness of resurrection. If the soul is indestructible then it seems that some reunion with the body is inevitable (*Summa Contra Gentiles* IV. 79–81). In Thomas's commentary on Paul's letter to the Corinthians, however, the argument is pursued in the opposite direction. If the body is *not* raised, then it becomes difficult to believe that the soul does survive, notwithstanding the philosophical arguments for thinking so; for how can something endure forever in an unnatural state? If the dead are not raised in their own bodies— something that cannot be accomplished by nature but only by the power of God—then human beings can only be assured of this life (*Super I ad Corinthianos* 15. 2. 924).

For Thomas Aquinas, death is not only the separation of body and soul but, for those who have persevered in charity, death is also the occasion of homecoming. The scheme of a journey towards an ultimate end or happiness is basic to the whole shape of the *Summa Theologiae*. The ultimate end of human life is the vision of God. The virtues and gifts of the Spirit move human beings towards their end on 'the way' who is Christ himself (*ST* IIaIIae 24. 4; cf. *ST* Ia 2; *ST* IaIIae 1; *ST* IIIa 1). While en route one receives the grace by which to merit a reward, by merit that is itself derived from the merits of Christ who was, at once, a wayfarer and a beholder: *viator et comprehensor* (*ST* IIaIIae 18. 2 ad 1; *ST* IIIa 15. 10).

When this life ends at death the human will ceases to be changeable and becomes fixed on whatever end has shaped its life while in the flesh. The destiny of the just is the beatific vision, which is a participation in God in whom all desire comes to rest. The life of heaven is not simply everlasting but is eternal. The damned, on the other hand, experience no true eternity, rather, their wills are subject to persistent and everlasting frustration, which is a fitting punishment for their own evil deeds.[44] Eternal life and everlasting death are, thus, not wholly symmetrical; nevertheless, Thomas wishes to argue that there is an underlying common cause for the fixity of their state, for the time of journeying is over and each person faces judgment for what he or she has become (*Summa Contra Gentiles* IV. 92–5).

Thomas is insistent 'against the error of certain Greeks' (*Summa Contra Gentiles* IV. 91; *Super ad Philippenses* I. 3. 36; *Contra errores Graecorum* 40; and elsewhere) that the souls of the righteous see God immediately after death, and the souls of the wicked are immediately punished. If there is no reason to delay reward or punishment, then it must follow immediately. But also, in line with the Church's practice of praying for the dead, he holds that there are many souls that need to undergo purgatory before they can enter bliss (*Scriptum super libros Sententiarum* IV. 21. 1. 1. 1).

---

[44] Eternity, which is *tota simul*, belongs only to God in whose life saints live. 'The fire of hell is called eternal because it is interminable (*interminabilitatem*), for in hell there is no true eternity but much time (*non est vera aeternitas, sed magis tempus*)' (*ST* Ia 10. 3 ad 2).

While the practice of praying for the dead, and especially of offering 'the sacrifice of the altar' for the dead, was already well established in the time of Augustine (*Confessiones* IX. 11; *De cura pro mortuis* 22) and Ambrose (*De excessu Satyri* 80, FR 5), the theological explanation for this practice was less well developed. It was Augustine himself who contributed most to the theology of purgatory and yet, strangely, it seems not to have been a question that really excited him (Le Goff 1984: 62). By the thirteenth century, however, the tentative speculations of Augustine had flowered into a vivid imaginative realm that held an important place in the piety of ordinary Christians (Le Goff 1984: 96 ff.).

In this later context Thomas is reticent and theologically precise in his understanding of purgatory (Ombres 1981). He distinguishes purgatory very strongly from hell, for those in purgatory have their will immutably fixed in charity. Purgatory is the removal of any stain, disorder, or impediment in the soul of one who possesses charity but is still unduly attached to lesser goods (*Summa Contra Gentiles* IV. 91). In this way the souls of those who were lazy or half-hearted about doing penance for their sins are not better off than the perfectly contrite. The souls in purgatory need to make satisfaction through suffering. Thomas is cautious as to the location of purgatory for it is a question that is 'not determined in Scripture and where reason alone is inadequate' (*Scriptum super libros Sententiarum* IV. 21. 1. 1. 2).

In another clear difference from his doctrine about what the separated soul can know by nature, Thomas holds that the souls of the saints in heaven obtain from the beatific vision a clear and certain knowledge of what is happening in the world. This allows them to pray for the living (*ST* IIaIIae 83. 4 ad 2). The souls of those in purgatory do not yet enjoy the vision of God and so do not have any direct knowledge of this world unless God grants it to them (*ST* IIaIIae 83. 4 ad 3). However, God does sometimes allow souls to appear in this world, so as to request that prayers be said to help them, 'as many saints attest' (*Scriptum super libros Sententiarum* IV. 21. 1. 1. 2). The soul of Thomas's sister appeared to him after she had died and asked him to be more fervent in praying for her as she was suffering in purgatory. Later she appeared to him a second time to say that his prayers had been effective and that she was now in bliss (a story attested in the earliest biographies, Gui 20, Tocco 44). The most effective of all prayers for the dead is the offering of the Mass, which was instituted to benefit the living and the dead (*Scriptum super libros Sententiarum* IV. 45. 2. 4. 3 ad 2; cf. *ST* IIIa 52. 8 obj. 2; *Lectura super evangelium Johannis* 6. 6. 964).

While they are safe from falling, the holy souls in purgatory are still wayfarers (*viatores*) and they exercise the virtue of hope for a happiness they do not yet possess (*ST* IIaIIae 18. 3). They are closer to heaven than the greatest of saints on earth, but they are not yet in a position to help others, for, in their suffering, they themselves need help (*Scriptum super libros Sententiarum* IV. 15. 4. 5. 2 ad 2). Purgatory is thus neither a temporary hell, nor is it a third destination. It does not disturb Thomas's great scheme of a journey towards the vision of God. The central theme in Thomas's writings on purgatory, which span from his commentary on the *Sentences* of Peter Lombard (1252–6 CE) to his sermons in Naples on the Apostles Creed (Lent 1273 CE), is the solidarity of Christian charity. If one is cruel who would not succour a friend who was in prison, how much more cruel is someone who will give no help to the soul of a friend who is suffering much worse pains in purgatory (*Collationes super Credo in Deum* 5). Prayer for the dead, like the prayers of the saints in bliss for those who are still on the way, expresses the communion of the members of the body of Christ.

The medieval Christian approach to death exemplified by Thomas Aquinas was shaped not only by philosophical reflection but by beliefs such as the last judgment, the beatific vision, the intercession of the saints in heaven, the punishment of the damned in hell; and by practices such as anointing and the viaticum (the last rites before death), the ritual of Christian burial, and the offering of the sacrifice of the Mass for the purification of holy souls. Such beliefs and practices inspire one to hope in death, and to fear the judgment more than death itself (*Collationes super Credo in Deum* 7). The grace of God makes the believer desire to depart and be with Christ, even while he or she still has a proper desire to be in the body. The saints still rightly fear death (*licet autem sancti naturaliter timeant mortem*), for it is a great evil, but they do not fear death excessively so as to fall into sin out of fear of death (*non cedunt timore mortis; Super II ad Corinthianos* 5. 2. 163). What orders all these reactions is the virtue of charity: wishing to remain in the body so as to serve God and neighbour, and fearing things in proportion as they are truly fearful, fearing to lose God more than life itself.

Thomas's theological understanding of death thus supplements, in a number of important ways, his philosophical portrayal of the separation of body and soul. The theological and philosophical approaches are combined and well integrated in Thomas's account of the relation of Christian hope and natural fear of death, and in his understanding of martyrdom. The meaning of death as destruction from the perspective of nature is allowed its full force, but it is placed in the context of a greater hope. The fearfulness of death is thus made relative to the hope of heaven and to the goods of acknowledging one's creatureliness and of serving God in this life. In regard to such issues Thomas integrates well the theological vision he receives from Augustine and the philosophical tools and concepts he finds in Aristotle.

Where the theological and philosophical approaches are less well combined is in Thomas's account of killing. Here there is certainly a theological context which is seen in the role played by the doctrine of creation (and the goodness of being), the doctrine of the dignity of the human person, and the doctrine of God's authority over life and death. Furthermore, Thomas succeeds in bringing clarity to issues such as the injustice of killing the innocent and the rights and wrongs of accidental killing, and he provides some important insight into the wrongness of suicide. Nevertheless, this clarity is gained at the price of introducing a sharp separation between the essential (natural) badness of death and the incidental (graced) reward that follows from death. This is problematic, for example, in the case of suicide. For, if death is redeemable, then the desire for death need not be a desire for extinction (as Thomas portrays it). In at least some cases, suicide may be an act of presumption (expecting heaven) rather than an act of despair (expecting extinction). Thomas's fundamental conclusion on the morality of suicide is not here in question, for the morally destructive character of suicide is shown by many converging philosophical and theological arguments. Nevertheless, the Christian understanding of suicide would be enhanced by a better integration of the theology of hope with the philosophical analysis of killing than Thomas provides in his account.

Where the separation of theological hope and philosophical analysis causes most problems is on the issue of actively welcoming death by withdrawing medical treatment as death approaches. Is it reasonable for a Christian, in the context of his or her approaching death, to desire that death come quickly so that the burdens of life may be over and so that he or she may be united to Christ? If it is reasonable, at least in some circumstances, to hope for death to come quickly, in what way may this desire properly inform practical decisions such as the decision to withdraw medical treatment? This was less of a practical problem in Thomas's day, as there was less that could be done, medically, for those who were dying. It is a much more pressing question in the modern context where there is much that can be done medically, and where decisions to withdraw treatment can cover a multitude of motives and intentions, some right and reasonable, others unjust or even suicidal. This poses a double problem for Thomas's analysis: in that he did not directly address this particular practical dilemma; and in that it is precisely on this issue that one needs to integrate an account of hope in death with an analysis of the wrongness of bringing death about.

The relative lack of integration of philosophical and theological themes in the writings of Thomas Aquinas allowed subsequent commentators to neglect the more specifically theological themes in his work on death. This has led to the abstraction and further isolation of a purely philosophical account of death, as 'the separation of soul and body'. Thomas's most influential work, the *Summa Theologiae*, was never completed, thus depriving posterity of a systematic account of his mature thought on death, judgment, heaven, and hell. Furthermore, in the sixteenth and seventeenth centuries, in the face of a suspicion of Augustinianism (both the Reformed Augustinianism of Calvin and the Catholic Augustinianism of Jansen), a reading of Thomas was developed that systematically separated nature and grace from one another as though they were independent spheres. Finally, in the nineteenth century, Thomas was promoted specifically for providing a response to the *philosophical* movements of the day. His philosophical works were studied meticulously while the commentaries on Scripture, which contain much of his most mature theology, have long been neglected. Servais Pinckaers (1995: 189–90) has argued convincingly that the core of Thomas's moral theology is the grace of the Holy Spirit and the theological virtues, but due to his extensive use of Aristotle many modern readers have been deceived into thinking of Thomas Aquinas more as an Aristotelian than as a Christian.

The twentieth century witnessed the development of a great variety of different approaches to Thomas's thought (McCool 1992; Kerr 2002). Some of these were more philosophical, some more historical, some more theological, and some mixed theological method with contemporary philosophy. Of particular interest is the German Jesuit Karl Rahner, who pursued a Thomistic theological method through engagement with Heidegger and other strands of German post-Kantian philosophy. Rahner sought to overcome that bifurcation mentioned in Chapter 4, which can be traced back all the way to Augustine, between a dogmatic account of death and a 'spirituality of dying'. Likewise he wished to overcome the separation of theology and philosophy which he perceived in the method predominant in the early twentieth-century Catholic theology, and which can be traced back to Thomas Aquinas.

Rahner wished to create a more integrated synthesis of grace and nature in the whole of his theology, but he was also particularly interested in developing a renewed theology of death. The resulting writings constitute perhaps the most creative and influential treatment of the topic of death by a twentieth-century Catholic theologian. The approach of Karl Rahner builds on and criticizes the approach of Thomas, who was himself building on and criticizing Augustine, as he was on Ambrose. Examining the work of Rahner thus offers a helpful way to extend our theological investigation of death into the late twentieth century. He provides a worthy interlocutor with whom to develop a contemporary Christian theology of death, through which to engage with some of the practical and existential issues that the approach of death presents for us.

6

Both Something Suffered and a Human Act: Death in the Thought of Karl Rahner

BACKGROUND TO THE THOUGHT OF KARL RAHNER

Between Thomas Aquinas in the thirteenth century and Karl Rahner in the twentieth there is a great dislocation of the tradition. The failure of the Church in the sixteenth century to hold within herself powerful reforming movements led to a schism and a bitter polemic in which the Catholic Church, to a considerable degree, defined herself over and against the Protestant reformers. The breakdown of feudal structures of society, the rise of the nation state, and a revolution in scientific thinking also distanced and, to an extent, alienated Christians from medieval patterns of thought and practice. At the same time, new rationalist philosophers, such as René Descartes, attempted to establish sure and indubitable foundations for the new scientific world view.

Each of these aspects of thought and society advanced still more radically in the late eighteenth and early nineteenth century. Hume in the English-speaking world and Kant in the German-speaking world discredited the very idea of attaining certain philosophical knowledge of the world as it is in itself (metaphysics as previously understood) and deemed God's existence inaccessible to the human mind. Scientific accounts of biological evolution and the application of historical and literary criticism to the Scriptures undermined the authority of the Church to disclose the true identity of the human being, or even the true historical identity of Jesus of Nazareth (Chadwick 1975). Society too was changing. The industrial revolution had brought people from village to city, loosening traditional and communal ties and fuelling uncertainty and desire for social reform. The failed revolutions of the middle of the nineteenth century exacerbated both fear of and desire for change and led the Church increasingly to identify herself with conservative forces of order and stability, thus alienating liberal and socialist political movements (McLeod 2000). The sort of violent anticlericalism which, in the Middle Ages, would have expressed itself as heresy, now took the form of 'scientific' agnosticism or atheism.

In the wake of the revolutions of 1848, Pius IX (Pope from 1846 to 1878) set the Catholic Church firmly against the forces of 'progress, liberalism, and modern civilization'.[1] In the face of a hostile modern world the Church presented herself as a supernatural authority. In this period devotion to the Blessed Virgin Mary and to the office of the Papacy both flourished and a growing number of religious orders opened schools and hospitals and sent missionaries to Africa, South America, and the Far East. Pope Leo XIII (1878–1903) was more confident that the Church could engage with the concerns of modern people and offer intellectual guidance. He saw the root of the problem in the diverse and eclectic character of philosophy taught in seminaries and, in his 1879 encyclical *Aeterni Patris*, he required that philosophy be taught in Catholic institutions according to the scholastic method of Thomas Aquinas. However, while Leo hoped to encourage creative intellectual engagement and Catholic solutions to modern problems, his successor, Pius X (1903–14) instituted a rigorous suppression of the heresy of 'modernism' attributed to a small number of Catholic intellectuals. The modernist crisis effectively smothered the emergent Catholic biblical school associated with Marie-Joseph Lagrange at the École Biblique and placed restrictions on dogmatic theologians and Catholic philosophers.

It was in this highly restrictive and intellectually fearful milieu that Karl Rahner did his first studies in philosophy while training for the priesthood as a member of the Society of Jesus (Jesuits). Born in 1904, he entered the Jesuits in 1922, three years after his

---

[1] *cum progressu, cum liberalismo et cum recenti civilitate*, Syllabus of errors n. 80, Denzinger (1953) para. 1780.

brother Hugo.[2] His early intellectual formation was strongly influenced by private reading of the works of Joseph Maréchal (1878–1944) and Pierre Rousselot (1878–1915), who had attempted use the thought of Thomas Aquinas to answer Kant on his own terms (McCool 1992: chs. 2–4, 1994: chs. 5–6; Weger 1980: 22–34; Rousselot 1935). In 1932, after initial studies and ordination Rahner returned to his hometown of Freiburg im Breisgau where he started working for a doctorate. There he found admittance to a prestigious seminar run by Martin Heidegger, who opened his eyes to new ways of reading ancient philosophical texts. Rahner's attempt to embrace contemporary philosophy was not received well by his (Catholic) supervisor, Martin Honecker; he was denied a doctorate in philosophy and was sent in 1936 to Innsbruck, where he rapidly prepared a doctorate in theology and started teaching at the University. In 1939 he published his offending philosophy dissertation under the title *Geist in Welt* (later published in English as *Spirit in the World*).

Geist in Welt is a study of the act of knowing constructed as a philosophical reflection on question 84 article 7 of the *prima pars* of the *Summa Theologiae* (an article examined in the previous chapter). This is a focal question for Thomas's account of the embodied understanding of the intellectual soul: whether the soul can understand anything without attending to some sense-image (*phantasma*).[3] Rahner saw in this article the necessity of some 'pre-apprehension' (*Vorgriff*) of being as such, as the condition of grasping any particular being. Rahner's philosophical method, following Maréchal, was to ask what conditions must be fulfilled in order for knowing to be taking place. He considered that the very ordinary act of knowing something presupposed an infinite background or horizon of being. Similarly, loving something presupposed a horizon of the infinitely lovely and lovable.[1] Rahner used a method somewhat similar to Kant's, but concluded not

---

[2] For biographical material cf. Vorgrimler 1965, 1986; Rahner 1984.

[3] 'This article [*ST* Ia 84.7] has been called the touchstone of Aristotelian-Thomistic realism—and rightly so. The most important aspect of the doctrine is found in the sentence "Hence it is obvious that for the intellect actually to understand (not only in acquiring new knowledge but also *in using knowledge already* acquired) acts of the imagination and other faculties are necessary" ' (Durbin 1968: 38 n. a).

[4] For discussion of Rahner's transcendental method, especially as developed in *Geist in Welt* see Ernst 1961: p. xiii n. 1; Lonergan 1963; Roberts 1967: 7–31; Bradley 1977; Vass 1989a: ch. 3; Phillips 1992; Parker 1999.

with agnosticism but confronted with a Mystery that is necessarily known as unknown (Vass 1989*a*: ch. 7). The idea of mystery and of the human subject as reaching out towards the divine in even the most mundane thoughts and actions continued to stay with Rahner throughout the course of his intellectual life. After the outbreak of war, the Nazis closed down the faculty at Innsbruck and Rahner was sent to do pastoral work in Vienna. When the war ended he moved to Munich, finally returning to Innsbruck when the faculty reopened in 1948. There he taught a series of courses on dogmatic theology that would be the basis of much of his later writing.

Until the mid-1950s Rahner had published relatively little, but from this time he began a period of prolific literary activity. He co-edited and contributed many articles to a new edition of Herder's great theological encyclopaedia *Lexikon für Theologie und Kirche* which started to appear in 1957. While working on the lexicon Rahner also started publishing his scattered talks and articles under the title *Schriften zur Theologie*, of which the first volume appeared in 1954 and sixteen volumes were to be produced before his death in 1984. To further the cause of speculation and debate within theology (a cause to which he was to remain committed) Rahner initiated a series of monographs, Quaestiones Disputatae, and in 1965 he was one of the founders of the theological review *Concilium*. Rahner also wished to present a coherent and systematic account of Christian doctrine, which he did in a series of theological lexicons of his own: in 1961 the *Kleines theologisches Wörterbuch*; in 1967 *Sacramentum Mundi*; in 1973 Herder's *Theologischers TaschenLexikon*; and in 1975 a concise *Sacramentum Mundi* in English—his *Encyclopaedia of Theology*. He also contributed to another great theological co-operative work, *Mysterium Salutis*, which appeared in 1976. The same year he published his long-awaited *Grundkurs des Glaubens*, in which he attempted an overview of his own thought including his understanding of death and eternal life.

These writings straddle the period of the Second Vatican Council (1962–5), which transformed the face of the Church, in particular in her attitude to 'the other' (other Christians, other religions, the secular modern world). A defensive attitude of confrontation had been maintained since the sixteenth century, but especially in the recent pontificates of 'the Pian Popes' (Pius IX, Pius X, Pius XI, Pius XII; cf. Kerr 1980*b*). This approach was reversed by Vatican II in favour of seeking dialogue, co-operation, and solidarity. Though the Council came as a bolt from the blue for most Catholics (whether as liberating or as traumatic), it was the fruit of work that had been going on for many decades. There were two main sources of creativity which would eventually break down the contrived uniformity of early twentieth-century Neoscholasticism. The first source was historical research into the detailed situation of Thomas Aquinas and his contemporaries—exposing the variety of opinions prevalent in the supposedly homogeneous golden age of scholasticism.[5] Further historical research into the sources for Thomas's own theology led to a new appreciation of the importance of the Fathers of the Church in their own right, and to a breadth of vision many felt lacking in contemporary Catholic theology.[6] Another important aspect of this historical research was a focus on the history of liturgy, which helped fuel the emergent movement for the reform of the liturgy. Distinct from such historical scholarship, a second source of intellectual creativity was the attempt to engage with contemporary philosophy and thus present the central tenets of Thomism in the language of modern people.[7] This latter way was exemplified by Karl Rahner and, from being a figure of suspicion in the 1950s, he found himself a theological adviser (*peritus*) to the Second Vatican Council and an internationally recognized Catholic theologian.

Rahner's interest in the theology of death is evident throughout his writings. The first volume of Quaestiones Disputatae (a series now numbering well over a hundred monographs) was on the inspiration of Scripture. The second volume was on the theology of death, *Zur Theologie des Todes*. Around this time Rahner also started writing articles and giving talks on Christian dying and the death of Christ

---

[5] Especially the pioneering work of Etienne Gilson, Marie-Dominic Chenu, Yves Congar, and Eduard Schillibeeckx.

[6] A project associated with Jean Daniélou and Henri de Lubac but also, in a different way, Hans Urs von Balthasar and Josef Ratzinger (Benedict XVI).

[7] One should also mention Joseph Maréchal, Bernard Lonergan, Edith Stein, Karol Wojtyla (John Paul II), and Dietrich von Hildebrand, and behind them the influence of Maurice Blondel, Edmund Husserl, Martin Heidegger, and Max Scheler.

(subsequently published in *Schriften zur Theologie*). Whenever Rahner had editorial control of a lexicon or encyclopaedia, he wrote the article on death himself. Whenever he edited pocket or concise versions of larger lexicons, his method was 'to discard all articles on subjects purely or largely of interest to those specialising in the individual disciplines, and to give pride of place to more inclusive and humanly relevant entries' (*Encyclopaedia of Theology*, p. v). Needless to say, he always retained an article on death. In *Mysterium Salutis*, where he had no editorial control, he was nevertheless asked to write the section on Christian dying, a sign that by this time he had become recognized for his contribution in this area.

Rahner's habit of returning to the subject of death in a series of lexicon articles in 1961, 1965, 1967, 1973, 1975, and 1976,[8] as well as significant articles written in 1957, 1959, and 1970,[9] allow one to trace the development of his thought over twenty years. However, before charting its future development, the best starting point for an initial understanding of Rahner's teaching is the 1958 monograph *Zur Theologie des Todes* (*On the Theology of Death*) which is volume 2 of the series Quaestiones Disputatae (henceforth QD2) This remained his most significant work on the theology of death, notwithstanding the fact that certain aspects were to be qualified or quietly dropped in his later writings.

AN EVENT CONCERNING THE HUMAN BEING AS A WHOLE

Characteristically, Rahner begins his investigation with a consideration of anthropology.

The order to be followed in our first meditation on death is suggested by the following consideration: death is an event which strikes man in his totality

---

[8] 1961 *Kleines theologisches Wörterbuch* (*Concise Theological Dictionary*); 1965 *Lexikon für Theologie und Kirche*; 1967 *Sacramentum Mundi*; 1973 *Theologisches TaschenLexikon*; 1975 *Encyclopaedia of Theology*; and 1976 *Mysterium Salutis* respectively.

[9] 1957 'Abgestiegen in Totenreich' ('He Descended into Hell'); 1959 'Über die christlich Sterbens' ('On Christian Dying'); and 1970 'Zu einer Theologie des Todes' ('Ideas for a Theology of Death') respectively.

(*den ganzen Menschen*), in a sense to be clarified later. Man is a union of nature and person (*Natur und Person*). (QD2: 13)

The division of the human being into nature and person is stated here as a given. These categories are not to be confused with the traditional resolution of the human being into soul and body, nor even of the Cartesian resolution of the human being into mind and mechanism. Rather, the form of Rahner's categories is clearly rooted in the German philosophical tradition issuing from Immanuel Kant. Kant's division of reality into the categorical world-as-it-appears and the transcendental world as-it-is-in-itself (but cannot be conceptualized) allowed him to safeguard human freedom by sheltering it in the pinions of the noumenal self, away from the attacks of deterministic science. Kant's vision continued to have influence through the series of reactions and counter-reactions of the German intellectual tradition (from Hegel and Schopenhauer to Husserl and Heidegger). Rahner sees the human being as *nature* in broadly Kantian terms, as the object of scientific investigation and knowledge, as passively subordinate to a web of necessary causes. However, the human being as *person* is essentially free and active.[10] The root of the distinction of nature and person is thus the phenomenon of human freedom.[11]

Having presented this distinction, Rahner goes on to apply it to the understanding of human death.

Death must consequently possess for [the human being] a personal and a natural aspect. In the doctrine of the Church, the natural aspect of death is expressed by saying that death is the separation of body and soul; its personal aspect by saying that it means the definitive end of our state of pilgrimage. (QD2: 13)

---

[10] A number of writers see theological anthropology as the key to understanding Rahner (Ernst 1961: p. xviii; L. Roberts 1967: 31; McCool 1975: pp. xxv–xxvi; Weger 1980: 35; Macquarrie 1984). Thus an implicit Cartesianism (assuming this is a bad thing) that some find in his anthropology threatens his whole theological project (McCool 1975: pp. xxv–xxvi.; Kerr 1981; Kerr 1997*a*: 7–16; Kerr 1997*b*: ch. 8). In an effort to defend the continuing relevance of Rahner, without necessarily endorsing his anthropology, others have stressed the ad hoc and eclectic character of many of his writings (Healey 1992; Kilby 1997: 51–2; Di Noia 1997). This chapter takes a position closer to that of Kerr than to that of Kilby.

[11] 'Just as man is both spirit and matter, liberty and necessity, person and nature' QD2: 30.

Thus, the division of the human being into person and nature allows Rahner to consider an aspect of human death which he regards as having been overlooked in the traditional description of death as 'the separation of body and soul'. Rahner does not, however, dispute the validity of this description. He does not dispute that it is the soul that gives life to the body, or that the soul continues to exist after death. This language of body and soul is not used in a clear or consistent way within the Holy Scriptures, yet it is almost universal in the Fathers of the Church and the later tradition which, at least at this stage of Rahner's intellectual development, is held to be determinative. The description of death as the separation of body and soul is acceptable, but only so long as it is recognized that this is only one among many possible descriptions. It is not a definition of the essence of death.

Nevertheless, as theologians, we may point out that this is a description and nothing more, and by no means a definition of death in its very essence (*eigentliches Wesen des Todes*) ... it is absolutely silent, for example, about the characteristic feature of death, that it is an event for man as a whole and as a spiritual person. (QD2: 17)

However, before examining the personal aspect of death—death as the completion of our earthly pilgrimage—Rahner goes on to examine the notion of the separation (*Trennung*) of soul and body. A question arises as to the relation of the separated soul to the material universe. One might reasonably think that a soul separated from the body no longer has any relation to the material universe. For a Thomist, the soul is not a second (subtle) body hidden inside the body, it is the form of the body, the animating principle of the living body as a unified whole. The soul is thus related to the material world *via* this particular living body. When the soul departs and the body decays there is no particular living body the soul is related to, and thus the soul seems not to be in any particular place. While a separated soul may still act (thinking and willing), it no longer acts in a particular place. Nevertheless, Rahner thinks that the doctrine of the separated soul ceasing to have any relationship with the material universe, becoming 'acosmic', is a prejudice due to Neoplatonic influences:

We tend to assume that the appearance of the soul before God, which, as faith teaches, takes place at death, is a contrary concept to the soul's belonging to the world, as though lack of relation to matter and nearness to God must increase in direct ratio. (QD2: 19)

As an alternative to this view, Rahner puts forward the hypothesis that 'the human spiritual soul will become not acosmic but, if the term may be used "pancosmic"' (QD2: 21).

The soul, by surrendering its limited bodily structure in death, becomes open towards the universe and, in some way, a co-determining factor of the universe precisely in the latter's character as the ground of the personal life of other spiritual beings. (QD2: 22)

In an effort to defend this view theologically, Rahner turns to the neglected topic of angelology. Angels are referred to in the Scriptures as principles or powers of the created order. Perhaps embarrassed by the subsequent tradition, Rahner does not allude to the way that the 'powers' of scriptural angelology came later to be identified with the eternal substances which moved the spheres in Aristotelian cosmology. Astronomy no longer invokes intellectual substances to explain the circular motion of stars or planets. The angels have become redundant in modern physics. However, Rahner still thinks that a proper understanding of scriptural revelation supports the view that there are angels who are the founding principles of the natural order. On the level of natural reason, Rahner appeals not to astronomy but to metaphysics to establish the need for a 'ground of the personal life of corporeal[-spiritual] beings' (*Grundes des personalen Lebens der leib-geistiger Wesen*; QD2: 22). If angels have an essential relationship to the cosmos as a whole—operating as the spiritual principles of the natural order—then there is nothing to exclude the possibility that human souls, after death, might come into the same sort of relationship to the cosmos as a whole.

The theological assurance of a natural, pancosmic relationship between the angels, as personal spiritual beings, and the world, makes it impossible to exclude, *a priori*, as an idea without parallel elsewhere, the possibility of some such relationship in the case of the spiritual, personal principle in man. (QD2: 23)

Thus the soul at death is freed, liberated, perfected, no longer confined by the particularities of an individual body (*abgegrenzten Leibgestalt*) but now opened out to a radical relationship with the cosmos as a whole (*das Ganze der Welt*). Yet, if this is so, how are we supposed to make sense of the resurrection of the flesh? Is the soul freed, only to be put in its prison once more? Rahner here points out the perfect plasticity (*vollendete Plastizität*) of the glorified body. The transfiguration of the body, which is accomplished in the resurrection, gives rise to a whole new form of corporeality that is the complete expression of the liberated spirit. 'In this way the glorified body seems to become the perfect expression of the enduring relation of the glorified person to the cosmos as a whole' (QD2: 26).

Thus the resurrected body catches up, as it were, with the new unhampered relation that the separated soul *already* enjoys with the material world. What happens to the soul in death is finally enjoyed also by the body in the resurrection, without prejudice to the soul's new-found freedom. Having thus redefined the notion of the separation of body and soul to include a new and unhampered relation to the material world, Rahner returns to the personal aspect of death. Death is not only the separation of two aspects of a natural living substance; it is also an event in the life of a person. With bodily death, the state of pilgrimage of the human being comes to an end. After death we are no longer *in via*, on the way, but our life shall have come to an end and been resolved, for good or ill. The Christian understanding of death has no room for a second chance after death, for more life of this sort beyond this life. Rather, this mortal life is the one, and the only one, on which our eternal destiny is founded.

This doctrine of the faith involves taking this earthly life with radical seriousness. It is truly historical, that is, unique, unrepeatable, of inalienable and irrevocable significance. Life is suspended between a genuine beginning and a genuine end. (QD2: 27)

Death is not merely the passage from one form of existence to another within a continuing temporal sequence. It is, rather, the beginning of eternity, the resolution and consummation of a whole temporally ordered life. All Catholic theologians are agreed that judgment comes with death, but it remains a point of debate, not stated explicitly in the sources of revelation, whether judgment is of itself an essential constituent of death, or whether it is linked to it extrinsically, though fittingly, by God's decree. From Rahner's viewpoint it is important to assert that death is, of itself and intrinsically, the moment of judgment. If this may be granted, then death can be seen as the intrinsic moment of completion and hence, self-realization for human existence.

> In death the soul achieves the consummation (*Vollendung*) of its own personal self-affirmation (*Selbstauszeugung*)... through its own personal act (*eigene personale Tat*). Death, therefore, as the end of man as a spiritual person, must be an active consummation (*tätige Vollendung*) from within brought about by the person himself, a maturing self-realization (*aktives Sich-zur-Vollendung-Bringen*) which embodies the result of what man has made of himself during his life, the achievement of total self-possession (*totales Sich-in-Besitz-Nehmen*), a real effectuation of self (*Sich-selbst-gewirkt-Haben*), the fullness of freely produced personal reality (*personalen Wirklichkeit*). (QD2: 30–31)

There is no denying that death is also the destruction of the human being as a living whole, something suffered rather than done, yet this primarily concerns death as a natural phenomenon, rather than as personal. Death must be regarded as at once 'an active consummation of the self *from within* and a passive submission to destruction *from without*' (QD2: 31). Furthermore, we should beware making an easy identification of suffering with the body and activity with the soul, for this would contradict the foundation of Rahner's understanding of death: that death is a phenomenon which affects the human being in his or her totality. Death is something the soul and body suffer together, and something achieved by soul and body while together. Every death must be both suffered and achieved, and these two aspects involve the human being in his or her totality.

THE CONSEQUENCE OF SIN

Death is described in the Scriptures as a consequence of sin, so that, had Adam not sinned, it seems he would have been under no necessity of death. Does this mean that he would have continued to live an endless this-worldly existence? Rahner thinks not; rather, he holds that, even had Adam not sinned, his life would still have come to an end.

It can confidently be said that he would surely have had an end to his life … In other words, Adam would have brought his personal life to its perfect consummation even in its bodily form through a 'death' which would have been a pure, active self-affirmation (*Selbstauszeugung*). (QD2: 34)

This would have been in effect a ' "death" without dying' (*der 'Tod' ohne Tod*; QD2: 34). In this way Rahner develops the view of Augustine and Thomas who both held that Adam's body was like ours—'an ensouled body'—but as a reward of a holy life his body could have been spiritualized and then Adam would have become truly immortal, as the saints are after the resurrection. His body was 'ensouled before but could have become a spiritual body when God so willed after a holy life' (*De Genesi ad litteram* VI. 23; *ST* Ia 97. 4). Thus, there is nothing novel in Rahner positing that, had Adam not sinned, he would have been glorified at the end of his earthly life, without death intervening. What is novel is the conclusion Rahner draws from this; if Adam would have had an end to his life, then having an end to one's life is a *good thing*: 'Not every aspect of our death can be considered a consequence of sin that ought not to have been' (QD2: 35).

From this point, Rahner goes on to state that, for *theological* reasons, it is necessary to hold that death has a natural essence that is neutral, being neither good nor bad in itself. This cannot be shown simply from the constitution of human beings as body and spirit; our actual constitution must also be placed in the context of our proper end or destiny. The decisive theological ground for proposing a neutral common essence for every death is that there must be a something that is capable of taking the meaning either of punishment for sin, or as dying with Christ. Death is capable of taking negative and positive values, therefore *in itself* it must have neither value, but must be a neutral common matter. The actual concrete death will always be positive or negative, one in which the neutral essence is resolved one way or the other. 'There must be in death, as it is an actual event for each individual, some common element, neutral, so to speak, which permits us to say that, in a true sense, all men die the same death' (QD2: 36).

What makes death a consequence of sin that should not be, is that it stands in the way of the complete bodily and spiritual fulfilment to which human beings were destined; this is true even of sinners. 'Death is something that ought not to be, because even the sinner still retains his orientation towards grace and eternal life as a real ontological feature characterizing the human situation. (QD2: 38)[12]

What, then, is it that allows death to take these diverse values, positive or negative? According to Rahner, it is death's character as simultaneously negative and positive; at once the spiritual self-realization and the biological catastrophe; at once fullness and emptiness that allows it to be resolved either way. Rahner calls this the veiledness (*Verhülltheit*) of death: the obscurity or darkness in which its character, either as damnation or as salvation, is hidden is a result of the fall.

Adam's 'death' would not have been hidden in darkness. His end would have been the perfection and preservation of the personal reality effected in life, an end undisguisedly (*unverhüllt*) and tangibly experienced. The fact . . . that death as a human act is [now] obscured by death as suffering, visibly manifests the absence of divine grace. Death, therefore, is the penalty of sin. (QD2: 42–3)

This obscure character also explains why it is possible to take so many different attitudes to death. Faced with a prospect that is darkly veiled, and being unwilling to accept the help of faith, there is a tendency to despair or alternatively to simply deny the obscure character of death. Death's obscurity can be denied by resolving the human person either materialistically or spiritually, so that the meaning of death becomes clear. Either it is a natural material event, or it is a simple spiritual liberation. Yet both these possible avenues do violence to the compound unity of the human being and

---

[12] This orientation towards an end which exceeds our natural powers, but which constituted the *de facto* situation of all human beings, saints and sinners, is what Rahner at other points calls the 'supernatural existential' (cf. McCool 1975: p. xxvi, ch. 9). It is that aspect of our actual existential situation constituted by the fact of our supernatural destiny.

the essential obscurity of death. The obscurity of death is faced properly when the person surrenders to the demand of God, and it is faced wrongly when the person attempts to make death an act of autonomy.

Death, because of its darkness, is faced rightly when it is entered upon by man as an act in which he surrenders himself fully and with unconditional openness to the disposal of the incomprehensible decision of God, because, in the darkness of death, man is not in a position to dispose himself unambiguously. Conversely, we can also say that mortal sin consists in the will to die autonomously. (QD2: 44)

Death as it actually exists is not the simple completion or fulfilment of the spiritual creature, but is mixed with darkness, obscurity, destruction, and judgment. Hence, 'man is rightly afraid of death' (QD2: 54). According to Rahner, this fact is not explained by metaphysical anthropology alone, for fear of death is not appropriate to a spiritual being. Yet it is explained by theology which points to a supernatural vocation for all human beings, a vocation that involves a transformation of the body, and that is radically contradicted by death as it is actually experienced. 'Because a creature belongs to God, it shrinks back, by a movement of its very essence, from this last mystery of emptiness, of finality, of nothingness, from the mystery of iniquity' (QD2: 55).

This terror of death must be admitted and cannot be avoided or abolished but only transformed by the light of Christ who overcame the darkness of the death of the cross and 'penetrated in death the very depths of the world, in order to give life to the world' (QD2: 55).

DYING WITH CHRIST

The starting point for an understanding of the death of Christ is the fundamental assertion that 'Christ died our death' *Christus ist unseren Tod gestorben* (QD2: 57). This is underlined by the explicit addition of the affirmation that, having died, he descended to the underworld.

This establishes the essential similarity of Christ's death with our own ... for such a descent into hell was regarded as an essential element in human death, at least according to the situation in the economy of salvation then prevailing. (QD2: 57)

This consideration of the character of Christ's death also raises a question with respect to the received understanding of how Jesus accomplished his saving work. The accepted Catholic account of the redemption is, with some modifications, that which was developed by Anselm of Canterbury in his *Cur Deus Homo*. The positive engine of human redemption according to this account is not the suffering that Christ underwent, but the infinite value of the love and obedience with which he suffered. The obedient actions of Jesus were pleasing to God and could be offered as a complete satisfaction for any offence caused by human sin. The weakness of this traditional account is that it fails to explain why Jesus had to die in order to satisfy the Father. It seems that some other act could have been done with the same infinite love and accomplished the same saving effect. Yet the Scriptures stress the saving character of the *death* of Christ, and not any other act. On the face of it there seems to be something in the character of death that makes it alone capable of restoring human nature. 'The efficacy of Christ's death consequently cannot be attributed to it as directly as this in its general quality as a moral act but only in its precise character as death' (QD2: 60).

Anselm's theory of 'satisfaction' fails to explain why we were redeemed precisely through Christ's *death*. Furthermore, according to Rahner, another shortcoming of this theory is that it makes death a purely passive occurrence and not, in itself, a human act. 'On this tacit but in reality questionable assumption, the redeeming act of Christ will not reside in his death as such, but only in his patient and obedient submission to it' (QD2: 61).

Yet, in order to have entered into the human situation to redeem it, it was necessary for Christ to take on the darkness of human death. In dying the death of sinful human beings Christ transformed the meaning of death, from a manifestation of sin to an expression of loving obedience to the Father. This becomes the proper culmination of his redemptive activity. This does not mean that the significance of his death is to be isolated from the significance of his life. It is rather that the manner of his death is seen as the culmination of his life, and hence his redeeming death can be thought of as present throughout his life.

Man's death, in so far as it is his own personal act, extends through his whole life. If this is so, it makes it easier to comprehend how the life and death of Christ in their redemptive significance also form a unity. His life redeems, inasmuch as his death is axiologically (*axiologisch*) present in his entire life. (QD2: 62)

Rahner also speculates that reconsidering the metaphysics of human death in this way might throw new light on the mechanism by which Christ brought redemption. Rahner considers that death opens the human soul up to 'an unrestricted relationship to the cosmos as a whole' (QD2: 63), like that of the angels to the world. When this is applied to the soul of Christ it becomes clearer how Christ could be 'inserted into this whole world in its ground as a permanent determination of a real ontological kind' (QD2: 63). The redemption is accomplished, according to Rahner, precisely by Christ's death and his descent into hell.

The basic images in our usual idea of hell include 'depth', something 'underneath', something 'more inward', belonging to the 'background', something 'more essential' (*Wesenhafteren*) and 'radically one' (*wurzelhaft Einen*). Thus we may suppose in general that when we think of man entering the lower world we think of him as establishing contact with the intrinsic, radically unified, ultimate and deepest level of the world . . . Consequently, if the reality of Christ, as consummated through his death, in his death is built into this unity of the cosmos, thus becoming a feature and intrinsic principle of it, and a prior framework and factor in all personal life in the world, that means that the world as a whole and as the scene of human actions has become different from what it would have been had Christ not died. (QD2: 64–5)

In this way—by using his 'pancosmic' theory of the separated soul—Rahner is enabled to give an explanation as to how the death of Christ actually effects a real change in the world: metaphysical anthropology sheds light on soteriology. Yet soteriology reflects back on anthropology: the death of a Christian cannot be considered separately from the death of Christ, for it has been transformed by Christ's death. By Christ's death, not only is the outcome of death changed (bringing eternal life), but the death itself is changed. 'A Christian in a state of grace dies a different death from that of the sinner. Not only is the final outcome in the next life reached through death, different for each, but the death itself is different' (QD2: 67). This fact has been overlooked by traditional scholastic Catholic theology, which has seen death purely in passive and negative terms. Yet in the New Testament 'dying in the Lord' is something positive, and indeed something which begins already in this life. 'These statements of the New Testament imply that physical death must be conceived as an axiological factor which dominates the whole of life, and also as an action' (QD2: 69).

To say this is not to make 'dying with Christ' a useful ethical metaphor, but is rather to identify the act of Christian dying as a principle of the Christian life. This in turn can only be understood because human death has been understood as a human *act* (*eine Tat*), and not only as something suffered.

We may even say that death is the culmination both of the reception and of the effecting of salvation, when we recall that death, as a human action, is precisely the event which gathers up the whole personal act of a human life into one fulfilment. (QD2: 69)

This identification of death in Christ as a principle of the whole Christian life, which culminates in a good death, is shown most clearly in the context of sacramental theology. The death in the Lord which we take on in baptism is the same death we actually die when our time comes.

We have only, too, to recall, as Eutychius (582 CE) said, that there occurs 'pragmatically' in death what had occurred 'mystically' at the sacramental heights of Christian life, in baptism and in the Eucharist, namely our assimilation to the death of the Lord. What occurs 'sacramentally' in these moments of culmination, happens 'really' in our death: the partaking (*Teilnahme*) in the death of our Lord. (QD2: 69)

Through the grace of Christ, Christian death is transformed so that the experience of emptiness and remoteness from God in death (still present even in Christ's death) is overcome by the faith in, hope in, and love of God. These principles of the Christian life do not just last until death but they change the character of death itself so that it is a different reality. Rahner considers martyrdom to be the reality that is sacramentally expressed in baptism, the Eucharist, and the anointing of the sick. He goes so far as to identify all Christian death with martyrdom and martyrdom with the life of grace as such. 'Baptism is the beginning of Christian death, because it is the initiation into the life of grace, by virtue of which alone death can be Christian. We may even say that the life of grace *is* Christian death' (QD2: 75).

Every Christian death has about it something of the character present in Christian martyrdom, yet also suffering in life shares some of the character of martyrdom, and indeed the character of death.

Suffering, in fact, is nothing else than that *prolixitas mortis*, that long-drawn out death, as St. Gregory the Great calls life which is subject to suffering leading to death. That is why, since baptism, companionship with Christ in suffering is the realistic accomplishment of companionship in death during life and both have their root in baptism. (QD2: 76)

MARTYRDOM

These considerations complete Rahner's sketch of a theology of death, yet at this point he chose to include, as a sort of appendix, an essay independently written on the subject of martyrdom. This recapitulates many of the same themes as the previous treatment, but gives a different focus and illuminates the topic from another perspective. It is, again, a topic he would return to in later writings, but the essentials are already here and form a proper complement to the foundation of Rahner's theology of death outlined above.

'Martyrdom is concerned with death' (QD2: 82). This is not an obvious or empty statement but an important and profound one. The New Testament concept of martyrdom is simply witness, and does not have the focal meaning of witness by blood that it comes to have from the second century. Why then do the concepts of witness and death become so closely identified? It is not simply that the time of the Early Church was one of intense persecution, so that witness often concretely meant witness by accepting death rather than infidelity. It is rather essential to martyrdom that, by it, the Christian identifies himself or herself with the offering of Christ on the cross. Death is essential to martyrdom as it was essential to Christ's sacrifice. 'Martyrdom has to do with death. In order to understand martyrdom, death must be understood. And so the mystery of death enters into martyrdom, and makes martyrdom itself a mystery (QD2: 83).

At this point Rahner returns to his thesis that human death cannot be understood only as a biological or passive event, or even as the separation of body and soul. Human death must be understood as a 'fully human and indissoluble unity of act and suffering' (QD2: 84). Therefore death as such has a voluntary aspect: 'Death is an act' (QD2: 84).

Death is not only *an* act it is 'the act of all acts' (*eine, nein* die *Tat*; QD2: 85). Admittedly the last moments of life may be unconscious, or death may take us by surprise, yet even in these cases death is present as an act throughout life. It is a sort of root principle present in all our lettings go, in all our orientation towards the dark fulfilment of physical death.

Because we die our death in this life, because we are permanently taking leave, permanently parting, looking towards the end, permanently disappointed, ceaselessly piercing through the realities into their nothingness, continually narrowing the possibilities of free life through our actual decisions and actual life until we have exhausted life and driven it into the straits of death...we die throughout life, therefore what we call death is really the end of death, the death of death. (QD2: 85)

Thus one's life moves towards death and the attitude one has to death must, of necessity, be shaped by decisions freely taken in life. 'He cannot avoid this death imposed on him as the work of freedom.' (QD2: 85) Human beings are under the necessity of freely adopting some attitude to death. This imposed freedom may not be welcomed; it can be hidden and denied, but it remains the deepest human reality. Freedom is shown in the accepting of death, to which life tends. So no human being should 'fear death like an animal' (QD2: 87), for this marks a failure to realize one's own transcendence. 'Wherever there is real liberty, there is love for death (*Liebe zum Tod*) and courage for death (*Mut zum Tod*)' (QD2: 87).

Yet it is not enough to love or welcome death. One must under-stand the true meaning of death, and thus of human existence, and welcome death as true human fulfilment. 'Man should not hurry towards a death which is the consummation of vacuity, a final emptying of life into meaninglessness, but towards a death which is the valid fulfilment of our existence' (QD2: 87). This can only be done by faith. For 'only by faith can this fall be interpreted as falling into the hands of the living God' (QD2: 87). Only by the grace of Christ can someone truly surrender himself or herself to God in death. Death always has, and cannot but have, the appearance of collapsing into emptiness, 'into the fathomless abyss'—this is the inescapable consequence of original sin. To have trust and confi-dence, in the face of death, that what appears to be emptiness is in fact one's fulfilment, can only happen through the grace of God in Christ. Thus every human being faces a radical choice between dying the death of Adam (emptiness) and dying the death of Christ (fulfilment).

Rahner is well aware that this radical dichotomy could be chal-lenged. What is one to say of those who have not heard of Christ but seem to live courageous and honest lives, even to the point of facing death well? Rahner here introduces his notion of anonymous Chris-tianity. Those who act well, even if they have not heard of Christ, do so only by the grace of Christ that comes to them invisibly. This grace is visible in the sacraments of the holy Catholic Church, but is not confined to that visible expression. The notion of a purely natural act that is honest and upright but not graced and supernatural is in fact an abstraction with no concrete historical reality. Again, here he invokes what is, effectively, the 'supernatural existential'. Once this is understood 'then the road is open to conceiving death as the comprehensive act of faith or unbelief, without having to reckon with the real possibility that it could be something less than the decision between the two extreme possibilities of human existence' (QD2: 96).

However, the act that takes place in death is veiled. Death itself leaves no one behind to attest to its action. We see the external action but not the inner principle by which it is done and the effect it has on and in the person. Martyrdom seems to present itself in some sense as the revelation of the true character of death: the revelation of death as a free act of Christian liberty. This is possible because martyrdom is a death that is freely accepted. It is a death that could have been avoided in the individual case. 'Then is revealed the love of death (*Todesliebe*) which a Christian must have' (QD2: 98). Though Rahner immediately adds the qualification: 'which he may not, however, carry into effect by suicide' (QD2: 98).

How, Rahner asks himself, is the death of the martyr exempt from the general rule that every moral decision remains ultimately enigmatic? To answer this question he turns, not to a deeper philosophical understanding of the person or of the act of dying, but rather, to the fundamental principle of Christian revelation. God reveals himself in his Church as holy, but this can only be done by the revelation of actual holiness in actual persons. Rahner has shown that dying is the act of the whole person, the act of a person *par excellence*. 'If the Church is indeed to be subjectively holy and if this holiness is really to appear as the work of God's grace, then, if anywhere, it must be seen in martyrdom' (QD2: 101). Martyrdom is a revelation of the possibility of a free death due to the presence of faith in God. 'Martyrdom is, therefore, Christian death as such' (QD2: 101). Martyrdom discloses what is so often hidden in the different circumstances and conditions in which Christians die, the essence of a death rendered a free act by faith. As such it belongs to the very essence of the Church, which is why the Church is always attested by martyrs.

Martyrdom is a sort of 'sacrament' of the reality of grace in the world: it is characteristic of Christianity as such. Other religions may encourage their adherents to die for a cause but only Christianity has a death as its focus (in the crucified Christ), hence also martyrdom was, from the first, seen as equivalent to baptism and the first cult of saints, after the apostles, was directed to the martyrs. In the official process of canonization of saints, martyrdom dispenses from the necessity to do other miracles, and this is because the manner of martyrs' deaths is itself God's testimony to them. Martyrdom shows forth the essence of death as Christian death, and simultaneously the essence of the Church as the place of God's grace. Therefore, only in Christianity is death faced as it should be. 'The essence of death appears in its purity only in Christian death' (QD2: 115). Yet this death, though fully visible in martyrdom, can be recognized only by one who, himself or herself, has already accepted this kind of death 'undergoing the same death spiritually in himself' (QD2: 115). Martyrdom is a witness to the faith, which can be an occasion of belief to those who see, but only if they themselves are moved by grace. Martyrdom is the best kind of death, which is itself the culmination and pinnacle of the whole Christian life. It is indeed the 'act of all acts':

It is, we have said, the highest personal event in the Christian life because, deriving from faith and furnishing a testimony to faith, in it the highest deed of man and its historical manifestation before the eyes of the Church and of the world coalesce into one, in an absolute (one might almost say 'supra-sacramental') manner. It is no wonder that throughout the history of the Church there have always been Christians longing for martyrdom and praying to God for this greatest of all graces. (QD2: 116)

Martyrdom makes visible what is true of every Christian death, which itself is the essence of human death as such: that death is an act as well as something suffered, and that such an act, when embraced freely, is the fulfilment of the whole person. When accepted in a Christian context, with a desire to imitate the Saviour and with faith in the God who saves through death, death itself becomes something to desire. That is, for Rahner, the difference between martyrdom and suicide. The suicide chooses death only as a means of escape, but the martyr loves death for itself, as a way of sharing in Christ's passion, and as a completion and offering of his or her whole life.

When [death] not merely 'happens' in the course of striving for something else and perhaps is not really envisaged through blind eagerness for something (flight from shame, something obstinately sought etc.), when death is loved for its own sake (*er selbst als solcher geliebt wird*) and explicitly, it cannot be but a good death. (QD2: 111)

LEXICONS AND OTHER INFLUENCES

Rahner's treatment of death in *On the Theology of Death* (QD2) divides the subject according to received categories such as:

● The universality of death;
● death as the end of our earthly pilgrimage;

- death as punishment for sin;
- death as the separation of body and soul.

These subdivisions can already be found in the treatment of death in earlier lexicons: in the Beker and Belte *Kirchenlexikon* of 1899; in the *Kirchliches Handlexikon* of 1912; and in the 1938 edition of Herder's *Lexikon für Theologie und Kirche*. Indeed, Rahner's own lexicon article for the 1965 edition of Herder's *Lexikon für Theologie und Kirche* keeps the same subheadings as the 1938 edition, at least for the section on official teaching (*Lehramt*).

It is clear that Rahner's early treatment of the theology of death has its roots in a well-established tradition of lexicon writing which shapes not only the general approach but the specific form and content of his thought. It is this very *specific tradition* that Rahner seeks to interpret with the help of his philosophical framework: a framework that combines the transcendental method of Kant with elements of the existential philosophy of Heidegger.

The acceptance of existentialist insights leads him to lay stress on the definitive character of death as an event affecting the whole person, hence his remark that 'death is an event which strikes man in his totality' (QD2: 13). In this regard Rahner is part of a larger movement in twentieth-century dogmatic theology. In the bibliography of his *Lexikon für Theologie und Kirche* article Rahner cites a paper of Hans Urs von Balthasar, 'Der Tod im heutigen Denken', written in 1956, two years before QD2. In this article Balthasar divides thought on death in every age into mythic-magical, theoretical, and existential. The first phase is supposed to have been exemplified by the ancient mythological systems of China, Mesopotamia, and Egypt; the second phase by the Greek conception of θεωρια. The Greek dialectic between Platonic and Aristotelian/Stoic accounts of the duality and unity of man, Christianized to a certain extent by the message of the resurrection, is supposed to have held sway until the nineteenth century. Then a third period of thought begins to emerge which does not understand the human being in cosmological terms, but regards the cosmos as to be interpreted by human beings. Yet the human person, the measure of all things, is now to be understood as essentially *mortal*, notwithstanding traditional beliefs about the immortality of the soul. 'Death affects the whole human being, body and soul, even if the soul does not become nothing' (Balthasar 1956). For this reason the next life must not be seen as more of the same, but death brings life to a definitive close. 'Eternal life is no second, other life than the temporal and finite life, this—in God—given eternal breadth and depth' (Balthasar 1956).

Here Balthasar seems to be echoing the forceful but rather opaque doctrine of Karl Barth on the impossibility of conceiving eternal life as a continuity of this life.

Its [the promise's] content is not, therefore his liberation from his this-sidedness, from his end and dying, but positively the glorification by the eternal God of his natural and lawful this-sided, finite and mortal being. (Barth 1960:3/2, 633)

Barth here, as elsewhere, has much in common with Heidegger, one of the few secular philosophers to whom Barth is willing to grant a degree of insight.

In this sense, whether taught by Heidegger and Sartre or elsewhere, no one today can think or say anything of value without being an 'existentialist'... their positive value is ... to introduce the subject of nothingness with such urgency. In this respect they reach a point unreached in much ancient and modern—and even Christian—literature. (Barth 1961:3/3. 345)

It is this understanding that Rahner is seeking to accommodate when he says that 'life is suspended between a genuine beginning and a genuine end' (QD2: 27). However, while Rahner, in common with many twentieth-century theologians, stresses the definitive character of the moment of death, his own understanding of death is at some distance from Heidegger's form of existentialism. There is very little trace of *Angst* in Rahner's account of death. He does make mention of the dread fear of death, in the context of the ambiguity of death that is the result of sin, but it is far from pervading his treatment as a whole. The stress of Rahner's treatment is on death as, of it very nature, a self-fulfilment (*Selbstvollendung*). The words fulfilment (*Vollendung*), end (*Ende*), finality (*Endgültigkeit*), and their variants are constantly repeated in Rahner's writings on death. Death is not primarily the threat of nothingness that Barth sees as the great insight of Heidegger and Sartre. Death is primarily a personal fulfilment, a death of one's own (*Der 'eigene Tod'*). Most fundamentally and characteristically for Rahner, death is the action of the person (*Die Tat der Person*).

This conception of death as a fulfilment of the person has more in common with the transcendental idealism of Kant than the existentialism of Heidegger.[13] Death, whether understood as the separation of body and soul, or as the end of the earthly pilgrimage, is not a threatening abyss but is rather, *of its nature*, a fulfilment of the human person, and, further, a fulfilment that the person himself or herself actively accomplishes. The darkness and ambiguity of death belong to what is external and incidental. In its inner and essential reality death is the final self-realization of the spiritual person. Rahner has taken the traditional category of death as the end of the earthly pilgrimage,[14] and made this the theological expression of the passage of the embodied spirit from temporal acts to its definitive and eternal act. The character of death as a fulfilment is a necessary corollary of Rahner's understanding of the person as spirit in the world. This accounts for the constancy of his interest in the theology of death and his constant insistence that human death itself is a personal act.

Also significant, though often overlooked, is the influence of Rahner's spiritual practice upon his philosophical understandings. His existential concern with a fundamental decision that pervades and transcends particular categorical decisions stems as much from the spiritual exercises of Ignatius of Loyola as from the writings of Immanuel Kant (Rahner 1965*b*: 11–17, 89–91; Dych 1992: 5–6). His practical attitude to death and dying, to martyrdom, and to self-renunciation have roots further back even than his Jesuit formation. The piety in which he was brought up and the stern influence of his mother, who lived to be over 100 (Vorgrimler 1986: 46–9; Rahner

---

[13] The extent of Rahner's debt to Heidegger is debatable. Rahner's only major criticism of an introduction to his thought published in 1967 was that 'Dr. Roberts overestimates [Heidegger's] influence somewhat' (L. Roberts 1967: p. viii). Vass also remarks that 'one suspects rather that [Heidegger's] influence can be reduced to a terminological saturation of Rahner's writings with oddities of Heidegger's language' (Vass 1989*a*: 27; cf. J. R. Williams 1971; Masson 1973; Kerr 1981: 376–7).

[14] The understanding of this life as a pilgrimage is architectonic for both Augustine's *De civitate Dei* and Thomas's *Summa Theologiae*, but, at least in the case of Thomas, this theological theme finds relatively little prominence in his philosophical considerations, shaped as they are by concern with the relationship of soul and body.

1984: 24–34), laid the groundwork (to invoke the most pervasive
of Rahner's metaphors) for his later theological reflections.

THE DEVELOPMENT OF RAHNER'S THOUGHT

The fundamental anthropological approach to death that Rahner
adopts in QD2 remained unchanged through his later writings.
Death is a reality that affects the human being as a whole and
throughout life the acting person must actively dispose himself or
herself to embrace death freely from God. However, this is not to say
that there is no development in Rahner's thought, far from it. The
lexicon articles from the *Kleines theologisches Wörterbuch* in 1961 to
Sacramentum Mundi in 1969 follow the thought and structure of
QD2, but they omit the speculative angelology and play down the
descent of Christ into hell as revealing the mechanism of the redemption. This may be due to the influence of the English Dominican
Cornelius Ernst, who criticized these aspects of Rahner's thought in
an article which appeared in the *Clergy Review* in 1959. Ernst took
issue with the reinterpretation of *Hades/Sheol* as the foundation of
the cosmos. He argued that Rahner was seeking to give to the descent
into hell the meaning that had traditionally been seen in the *ascension*
of Christ into glory. This was untenable on exegetical grounds and
doubtful on theological grounds.

The death itself is the ultimate kenosis, the emptying. 'The heart of the
world' is not the *inferiores partes terrae*, the *inferni* to which Christ descended, but above all the heavens; and he ascended there to fill all things.
The Death was the ultimate emptying, so that all might be filled with the
Spirit of the risen Christ. (Ernst 1959: 600)

This article seems to have a great impact on Rahner. Ernst is well
known to Rahner: he translated the first volume of *Schriften zur
Theologie* into English as *Theological Investigations* and wrote the introduction for it; later, Ernst would be among the co-editors of English
edition of *Sacramentum Mundi*. Rahner's *Lexikon für Theologie and
Kirche* article on death has a bibliography of twenty works, only two of
which are not in German: an article that he had already cited in the

introduction to QD2 and Ernst's *Clergy Review* article. However, while Rahner may accept Ernst's criticisms, he does not explicitly retract his earlier opinions. Rather, he becomes more circumspect about expressing any views on Christ's descent into hell and less confident of his identification of *Sheol* with the spiritual ground of being.

This is the first move away from QD2 in his later lexicon articles. A further and more marked shift in Rahner's thought comes in 1970 in a paper entitled 'Zu einer Theologie des Todes' which he delivered to a theological conference in Regensburg that year. In this paper, Rahner first sets aside various issues that had previously been considered central to the theological treatment of death, as evident in his own lexicon articles of the 1960s, issues such as the universality of death and the relation between sin and death. Then he begins a long digression on the character of religious language, especially the language used in discussing death and life after death. Rahner defends a duality between 'the form of language' and 'that which is actually signified by it'. This duality cannot be overcome by any purified or technical language, for all language relies upon some link with perception and imagination, what Thomas Aquinas called *conversio ad phantasma*.[15] Thus Christian language about death is also inevitably enmeshed in spatial and temporal images of heaven 'above' or of life 'after' death. According to Rahner, there is no need for embarrassment about this feature of religious language because it is in fact shared with *all* language, even scientific language. Here he appeals to the fact that the model of light as a wave and the model of light as a particle must both be used to describe the behaviour of light, according to the circumstances. In order to do justice to reality, it is necessary to invoke models relying on incompatible imagery. Having set out these remarks about the character of language, Rahner finally makes his first major point concerning death. Death is the end of temporal existence so that, strictly speaking, there is no further extension in time 'after' death.

It is obvious that death is in this sense the absolute end of the temporal dimension of a being of the kind to which man belongs ... Life 'after death', on the contrary, is something radically withdrawn from the former temporal

---

[15] *ST* Ia 84. 7; this is the same doctrine Rahner appealed to as the basis for his transcendental philosophy in *Geist in Welt*.

dimension and the former spatially conceived time, and a state of final and definitive completion and immediacy to God. (1970: 174)

The conception of eternal life as a continuation of more temporal life after this life, a 'change of horses' (quoting Feuerbach), is confused and mistaken. The beguiling attractiveness of such a mistake is due to the force of the mythological language with which death *must* be described, but not due to the reality as such. In a similar way, Rahner does away with the 'intermediate state' when the soul exists separately from the body during the time between death and the general resurrection. According to Rahner, statements about the 'continued existence of the soul after death', about its 'separation from the body' and about 'the resurrection of the body' should be regarded as 'the same state of affairs ... being pointed to by means of different conceptual models'.

From asserting confidently (in 1958 in QD2) that the separated soul becomes 'pancosmic', to becoming reticent about such speculations (in the lexicon articles of 1961–9), in 1970 Rahner loses confidence even in the ancient categorization of death as 'the separation of body and soul'. Instead he treats this description, and the language of bodily resurrection, as useful mythology to express what cannot be expressed in simple univocal terms. Christian hope is recognition of the inconceivable (in the words of Anselm of Canterbury *rationabiliter irrationalia cogitare*). This emphasis on the limits of language and the limits of knowledge is evident in all his later work on death. In a paper given in 1975 on the intermediate state, Rahner concedes that: 'in my view, the idea of the intermediate state contains a little harmless mythology, which is not dangerous as long as we do not take the idea too seriously and do not view it as binding on faith' (1975a: 123). When asked in 1980 (in an interview published in 1983a) about the view he put forward in QD2, twenty-two years earlier, he says that his whole theological attitude has since 'moved in the direction of admitting that we do not know this or that'. He now recognizes a 'legitimate Christian scepticism' in this area so that 'without having all the answers already' we have instead to trust in the incomprehensibility of God. Also in that interview in 1980 Rahner says that he sees himself in the Thomist metaphysical tradition that stresses the radical unity of matter and spirit. However, he does not think that Thomas was radical *enough* in this regard and so he tried to go further, first with his concept of the 'pancosmic' soul and later by abandoning any conception altogether that involved a separation of soul from body.

While Rahner shifts his view on the state of the separated soul and the confidence with which one can rely on traditional language, he remains resolute in his most fundamental understanding of death. Death is an act, the culmination from within of a personal life and, as such, a fulfilment. This was clear in 'Zu einer Theologie des Todes' (in 1970) and was still so in the interview given in 1980. Rahner's last mature systematic presentation of the theology of death is given in his *Mysterium Salutis* article 'Das christliche Sterben' (1976). As he had done many times before, Rahner first presents what he sees as official magisterial teaching about death. Death is a punishment for sin; it is the occasion of our final determination for or against God; and it is universal. Rahner then sets out on a defence of the view that death is the close of the history of freedom and, further, that it is 'a *consummation of freedom* from within'. This, he thinks, must be attributed even to the Old Testament account of death as descent into *Sheol*—if we are to escape the charge of positivism about revelation or the charge that the teaching about *Sheol* was mistaken and had to be *corrected* by belief in the resurrection.

The basic structure and argument of this most mature reflection on the topic: death as the consummation of freedom from within, death as a manifestation of sin, and death as dying with Christ, follows closely the thought of *Zur Theologie des Todes* eighteen years previously. However, there is a greater degree of subtlety in the later article and an awareness of some of the criticisms to his position levelled over the years. The consummating act of freedom is seen in the later piece, not as *pure* activity, but in a dialect of active and passive, self-determination and disposability. It concerns the paradox of free renunciation. So also the fulfilment of death as dying with Christ is not regarded as a kind of natural self-fulfilment but is emphatically work of God's grace. Nevertheless, these nuances do not obscure the fundamental elements of continuity in Rahner's thought on death throughout his writings.

AMBROSE REDIVIVUS?

Rahner attempts to overcome a dichotomy between philosophical accounts of death and the spirituality of Christian dying. This dichotomy can be traced back through Thomas Aquinas to Augustine and has its roots in his acute but incomplete critique of Ambrose. Before assessing the positive contribution of Rahner, we would do well to ask whether, in criticizing Thomas and Augustine, Rahner's approach inadvertently revives some of the mistaken approach of Ambrose.

Like Ambrose in the fourth century, Rahner in the twentieth century creates a synthesis of philosophical and scriptural themes to shape an understanding of dying-with-Christ. In the case of Ambrose, the Platonic conception of freeing the soul from the body, first by philosophical contemplation and asceticism, and finally by death, is synthesized with the 'mystical' death of the Christian in baptism and the Christian desire 'to depart and be with Christ' (Philippians 1: 23). In the case of Rahner the transition from time to eternity, and from particular acts to a complete self-defining act is synthesized with death as judgment and the end of one's earthly pilgrimage. Whereas for Ambrose it is *separation* from all that is worldly and sinful and corrupt that forms the bridge between philosophical and theological ideas of death, for Rahner it is *finality*: death is essentially the defining moment for a human being because it is the moment in which a whole life is summed up and brought to judgment. Judgment here is not thought of as the imposition of a transcendent and sovereign judge, but as the necessary corollary of the fact that life is finished and done; judgment is simply the realization that when one's time of becoming is no more, then one will be what one has become. For Rahner, judgment is not added to death by providence, but is an intrinsic aspect of death as our end.

It is difficult to escape the impression that Rahner here confuses two quite distinct senses of 'end'. By end one can mean the aim or fulfilment of something, as when something is described as a means to an end. This sense of end, corresponding closely to the Greek τελος, is essential to the understanding of human action, notwithstanding its absence from modern physics (C. Taylor 1964; Jonas 1966). Related to this, but distinct from it, is the narrower sense of an end as the terminus, the fact of having come to a stop. A terminus may be the aim of a process, as is generally the case with a journey, but it may be a stop without being a fulfilment. If a process is brought to a premature end through the action of external forces, if a train crashes before it has reached its appointed destination, then the journey has reached an end in one sense, but not its end in the sense of its τελος. It is not legitimate to conclude that, because death brings life to a stop, it therefore brings it to a fulfilment. Indeed, the difference between death in the case of Adam, and death in the case of contemporary human beings, seems precisely to be that for Adam the end of life would have been a perfect fulfilment, whereas for contemporary human beings death brings a terminus without bringing fulfilment.

Rahner and Ambrose lived in very different intellectual and cultural environments but there are certain formal points of similarity between modern German critical Idealism and ancient Greek Neoplatonism in their attitude to mind and matter. Thus, in some ways, early Rahner can be seen as recapitulating the theological vision of Ambrose. This is shown by Rahner's comments about the separation of body and soul and about angelology. In 1958 Rahner argues that it is a Neoplatonic prejudice to think that closeness to God must mean distance from matter (QD2: 19). However, a prejudice that Rahner did not examine was the belief that death necessarily brings the soul nearer to God. This is in some tension with the view expressed in several of the Psalms that death takes the person further from God (Psalms 6: 9, 30: 9, 49: 4, etc.). On this point Rahner seems to show his idealist colours. He thinks that without the body the soul is free, opened up to the cosmos as a whole, fulfilled. This free and fulfilled relationship is akin to the relationship the angels have with the material world. It is heavily ironic that, while Rahner's putative wish is to emphasize the intrinsic relationship between the human soul and the material cosmos, his model is explicitly an angelic one!

Rahner is strongly resistant to the view that death is, in itself, a bad thing. However, unlike Ambose, he is also reticent about saying that it is simply a good thing. At several points he claims that death has a neutral reality that is neither good nor bad. This must be so, he thinks, so that the good and the bad can be said to die the same death. 'There must be in death . . . some common element, neutral, so to speak, which permits us to say that, in a true sense, all men die the same death' (QD2: 36). This seems to be based on the idea that, if something can have the properties of goodness and badness, then in itself it must be neither good nor bad. This is similar to the argument criticized by some commentators on Aristotle.

The idea that what changes must be something that doesn't change precisely because it is what changes, is very like the idea that what has predicates must be something without predicates just because it has predicates: both being based on inadequate reading of Aristotle. (Anscombe 1981*d*: 57)

Something that can be either good or bad is not necessarily neutral in itself. It may be good in itself, but become bad because of context or circumstances (like food that is poisoned) or it may be bad in itself, but good could come from it indirectly (as debt and hunger might bring a prodigal son to his senses). That death can be the *occasion* both of good and of evil does not mean that it cannot be either good or evil in itself. In fact, despite such passages, Rahner generally seems to hold that the true and inner meaning of death is positive but that, due to the fall, it now has a negative aspect and has the possibility of a negative outcome.

Like Ambrose, Rahner (at least in 1958) holds that the soul, *as such*, is better off without its body and that the resurrection of the glorified body involves the production of the sort of body which can allow the soul to *continue* to enjoy the freedom it *already* enjoys in its separated state. Both conceive death as bringing with it a freedom and a natural spiritual fulfilment that is not possible for the soul when confined to the limits of the earthly body. Rahner's consistent attempts to interpret *Sheol*—the underworld of the Old Testament— as some sort of positive reality rather than a gloomy imprisonment stem from a genuine insight: that *Sheol* or *Hades* is none other than death itself, presented mythologically. If death in itself has some positive note (as finality or consummation), then it is necessary for Rahner to find this aspect in *Sheol.*

Otherwise the ancient doctrine of *Sheol* could have no *positive* meaning for us, but would raise the unanswerable question as to why it had not been simply erroneous even in its earlier form. The later teaching in the Old Testament and particularly in the New on an eternal life of a positive character could not be understood as a radicalization of what was really meant by the doctrine of *Sheol*, but would be merely additional. (Rahner 1976a: 240)

However, it is very doubtful on exegetical grounds that such a positive aspect to *Sheol* can be found. Further, inasmuch as there is a developing hope in the Old Testament it is precisely hope in a resurrection from death, that is, from *Sheol*, not a 'radicalization' of the true meaning of *Sheol*. The gates of death have been broken down, but the land of the dead is, as such, the land of gloom and deep darkness. This aspect of the teaching does not change. Far from being erroneous or misleading, the 'ancient doctrine of *Sheol*' reveals the true character of death in itself, a doctrine which remains relevant even for those for whom death has been overcome. Rahner's desire to reinterpret *Sheol* as something positive (attempted in different ways from 1958 to 1976) stems directly from a desire to see death, in itself, as something positive—for *Sheol* is nothing other than the land of the dead. It is this conflation of descent to the dead with ascent to glory that Ernst had already astutely identified in his critique of Rahner's theological conception of death (Ernst 1959: 598–600). The conflation of Jesus' descent into hell with his ascent into heaven is but the Christological expression of his wider anthropological scheme. Death, for Rahner, *is* liberation and eternal immediacy with God, it is only accidentally through mortal sin that it may fail to be this. Here Rahner's closeness to Ambrose is most evident.[16]

Inasmuch as Rahner, especially early Rahner, repeats the formal scheme of Ambrose and makes death a *natural* good for the human being, his account is open to the same set of criticisms. It fails to value sufficiently the unity of body and soul in this life. It conflates death with eternal life and conflates descent among the dead with ascension into heaven. It fails to present death as an evil, not only against a supernatural background, but also by nature; for the human

---

[16] Kelsey (1997: 370 n. 4) contrasts the attitude of Rahner to death with that of Jüngel and finds, 'one more version of the conventional Roman Catholic/Protestant theological polarity'. Yet the same theological fault line also runs between different schools within the Catholic tradition (e.g. between Dominicans and Jesuits, represented by Ernst (1959), Schillebeeckx (1962a, 1962b), Kerr (1997b), McCabe (1987) on the one hand and Rahner (QD2 etc.), Lonergan (1963), Boros (1965) on the other) and between different individual Catholic theologians at least as far back as Ambrose and Augustine.

being is at once spiritual and animal.[17] It fails to bring out the force of the analogy between mortal sin, physical death, and 'the second death' of everlasting damnation (cf. Augustine *CD* XIII. 2, 12).

DEATH AS A HUMAN ACT

There is, however, a further point that is peculiar to Rahner and absolutely central to his account. This is the claim that death is a human act. Rahner's understanding of the human being as spirit and matter, person and nature, revolves around the category of free action. What is spirit and person is that which acts of itself, and what is matter and nature is that which is acted on from outside. Thus to say that there is a personal aspect to death, which one must say if one acknowledges death as a reality that affects the whole human being, is to say that death is a free act. Human beings are under the necessity either to freely die well or to freely die badly— either accepting death by grace from God or rejecting God in death. Thus, for all human beings, death must be either dying-with-Christ or mortal sin. At this point Rahner's doctrine of 'anonymous Christianity' is invoked to explain how those outside the visible life of the Church could still face the choice of grace or sin in death. Because 'death is in fact the whole action of [the human being's] life', it is possible to say that 'the life of grace *is* Christian death' (QD2: 75; emphasis in the original) and, concomitantly, that 'mortal sin *consists in* the will to die autonomously' (QD2: 44; emphasis added).

Rahner constantly invokes a duality of inside and outside to account for the fact that the *act* of death is obscured by the passivity of death considered purely from the biological point of view. Death is an act. Yet how are we to conceive of death as an act in the case of sudden and unprepared death? In this case, says Rahner, it is the underlying disposition of willingness to let go which is the act of

[17] Dread of death is something 'metaphysical anthropology cannot explain' because 'man as a spiritual being is immortal' (QD2: 54). According to Rahner, revealed doctrine is necessary to make sense of fear of death on the basis that death is out of keeping with God's original plan and out of keeping with final destiny for the human person in the bodily resurrection.

death axiologically present throughout life. But why consider this disposition towards death present during life as being the 'act of dying'? Is there not a problem with locating any act at the moment of death itself? Ladislaus Boros (1965) developed Rahner's idea of an act of death by making the act something that transcended all temporal human acts. He supposed that the situation of the soul *between* this life and the next created a unique opportunity and a uniquely clear vision in which one could consciously resolve the whole of one's life either for or against God. Only in the moment of death was it really possible to define one's whole existence in this way.

The problem with the account that Boros gives is that particular earthly acts of sin or repentance are robbed of their eternal significance. This is not just because they could be superseded by similar acts, as an act of despair could be followed by a final act of repentance, or vice versa, but because all temporal choices would be subject to the single and only properly informed choice *in* death. Life would become a preamble to death, which would be the only true arena of decision and self-definition. It is important to note that Rahner explicitly rejects this view of a uniquely transcendental moment of choice in death (1976a: 230). While there is an act of dying, this does not happen *between* this life and the next. It happens in life. Indeed, it may not happen immediately before death but may happen much earlier. The reality of sickness as a *prolixitas mortis* gives ample scope for an act of handing oneself over before death, whereas, at the moment of physical death, someone might not be able to make any conscious decision. Rahner here gives a central place to a theme in the life of grace that had been relatively neglected by Augustine and Thomas: the theme of dying-to-self or dying-to-sin, throughout life, as the necessary corollary of finding new life from God in Christ. However, even here, Rahner's wish to distinguish a transcendent 'act of dying' from mundane temporal acts presents difficulties analogous to the problems faced by Boros. If the 'act of dying' is separated too much from individual acts in this life, then individual acts lose their significance. On the other hand, if an individual act of spiritual submission can constitute the 'act of dying' (and this is supported by taking the act of dying to be any act informed by faith, hope, and love) then why claim that there is something unique or transcendent about physical dying?

This raises the question of whether Rahner is correct to see physical death as itself an act. Throughout his writings he is insistent that death itself is not only something suffered (*erlitten*) but also something done (*getan*). '[On the] questionable assumption [that death itself is not done but only suffered], the redeeming act of Christ will not reside in his death as such, but only in his patient and obedient submission to it' (QD2: 61).

In his early work Rahner had tended to identify the *suffering* of death with what was external and categorical and the *action* of dying with what was internal and transcendent. For this reason death as such appeared to be an act of fulfilment and self-definition. Later he came to stress that such an act was not possible without the help of God's grace, but, even so, grace seemed to build on natural desire, and not, as Thomas held, to be set against it. More significantly, in his later writings, Rahner came to acknowledge more openly the negative aspects of death from a naturalistic point of view, and the dialectic of activity and passivity involved in the 'act of dying'. The act of dying is to be understood as an act of self-renunciation, indeed the complete act of self-renunciation, and thus involves the paradox of self-fulfilment only through self-emptying. The acknowledgement of this paradox of emptying (in death) so as to be filled (by the new life) differentiates the approach of mature Rahner from the earlier, more Ambrosian, approach to death as self-fulfilment.

Both these point are very well taken and help to give a better understanding of what is involved in the 'act of dying'. The act in question is the act of willingly handing over one's life to God if it is so demanded. This is seen most explicitly in Jesus' death and in the deaths of the martyrs who 'loved not their lives even unto death' (Revelation 12: 11). However, the action involved here is not the cause of physical death. The act of dying-to-self is the action of renouncing one's life, that is, the action of not clinging to life when love demands clinging more obstinately to a greater good. The continual self-renunciation demanded by the Gospel is necessary because the circumstances of this corrupt world and the fallen character of the human heart present one with good things that, if followed, would deflect one from final blessedness. In the current human state, therefore, every action of grace must involve some denial of the old self.

The act of complete self-renunciation demanded by the Gospel is seen explicitly in the martyrs and is required implicitly in every Christian life. However, while martyrdom is a demonstration of the extent of love of God by overcoming even the natural love of life, the death itself is not the martyr's action. The would-be martyr may hand himself over only to be released because of some amnesty; the causing of death is not in his or her hands, but in the hands of another. Physical death is always something suffered, even if, in the case of the martyrs, they suffer willingly. Consider the case of suicide: the suicide is both the one who kills and the one killed: both perpetrator and victim. Yet there is no 'act of dying' (in Rahner's sense) here but only an act of killing and a death that is suffered. The act of renunciation, by which death is willingly accepted, is never as such the cause of death, so the phrase 'act of dying' is one that should be treated with extreme caution. Nevertheless, Rahner is right to see the renunciation of life by the martyrs as the completion of that dying-to-self which is a necessary part of accepting the grace of God. In this context martyrdom can be understood as something desirable because it makes of death (which would come anyhow, one way or another) a means of expressing love of God. Yet, even in this case, death itself is not an act of fulfilment nor is it to be seen as something desirable in itself, but circumstances have arisen that require, or at least allow, life to be forfeited for the sake of holding fast to a God.

If anything is to be thought of as something endured or suffered it is death. Death dissolves the human being into a corpse and a separated soul. It is the limit of earthly life and action, the cessation of temporal freedom. Unless one places the real person and the real decision outside the temporal realm, as Boros attempts to do, then death, so far from being in itself an act, is the undermining of free temporal activity. Judgment takes people where it finds them. Human beings do not come to a consummation as a maturing from within—as could have been true of Adam—but one's life is cut short and it is prior actions and attitudes in life, not any act 'in death', that counts for or against one. Physical death is a terminus but not a τέλος. Nevertheless, death is an event for which Christians are urged to ready themselves, even though it may come suddenly. The saints are asked to 'pray for us now and at the hour of our deaths' in the recognition that the hour of death brings the last chance, either for sin or for repentance. Furthermore, precisely because death is the last and greatest natural deprivation, the act of accepting death is the last and greatest act of surrender of the person to God.

Rahner makes a real contribution in reviving discussion of dying-to-self in the context of the approach of physical death. Among his later works, 'Dimensions of Martyrdom' (Rahner 1983*b*) is the most subtle presentation of the relation of activity and passivity in martyrdom and finally escapes any 'love of death' of the sort evident in QD2. Nevertheless, if dying is to be described as an act, this act of dying needs to be distinguished more sharply than Rahner generally does from the causing of death (i.e. from killing). Most of what Rahner wishes to say about the finality of death and the need to be properly disposed towards death can be said without talking of an act of dying. Thus, while accepting Rahner's insight, it seems better to follow the terminology of Schillebeeckx (1962*b*: 335) and say that 'death is not an act but the attitude of mind in which we accept death can give it the value of an act.'

THE LIBERTY OF THE SICK

Though primarily a philosophical and a dogmatic theologian, Rahner several times entered into discussion concerning matters of moral theology. The first and most important reason for this was to express the implications of his existential approach to theology (1959*c*: 220 ff.; cf. Wallace 1963; Nelson 1987). His concern with theological anthropology could not be without moral import. This needs to be stated, for, since the Council of Trent, Catholic moral theology had become a recognized discipline with its own area of competence, a competence which Rahner certainly respected.[18] His concern with particular moral matters never strayed far from the central theological and anthropological principles involved. He did not seek to usurp the role of the moral theologian by addressing in detail particular practical issues but sought to enrich the method and approach of moral theology.

---

[18] 'We must... hope that the moral theologians will clarify the problem further in the future.' (Rahner 1977: 111).

Like many others, Rahner was concerned that, in the pre-Vatican II moral theology of the manuals, a model of universal moral law and particular application had narrowed the proper scope of moral theology. Wishing to distance himself from 'situation ethics', which would deny any validity to universal moral norms, Rahner nonetheless thought these moral norms insufficient to express all the particular obligations and responsibilities that might fall on individuals precisely as individual (1959c: 217–19, 222–3). The particularity of divine call and of the spiritual gifts is an aspect of the Christian life that needs to be integrated within a moral vision. Rahner is representative of a broad ecclesial movement in voicing his desire for a moral theology reintegrated with existential, spiritual, and sacramental theology.

Central to Rahner's particular moral understanding is the status of human freedom as the defining human moral characteristic. He does not accept the false dichotomy between internal freedom and external moral law but seeks to place freedom itself at the root of moral reflection. Being unwilling to place fundamental restrictions on freedom in the face of nature, or even of supposed divine prerogatives, he is much slower than others to find anything intrinsically, absolutely, or universally wrong with practices such as contraception, genetic manipulation, or euthanasia (Rahner 1968b, 1968c, 1977 respectively). In the last case he is clear that the tradition and present teaching office of the Church have taught that it is never licit directly (intentionally) to kill an innocent person. 'It is true that, according to the general Christian and Catholic view, it is not objectively and morally legitimate to will an action which is aimed directly at causing the death of the sick person' (1977: 110).

Nevertheless, Rahner finds no grounds for distinguishing direct from indirect killing which amount to more than a rule of thumb (*Faustregeln*). He is unwilling to set limits to the scope of human freedom but seeks to show how true and unlimited respect for human freedom should be the guiding principle in our actions. Explicit in this view is the claim that merely unconscious life can have no real personal worth. What gives life human worth is not the biological but the personal, which transcends the merely biological. If the act of suicide, for instance, cannot, in general, be regarded as a legitimate expression of freedom, this is not because the scope of freedom is limited by respect for biological life, but must be because the act of suicide in fact curtails human freedom in some way. Rahner's concern with freedom in dying leads him to assert very strongly the right to choose the manner of one's death, the right not to be placed under pressure to accept the benefit of priest or of last sacraments, and the right to choose one's own doctor.[19] These particular rights are part and parcel of one's right to *control* one's dying—in marked contrast to that popular Catholic piety that would condemn euthanasia precisely because it seems to involve the desire to exercise undue control in the face of death. Death is a human act and should occur in the most free and active manner possible. This is the root of Rahner's objection to deliberately cutting life short.

Because, and in so far as, death (or the act of dying) is a special situation for liberty in the theological sense, man has the right, and even something of a duty, to mould the situation in such a way that it offers as many opportunities for liberty as possible, even in an empirical, sense... The alleviation of pain is not merely important for the patient's physiological and psychological well-being. It is also important in the struggle for the greatest possible area of liberty in the theological sense—an area where a history of salvation may be played out. (1977: 106–7)

Yet, while he clearly wishes to uphold the traditional prohibition against self-killing, the rationale he gives is not comprehensive enough to justify more than a general rule of thumb, as he tacitly acknowledges. Traditionally, direct killing has been distinguished from indirect killing using the concept of intention.[20] What is ruled out, according to the traditional norm, is intentional self-killing, except

---

[19] He regards the requirement to chose one's own physician as quasi-absolute, which is very curious given that he does not regard life and death themselves in this regard and given that the social provision of medical care seems archetypally a matter of prudence and the weighing of contingencies.

[20] The importance of intention for Catholic moral theory has led to a considerable literature on how to deal with foreseen but unintended consequences of actions. This is often discussed in relation to the so called 'principle of double effect' (Watt 2000: 39–43; Keown 2002: 20–9; Anscombe in Geach and Gormally 2005: 207–26). The present enquiry is not a treatment of the technical principles of intention and action, important as these clearly are in decision making. Rather, it is a treatment of the theological meaning of death, dying, and killing. It is hoped that this enquiry will illuminate the deeper human context and in this way help situate and so guide those decisions that relate to the approach of death.

on the express command of God. What makes suicide sinful is that it is direct or intentional so that one's mind is set on death. However, it is difficult for Rahner to acknowledge that there is something inherently wrong with making death our aim because he has previously argued that death is to be 'loved for its own sake' (QD2: 111).

It seems that, just as Ambrose had difficulties distinguishing suicide from martyrdom, so Rahner faces a similar problem. Because, even in his later writings, the act of dying is an act of self-definition and fulfilment, it seems to him that it is only the existence of certain rules about which there are 'theoretical obscurities' (1977: 111) that makes the aim of dying unlawful. According to Rahner, the clarification of these rules might bring with it 'considerable restructuring' (1977: 111) of the answer to this problem. That is to say, the current manner of structuring the problem of euthanasia is deeply flawed. Thus, while he admits that the general Christian and Catholic view excludes any action 'which is aimed directly at causing death' (1977: 110), he is still happy to assert that the sick have a 'right to die' (1977: 110) which grounds their right to refuse treatment. However, his language here is unhelpful and ambiguous. The sick do indeed possess a right to refuse inappropriate treatment and, as death approaches, many forms of treatment may become less appropriate. Presumably there is a also human right to make a good death, whatever this involves, and also to receive reasonable assistance in this last human task, but to describe this right as a 'right to die' is to invite confusion with the asserted right to *bring about* death in the name of mercy—a 'right' that Rahner in fact rejects.

THE MODERN PROBLEMATIC

Despite the advances Rahner makes in certain areas, there remain difficulties with other motifs in his thought on death; it seems that he is wrong to assert, especially in his earlier work, that death is itself a fulfilment or an act of self-realization. Though final human fulfilment and self-realization come after death, and through the accepting of death, death itself is the *occasion* and not the *cause* of this finality. It is God who gives us the grace to die well, and who brings life from death, while death of itself is sterile.

Although Rahner's systematic account of death cannot be accepted as it stands, he makes a substantial contribution to systematic theological thought about death. Like Ambrose, he integrates sacramental and ascetical theology with a theology of martyrdom to produce a consistent and *theologically* rich account of Christian death. Like Augustine his view develops and he becomes increasingly critical of an unduly positive account of death. Like Thomas, he begins with an account of how human death affects the human person, not only considered as body and soul but also considering human action and the final end of human life.

Rahner's contemporary philosophical concern with death as the absolute limit of earthly existence, and his refusal to portray eternal life as an ongoing continuation of life, constitute genuine modern insights. The proper consideration of death as judgment and as resolution (for good or ill) always stood uneasily with an account of death as the separation and subsequent continued existence of the immortal soul. If there is no great discontinuity in death, why need judgment come at the moment of death? Why are reincarnation and post-mortem repentance so strongly to be resisted, as they clearly always have been within the Catholic tradition? Rahner's claim that death must be understood to affect the whole human being, body and soul, and that judgment is intrinsically and not accidentally involved in death, must surely be accepted. In this sense, one needs an *existential* theological account of death. This stance is by no means unique to Rahner (similar claims can be found in Ratzinger, Balthasar, Barth, and Jüngel), but he should be credited among those who have taken up and vigorously expounded what is a very important turn in modern theological thought.

Rahner's attempt, later in life, to develop a 'legitimate Christian scepticism' (1983*a*) about the character of the next life, and his distinction between the language used about death and the reality referred to, expresses another valuable insight. Rahner is surely right to say that some imaginative (and, therefore, spatio-temporal) picture is necessarily involved in any conceptualization, no matter how metaphysically purified. The force and the importance of mythological presentations of theological topics such as death and eternal life must be used but simultaneously must be criticized by a negative—one might say an *apophatic*—way of understanding.[21] This is analogous to the situation with scientific understandings, which also require adequate imaginative accompaniment. However, while it is true and important to say that all scientific knowledge requires some grounding in sense experience, one should push Rahner a little here and say that theological understanding, of necessity, stands at the very edge of human understanding (McCabe 2005: 146; Anscombe 1981e: 109). The irreducible aspect of mystery present when talking of life beyond death is different in kind from the ubiquitous element of mythology and metaphor found in other areas of human knowledge. Death simply *is* more mysterious than other more mundane realities that human beings encounter.

Rahner's aim is to integrate doctrinal theology with spirituality, theological with philosophical method, ancient truths with modern insights. Of all the areas of theology that concern him, the theology of death is the one he returns to most often. His approach to the issue of 'the liberty of the sick', while flawed, represents an important and much needed effort to renew moral theology on end of life issues by turning to fundamental questions of philosophy and theology. The following chapter, which is the last, will revisit this issue and others discussed at the outset of this study, and will seek to illuminate them by drawing on our critical exploration of the thought of Ambrose, Augustine, Thomas, and Rahner.

[21] While this apophatic attitude may be the cause of some anxiety (Meynell 1980; Kerr 1980a; Hebblethwaite 1979; Lash 1978), it should not be taken as a repudiation of hope of life beyond death, but rather as an expression of our inability to know the essence of the beatitude which awaits us (cf. *ST* IaIIae 5.3, Ia 12. 11). One should beware treating Rahner's awareness of the irreducibility of mythological elements in eschatological language as a wish for demythologization (e.g. Burnes 1994) in a similar manner to that proposed by Bultmann; neither should one turn what are tentative speculations in Rahner into new certainties (e.g. Dych 1992: 144): such approaches contradict Rahner's express intentions (1960; 1975a; 1976b: 431–4; 1983a).

7

Final Reflections

REVIEWING THE CENTRAL ARGUMENT

Examination of the thought of Ambrose, Augustine, Thomas, and Rahner shows them to constitute a single extended argument on the theology of death.

Ambrose of Milan provides the starting point for this argument with his work on the good of death (*De bono mortis*). He deserves credit for devoting attention to the question and for constructing an explicitly Christian account of death. Augustine, and through Augustine much of the later Latin tradition, benefits greatly from this account, both from those elements which he accepts and from those elements that he criticizes.

Ambrose first distinguishes different senses of death present in Scripture, some good, some bad. At first glance it would appear that bodily death is neither unequivocally good nor unequivocally bad, for it is harmful to those who are consigned to hell, but beneficial to those who reach heaven. Nevertheless, Ambrose is not content to analyse death only in terms of its outcome for the dead. The death of the body has a significance in its own right, as the separation of body and soul and as a consequence of the fall. In this light, according to Ambrose, the death of the body should be understood as something in every way good in itself, *omnifariam igitur mors bonum est* (*BM* 4. 15), even if it brings suffering to the wicked. For death always gives rest to the body and freedom to the soul, and provides the final remedy for the hardships of life that God imposed as a punishment on the children of Adam and Eve. It is not the fault of death that the wicked die in sin and merit punishment. Having characterized bodily death in this way,

Ambrose is able to relate bodily death to the positive meaning of dying with Christ in baptism.

While Augustine of Hippo comes to the opposite conclusion with regard to the inherent goodness of death, arguing that death is, in itself, never a good thing, *nulli bona est* (*CD* XIII. 6), he nevertheless agrees with Ambrose in many other respects. Indeed the contrast between the two would not be so striking were they not to share so many common assumptions. Like Ambrose, Augustine holds that the word 'death' is used in several different senses, some positive and some negative. Like Ambrose, Augustine is not content to characterize human bodily death as a neutral event whose meaning in a particular case is determined purely in relation to the final destination of that soul. Again, with Ambrose, Augustine considers the key to the inherent meaning of death to lie in the description of death as the separation of body and soul and in relation to the fall of Adam. However, while Ambrose regards the separation of body and soul as good for the soul, Augustine regards it as bad for the soul. Ambrose's account relies upon a negative estimation of the status of the body, a view strongly influenced by Platonism. Augustine, while retaining a high respect for other aspects of Platonic philosophy, comes to reject this view of the body, and to develop a much more positive account of the natural union of body and soul. This affects his thought on a variety of areas, from suicide and fear of death to virginity and marriage.

While Augustine emphasizes the natural union of body and soul, the goods of marriage, and the place of the emotions within the good life, and thus criticizes Plato at several points, he is not able to call upon any alternative philosophical system to assist him. In the thirteenth century, Thomas Aquinas fuses the theological vision of Augustine with the philosophy of Aristotle. In Aristotle, Thomas finds a philosopher who is far more able than Plato to defend the goodness of the body and the natural union of body and soul. While Augustine occasionally makes reference to the natural appetite of the soul for the body and to the naturalness of fear of death, he does not develop any systematic account of nature. Thomas makes up for this deficit by critical use of the philosophy of nature propounded by Aristotle. The effects of this are seen, for example, in Thomas's discussion of the naturalness of death (*ST* IaIIae 85. 6), which represents an important advance, in certain respects, on that of Augustine. However, while Thomas's account of death is clear, and involves both theological and philosophical approaches, it suffers from a relative lack of integration, especially with regard to a separation between the theology of hope and the philosophical analysis of killing. This separation of theology and philosophy was exacerbated in subsequent centuries. Paradoxically, the continuing and welcome revival of interest in Thomas Aquinas as a philosopher brings with it a potentially distorting effect: concentration on purely philosophical aspects of his thought can obscure the theological perspective. Yet theology plays an important role in shaping Thomas's thought in general, and his account of death in particular.

Karl Rahner seeks to remedy this problem by drawing upon existentialist, post-Kantian philosophy, and by revisiting the question of the specifically theological meaning of death. The key to his thought is his emphasis on the personal aspect of death. While not denying that death involves the separation of body and soul, Rahner thinks this description fails to capture the distinctively human character of death as a free act and as the end of our earthly pilgrimage (*QD2*: 13). Rahner does well to bring out an important aspect of the theology of death that was relatively neglected by Augustine and Thomas, at least in their systematic treatments of the subject. He also revives some important themes found in Ambrose in relation to dying in baptism and to martyrdom. However, while Rahner represents an advance in some respects, he also seems to revive Ambrose's thesis that death is essentially something positive. Nevertheless, there is a development in Rahner's thought over time and he becomes increasingly critical of some of the positions he defended earlier in his life. His writing on euthanasia and on the liberty of the sick contain elements in continuity with his early thought, and reminiscent of Ambrose, alongside elements of critical of his early thought, and reminiscent of Augustine. Seeing Rahner in relation to Thomas, Augustine, and Ambrose thus helps identify where Rahner is breaking new ground, where he is building on earlier insights, and where he is perhaps repeating earlier mistakes.

The aim of this final chapter is to present a coherent theological approach to death, drawing on the work of these four thinkers.[1] This

---

[1] As the chapter relies on the work of previous chapters, to avoid repetition, it often presents arguments in a concise form. If at some points the discussion seems

is set out in relation to the practical realities of grief, fear, and hope in the face of death, and in relation to bringing about death, either one's own or someone else's. In this context we will consider the vexed question of withholding and withdrawing treatment from those who are approaching death and conclude with the question of what it means to make a 'good death'.

GOOD GRIEF

It is fairly clear that, if there is no hope of life beyond the grave, no rest or reward for those who have gone, no hope of final reunion 'in the next life', then death is in general a grim prospect. In the words of Blaise Pascal, 'the last act is bloody, no matter how fine the rest of the play. They throw earth over your head and it is finished for ever' (1966: 165). It is on the assumption that there is nothing awaiting us that the preacher says, 'a living dog is better than a dead lion, for the living know that they will die, but the dead know nothing, and they have no more reward; but the memory of them is lost' (Ecclesiastes 9: 4–5). Without hope of life beyond death, what is lost in death is lost irretrievably, like stolen property that will never be returned. The fact that death is the 'common lot' of human beings (FR 4) is little consolation to someone who has lost a loved one. Philosophers, in an attempt to avoid being touched by life's vicissitudes, have sometimes sought to cultivate a detachment from the world by making 'a decisive break from this whole world-order', as Plato advocated, or else have attempted to 'minimize our exposure to the slings and arrows' as Epicurus and the Stoics sought to do, albeit in different ways (Tugwell 1990: 72). However, it seems either that these attempts fail to assuage the loss of a true love,[2] or else that they represent not a noble achievement

---

truncated, the reader should refer back to the relevant section of a previous chapter where this part of the argument is treated in more depth (e.g. see ch. 5 for a more detailed discussion of Thomas Aquinas on suicide).

[2] As the grieving philosopher remarks to Prince Rasselas, 'What comfort can truth and reason afford me? of what effect are they now, but to tell me, that my daughter will not be restored?' Johnson and Enright (1977: ch. 18).

but a failure in humanity. Augustine, talking about the horrors of war, comments that 'a man who experiences such evils, or even thinks about them, without heartfelt grief, is assuredly in a far more pitiable condition, if he thinks himself happy simply because he has lost all human feeling' (*CD* XIX. 7). In the face of irredeemable loss, what proper human reaction is there but inconsolable grief?

In contrast to such unrelenting sorrow, Christians have from the very first exhorted one another 'not [to] grieve like those who have no hope' (1 Thessalonians 4: 13). In contemporary popular piety, derived from Christianity, death is often present as 'nothing at all' or as just like 'slip[ping] away into the next room'.[3] More than this, within the Christian tradition, death has been presented even as a joyful prospect, a release from the miseries of life, a safe harbour from the storms of temptation, an end to sin, and the gateway to heaven (*BM* 2. 4–7). Ambrose reflects a Christian approach to death which is still evident in the twenty-first century. It is in a similar tone that the early Rahner describes death as 'the fullness of freely produced personal reality' (*QD2*: 31).

Ambrose is helpful because he gives clear expression to this approach: life is regarded as a prison sentence; death is our liberation. Indeed it would be more rational to follow those apocryphal tribes who, according to Ambrose 'mourn at the birth of human beings, and keep festival at their deaths' (*FR* 5). It is perhaps at this point that the perverseness of this approach is most evident. Can it seriously be claimed that it is properly human to mourn the birth of a child and to celebrate a child's death? Has there ever been a tribe who have lived like this? Those who exhort a bereaved friend to be joyful seem to add insult to injury, as the proverb wisely tell us, 'he who sings songs to a heavy heart is like one who takes off a garment on a cold day, and like vinegar on a wound' (Proverbs 25: 20). Such well-meaning exhortations also contradict the advice of Paul to 'rejoice with those who rejoice, weep with those who weep' (Romans 12: 15). To be sure, both Ambrose and early Augustine realize that it is natural and human to grieve, and they are eloquently in their own expressions of grief. Nevertheless, they tend to see any expression of grief as weakness

---

[3] 'Death Is Nothing at All' by Henry Scott Holland (1847–1918); see also 'A Parable of Immortality' by Henry Jackson van Dyke (1852–1933).

or irrationality out of accord with reason or with faith (*Confessiones* IX. xii. 31; *FR* 7).

The approach of the later Augustine and that of Thomas Aquinas accepts grief not only as natural but also as rational and appropriate. From this perspective, death is a terrible separation even for those who hope for reunion in the life of the world to come. The souls of the dead are currently alienated from the world and have no more communication with those who remain, until the final defeat of death and the redemption of all things. Augustine's assertion that the dead know nothing of what occurs in this world, unless God specially reveals it to them (*De cura pro mortuis* 16–21) is taken up in Thomas's account of the severely limited powers of the 'separated soul' (*ST* Ia 89 see also Rousseau 1979; Geach 1961: 100; Davies 1992: 216–17). Death is loss and brings about a radical exile. In this respect Rahner, especially the early Rahner, is mistaken in construing the underworld of *Sheol* as something positive, or in seeing death as such as liberation for the soul. These views represent a strand of Rahner's thought which has not wholly freed itself from that Neoplatonic prejudice which he rightly criticizes in others (QD2: 19). Death is painful and the loss it brings is real, even if it will not last forever.

The understanding of Augustine and Thomas that death brings loss and exile is deepened further by their awareness of the neediness of the dead. The neediness of the dead is related to the Christian doctrine of judgment and of the process of purging that remains even for those whose sins have been forgiven (a process mythologically represented as a place: 'purgatory'). Both for Augustine and for Thomas there is meaning and merit in praying for the dead in their transition from this life to the next. The usefulness of praying for the dead does not include those who are damned and beyond help, nor those who are so holy that they have no need of help (such as the martyrs). Nevertheless, there is no certainty that any particular person is damned and only of a few is it revealed that they are already in heaven. So, in general, prayers should be offered for all those who depart on the assumption that they need our help. Among these prayers central is the offering of the Eucharist (Augustine, *Confessiones* IX. 11; *De cura pro mortuis* 22; Thomas, *Scriptum super libros Sententiarum* IV. 45. 2. 4. 3 ad 2; cf. *ST* IIIa 52. 8 obj. 2; *Lectura super evangelium Johannis* 6. 6. 964; see also Ambrose, *De excessu Satyri* 80; *FR* 5).

The effect of praying for the departed is either that they receive much-needed help or, if they have no more need, at least that a bond of love is expressed. It is with good reason that Thomas likens praying for the dead to visiting a friend in prison, for it is an expression of solidarity with one who is alienated from the world. (Note the striking contrast with Ambrose, for whom this life is prison and death is liberation.) At a psychological level, the practice of praying for the dead provides a strong expression of hope, without disguising or denying the reality of loss. It also coheres well with the scriptural portrayal of *Sheol*, the land of the dead, as a place of darkness and exile, the valley of the shadow of death, but one from which a Christian firmly hopes to be redeemed.

While praying for the dead remains an important element of Catholic sacramental practice, there has been a noticeable shift in popular attitudes among Catholics, at least in the West, since the Second Vatican Council (1962–5). The liturgical reforms implemented by the Council sought to emphasize the joyful hope that Christians should find, even in death. Hence white vestments, previously reserved for funerals of young children, were permitted more generally. Hence also black vestments, previously the norm for masses for the dead, were discouraged in favour of purple. The liturgy also suppressed elements, such as the singing of the *Dies Irae* ('the day of wrath'), which spoke too fiercely of judgment (Duffy 2004: 116–25). A common practice which has since emerged at Catholic funerals, and one certainly beyond the intentions of the Fathers of the Council, is for the sermon to comprise a eulogy on the good character of the deceased, a celebration of his or her life, rather than an exhortation to pray for him or for her.[4] In the context of what has been said so far, it seems that the hope emphasized by the Council has been reinterpreted through a particular theology of death implicit in popular piety, one that echoes the approach of Ambrose of Milan. Death is then portrayed as a positive good, at least for the person who died. However, if all elements of judgment and of lament

---

[4] Ironically, this shift has occurred at the same time as there has been a growth of interest among Anglican and other Reformed Christians in the doctrine of purgatory (generally as expressed in a patristic or Eastern Orthodox terms) and in the practice of praying for the dead (Lewis 1984: 159–60; Cross and Livingstone 2005: 459–60, 1358–60).

are suppressed, if purgatory is no longer mentioned, and the dead are assumed to be already in heaven and in no need of prayers, then there is a danger that the reality of death will effectively be denied. This would distort the Christian message of hope in death, which finds the confident hope of the resurrection only through the reality of the cross.

Christians should not grieve 'like those who have no hope' (1 Thessalonians 4: 13), but this is not to say that Christians should not grieve at all. The idea that Christians should not grieve at all would not only place a severe psychological burden on those who are denied an opportunity to express their grief. It would also represent a mistaken theology that distorts the Christian attitude to the body and to other created goods. One of the benefits of studying the theology of Ambrose is to see how the valuing of this life and of the body requires that death be regarded as a loss. In this context we can see how the modern acknowledgement of grief and the necessity of a process of grieving corresponds to a Christian understanding. Some have criticized Kübler-Ross (1969) and others for seeking to describe the proper phases of grief and consolation without having a firm basis for hope. Without such a basis the 'acceptance of death', which is ultimately being advocated, could represent a subtle denial of the reality of death or even amount to a dangerous romanticization of death (Branson 1975; see also P. Ramsey 1974). Rahner was astute in realizing that both the materialist and the spiritualist deny the obscure and frightening reality of death (QD2: 44), and that this denial could have a detrimental effect on how we approach death. Nevertheless, whether or not there can be a proper acceptance of death for those without hope, there certainly can and should be an acceptance of death for those who do have hope. Indeed, it is arguable that the Kubler-Ross stages of grief, or something analogous to them, make *more* sense in a theological context of redemptive hope than they do outside such a context.

The present work is an enquiry into theological approaches to death rather than the psychological mechanisms of grief, but it provides a context within which such mechanisms may be evaluated. Death violently separates soul from body and cuts life short. It deprives those who remain of the fellowship of the departed and it leaves this world the poorer. It is completely appropriate for Christians to feel sorrow and even anger (McCabe 1987; Duffy 2004: 116–24) at the loss of a friend. It is appropriate also that these feelings be expressed with tears or cries, as Jesus wept over the death of Lazarus (John 11: 35), though with the caveat that how people express emotions varies to an extent between cultures and also between individuals in any particular culture. In sum, there is a rightful place for grief, a good grief, even for a Christian. Augustine teaches us that death is something with which we have to contend, and indeed that the difficult and painful process of contending with death is a means through which we are brought to our final joyful end.

FEARFUL HOPE

What has been said of grief over the death of another is also true of fear in the face of one's own death. Death, of itself, is grievous and fearful. The Christian message that believers should not grieve 'like those who have no hope' (1 Thessalonians 4: 13) means not that believers should not grieve at all, but rather, that their grief should be tempered with hope. So also the message that believers should not fear 'those who kill the body but cannot kill the soul' (Matthew 10: 28) does not mean that there is no right or proper fear of death, but that fear of death should be tempered by hope, and by love. This is affirmed in different ways by Augustine, by Thomas, and by Rahner.

Augustine provides three reasons why we should expect some residual fear of death even among those who desire to depart and be with Christ. In the first place, as death destroys the natural union of body and soul, human nature naturally recoils from it. Even Jesus shows this aversion to death and suffering as he prays in the Garden of Gethsemane contemplating his forthcoming crucifixion (Matthew 26: 38). The reason that the martyrs are admirable is precisely that they overcome this natural love of life for the sake of the Gospel. If someone were so jaundiced and dejected that he had no desire to live then his willingness to die would not count as any great sacrifice.

In the second place, quite apart from the question of whether or not fear is appropriate in the face of death, Augustine is wary of the perfectionism implicit in the claim that it is possible to eradicate the fear of death completely. He sees that the perfectionism of the Donatists and the Pelagians leads believers either to hide their faults or to despair, whereas the Gospel requires believers to confess their sins (1 John 1: 8–10). Augustine thus envisions the Christian life as an ongoing struggle with sin. It is important for Christians to cultivate a lively hope in the life of the world to come, and to desire to be with Christ, but it is unrealistic to aspire to be without any fear in the face of death. Such weaknesses are part of this mortal life and will not be wholly overcome until the perfect state of the resurrection. It is for both these reasons, according to Augustine, that Jesus says to Peter that he would be led, 'where you do not wish to go' (John 21: 18 quoted in *In Joannis evangelium tractatus* 123. 5; *Enarrationes in Psalmos* 69. 3; 90. 7).

Thirdly Augustine sees something beneficial in this struggle with death. If there were no fear of death, and no sense of human fragility (both physical and moral), then human beings would not so readily realize their need for God's grace. This is part of the reason why there is wisdom in calling to mind the prospect of death. Closely related to this theme is the threat of judgment in death. Jesus does not simply tell his followers not to fear death. He tells them 'Do not fear those who kill the body but cannot kill the soul; rather fear him who can destroy both soul and body in hell' (Matthew 10: 28). Jesus here distinguishes the fear of death from the fear of judgment, and advises that judgment is more to be feared than bodily death. However, as judgment comes with death, it could also be said that part of the appropriate fear of death is fear of judgment.

Thomas Aquinas reiterates the assertion of Augustine that fear of death is natural and adds to this the claim that, not only is a certain fear of death excusable, but that the failure to fear death sufficiently could even be a sin (*ST* IIaIIae 126. 1). We fear to lose what we love. Hence a lack of fear can be due to a lack of love. Someone who throws his or her life away for no reason, who does not appreciate the value of his or her own life, both in itself and for others, fails to love. As it is sinful deliberately to destroy one's own life, so it is sinful to fail to take sufficient care of the life we have been given. Thus the acceptance of death must occur within the context of a proper love of life. If bodily life can be loved too much, when it is preferred to obedience to God, it can also be loved too little, when it is not appreciated as a gift from God.

In line with this tradition, Rahner also affirms that 'man is rightly afraid of death' (QD2: 54). However, he does not trace this inherent fear to the unnatural separation of body and soul (as Augustine and Thomas do) but to the supernatural vocation of human beings which is contradicted by the reality of death as it is presently experienced.[5] He is adamant that 'this terror of death must be admitted and cannot be avoided or abolished' (QD2: 55), for to do so would be to deny this supernatural destiny. Only in the light of Christ who overcomes the darkness of the death can the fear of death be transformed into hope without avoidance or denial. Fear of death, for Rahner, is most fundamentally a fear of uncertainty and ambiguity, a fear of putting oneself utterly at the hidden and incomprehensible mercy of God.

Rahner's approach is in harmony with that of Augustine and Thomas, but Rahner makes it easier to see how the continuing fearfulness of death is reconcilable with the hope of the Gospel. His argument is that the fearfulness of death is in fact rooted in the hope of final happiness. If human beings were not created for eternal life and did not experience this call to something more than mortal life, then death would seem natural and fitting. The human experience of mortal fear would then appear irrational and without foundation, something simply to be abolished by human effort or by philosophical reflection. However, if one believes that human beings are created for a supernatural destiny, then it is for good reason that they recoil from death, which to all appearances is a contradiction of this destiny. Fear in the face of death, and the right response to this fear, is not comprehensible purely within the categories of nature and natural reason. Fear is provoked by the mystery of hope that appears as destruction and that requires an abandonment of will (a spiritual dying) to entrust oneself to the mercy of God. Christian

---

[5] 'Because a creature belongs to God, it shrinks back, by a movement of its very essence, from this last mystery of emptiness, of finality, of nothingness, from the mystery of iniquity' (QD2: 55).

hope thus does not deny a rightful fear in the face of the dark mystery of death but rather implies and encompasses it.

Christian hope affirms both the need and the difficulty of acknowledging one's own approaching death, even for a Christian.[6] At this point, as with the discussion of the stages of grief, there is a possibility for theology to come into fruitful dialogue with contemporary psychology. However, again as in regard to grief, theologians should be cautious about attempts to be reconciled with death outside a context of hope. Furthermore, as the later Rahner increasingly emphasized (Rahner 1983*b*, cf. *ST* IaIIae 62. 1; *ST* IIaIIae 17. 1), the hope we need to approach death well is a work of grace. What it is to approach death well, to make a 'good death', is a question that will be discussed further, after discussion of withdrawal of treatment. However, before this is can properly be addressed, it is necessary to turn from reflection on the approach of death to reflection on the deliberate ending of life: from dying to killing.

KILLING

Death is something that will come to every human being. Hence it is that Ambrose, Augustine, Thomas, and Rahner all discuss death in relation to Adam, the first and archetypal human being (for example *FR* 37; *CD* XIII. 15; *ST* Ia 97. 1; QD2: 34 respectively). The origin and meaning of human death is set out in the second and third chapters of the book of Genesis, wherein is found that most memorable phrase, 'You are dust and to dust you shall return' (Genesis 3: 19).

It is noteworthy that the first death recorded in the Scriptures, immediately after the eviction of Adam and Eve from the Garden, is the fratricide committed by Cain (Genesis 4: 8; cf. John Paul II 1995: 7–9). If, from a Christian perspective, death has its origin in sin, then there is something archetypal about the sin of murder, considered as the killing of a brother. Even before the giving of the Law, the

---

[6] Rahner in his old age confesses that 'I often think about death every day and feel it in my bones', yet he consoles himself with the thought that 'fear of death is a good thing' (Vorgrimler 1986: 137).

prohibition on shedding human blood is included in the covenant God makes with Noah (Genesis 9: 5–6, in language that echoes Genesis 4: 10–15). This prohibition is reiterated in the injunction, 'you shall not kill' (Exodus 20: 13), one of the Ten Commandments, the foundations of the Law of Moses. This commandment is included by Jesus in his summary of the fundamental requirements of the Law (Matthew 19: 18; Mark 10: 19; Luke 18: 20). Nevertheless, in spite of, or perhaps precisely because of, the deeply rooted character of the prohibition on homicide, it is not straightforward to articulate the reasons for it. 'The prohibition [on murder] is so basic that it is difficult to answer the question as to why murder is intrinsically wrongful' (Anscombe in Geach and Gormally 2005: 266).

Augustine begins his consideration of homicide with the commandment against killing and his discussion is thus framed by the theme of divine authority (*CD* I. 20 ff.). In general, human beings have the authority to kill non-human animals but not the authority to kill human beings (themselves or others). The exception to this is when God delegates authority to rulers to execute wrongdoers and when he directly commands individuals to kill, as he did with Abraham. On this account there seems no limit to what God could command by way of killing, only a limit on what killing may be done without God's command. Nevertheless, while on the face of it Augustine's account of homicide may seem excessively arbitrary and related only to divine commands, this account needs to be understood in conjunction with his theological analysis of death later in the *De civitate Dei* (*CD* XIII).

Human death is unique in being a consequence of sin. There were angels who sinned but angels do not have bodies and hence do not undergo bodily death (*CD* XIII. 1). Non-human animals die, but they do not sin and death for them is natural (*De Genesi ad litteram* VI. 22). Only human death is due to sin, in that death could have been avoided had Adam not sinned. It follows from this that only human death is a punishment for sin. Augustine regards human life as a blessing, even after Adam's fall, and human death as a punishment due to the fall. As a punishment, death is something painful to soul and body and is not good for anyone (*CD* XIII. 6). For Augustine, then, the legitimacy of killing human beings is bound up with the authority to punish. It is wrong to bring about death unless this is imposed by a legitimate authority as a just punishment. Augustine's account of killing is thus informed by these two theological themes, death as punishment and death as something bad both for body and for soul. The prohibition on homicide without divine authorization is thus universal because death is a punishment imposed universally by God and because, considered in itself, death is universally bad.

Thomas's influential treatment of homicide (*ST* IIaIIae 64) takes as his starting point Augustine's discussion in *De civitate Dei*. Thomas starts with the question of animals, defending the argument that non-rational animals are by nature ordered to human use. Here he appeals not only to Augustine (*CD* I. 20) but also to Aristotle (*Politica* 1. 8. 1256b). From the beginning of the discussion, Thomas uses the idea of natural order, understood in broadly Aristotelian terms, to complement his discussion of divine authority. The discussion that follows invokes the categories of human dignity and of existing for one's own sake to explain why, considered in itself, it is always wrong to kill a human being. However, in relation to the execution of wrongdoers (*ST* IIaIIae 64. 2), Thomas makes two claims: that the good of the community takes priority over the good of the individual for 'every part is naturally for the sake of the whole'; and, more crucially, that the wrongdoer, by sin, falls away from human dignity. It was argued in Chapter 5 above that there are problems with both of these claims. Nevertheless, what is significant for the present discussion is that neither Thomas's account of what is wrong with killing human beings nor the exception he makes for killing wrongdoers relies on appeal to divine authority. Rather killing requires (divine) authority because of the nature and dignity of the human being. Thomas follows Augustine in allowing that God could authorize someone to kill the innocent, as God apparently did in the case of Abraham (*ST* IIaIIae 64. 6 ad 1), but this claim does not play a central role in Thomas's treatment of homicide. The key point for Thomas is that, in itself, it is always wrong to kill a human being on account of the dignity of human nature (*ST* IIaIIae 64. 6). Implicit here is the understanding shared by Augustine and Thomas that human death, in itself, is bad for both body and soul. We might add to this with Rahner that it also stands in contradiction to the supernatural destiny of human beings. It is for these reasons that killing is an affront to human dignity.

SUICIDE AND MARTYRDOM

While there are Christian writings from as early as the second century which explicitly condemn suicide, it is Augustine who develops the first extended treatment of suicide. He argues that the commandment 'you shall not kill' applies equally to killing oneself as to killing another, 'for to kill oneself is to kill a human being' (*CD* I. 20). Augustine holds that killing can only be justified if it is authorized by God. It is true that this can apply to suicide, if the person is secretly commanded by God to kill himself, '[as] we are required to believe in Samson's case' (*CD* I. 25). However, Augustine does not believe that suicide can be justified by any other reason. Suicide is emphatically not justified by such motivations as escaping from temporary troubles, avoiding temptation to sin, avoiding complicity in another's sin, expressing grief over past sins, or gaining a better life after death. Apart from the direct command of God, the human individual has no right to take his or her own life.

Thomas builds on the understanding of Augustine in his analysis of suicide. Whereas Augustine considers the motivations that seem to justify suicide, and finds all of them wanting, Thomas seeks to understand more deeply the reasons why suicide is prohibited. Suicide is wrong for three reasons: because it is self-destructive; because it is unjust to the community; and because it is a sin directly against God.

Thomas starts with the proper love of self that all beings ought to have. Suicide might seem compatible with self-love, as it clearly seems attractive to some people as an escape from hardships which are difficult to bear. However, such an act represents either a failure to value the good of life or a failure of courage to hold on to it. Furthermore, there is no guarantee that someone who leaves this life by his own hands will find eternal rest, for 'the passage from this life to a better and happier one is subject not to man's free will but to the power of God' (*ST* IIaIIae 64. 5 ad 3).

In the second place, while suicide is directly an act of self-harm, it is indirectly harmful to relations and loved ones and to the wider society, in the same way that murder is an injustice not only to the person killed but also to those who are bereaved and to society as a whole.

In the third place suicide is the deliberate destruction of a living creature who is made in the image of God, and hence an offence against the creator. Some claim that, if life is indeed a free gift from God, than the recipient may do as he or she wishes with it (Battin 1994: 217). However, as Nigel Biggar makes clear, it is necessary to take due care of any valuable gift, 'both because of its intrinsic value and because of its status as a gift' (Biggar 2004: 25). Furthermore Battin's way of framing the question seems to imply that human autonomy and the human good make sense over and against God. However, if the world is indeed created by God, then no good can come of seeking independence from God. It is like cutting the branch on which one is standing.[7]

Given this deeply rooted rejection of suicide within the Christian tradition, a key question for the theologian is how to understand the self-sacrifice of the martyr. It seems that the martyr is honoured precisely for voluntarily laying down his or her life willingly: 'Greater love has no man than this, that a man lay down his life for his friends' (John 15: 13). However, if the voluntary embracing of death is praised in the martyr, how can it be rejected always and absolutely in the case of suicide? It is true that Augustine and Thomas give one exception to the prohibition of suicide, when God commands one to kill oneself, as Augustine believed occurred in the case of Samson. Nevertheless, martyrdom is not restricted to those men and women who have received a private revelation from God. Rather martyrdom is obligatory for those faced with a choice to sin or to be killed.

In the introductory chapter of this book mention was made of the work of Droge and Tabor (1992), who conflate martyrdom with suicide under the category of 'voluntary death'. This modern conflation has its origin in the work of Durkheim (2002), first published in 1897, but even in the ancient world, when the categories of suicide and martyrdom were generally held to be distinct, there was sometimes disagreement in relation to particular cases. This is evident from the disagreement of Ambrose and Augustine over the suicide/martyrdom of Pelagia.

---

[7] '[T]here can be no such thing as being independent of God, whatever my freedom means it cannot mean not depending (in the creative sense) on God' (McCabe 2005: 11) A related metaphor of the foolishness of kicking against the ground is given by Geach (1977: 83).

Augustine deserves credit for bringing greater clarity to this distinction, even to the extent of taking issue with popular piety. A martyr is not someone who seeks death but someone who remains faithful to the truth even in the face of death. The death of a martyr is free and voluntary in the sense that he or she could have sinned to avoid being killed but freely chooses not to sin. However, in another sense martyrdom is forced, for martyrdom is the result of unjust persecution and the martyr accepts to be killed only because the alternative is sin. 'It was then said, "If you break the commandment you will certainly die." Now it is said, "If you shrink from death, you will break the commandment"' (*CD* XIII. 4). The martyr is killed but is not a killer. It is the persecutor who is the killer. In contrast, the suicide is both killed and killer. Thomas reinforces this distinction with his definition of martyrdom as 'the right endurance of sufferings *unjustly* inflicted' (*ST* IIaIIae 124. 1; emphasis added).

Both Augustine and Thomas are cautious about the enthusiasm that some Christians have shown for martyrdom. This is in part because wishing for martyrdom involves wishing that someone else commit a great injustice, but it is also because the courage of martyrdom is a gift from God which should not be presumed. For Augustine, the essence of martyrdom is submission to the mysterious will of God, free submission which is itself possible only by the grace of God. In contrast, it seems to Augustine that some of those who seek martyrdom, such as the Donatists, are conceiving martyrdom as a human achievement.

It has been noted that, at certain points, Rahner's approach to death seems to share some of the weaknesses of Ambrose's approach. Death is seen as a good thing and hence as something desirable. Rahner thus states with approval that 'throughout the history of the Church there have always been Christians longing for martyrdom' (QD2: 116). Indeed, for Rahner the problem is more acute because he repeatedly describes death as a free action from within. According to Rahner, martyrdom reveals 'the love of death' which a Christian must have (QD2: 98). It is then difficult for him to justify the immediate qualification, 'which he may not, however, carry into effect by suicide' (QD2: 98). Hence at certain points Rahner is less clear or helpful than Augustine or Thomas. Nevertheless, Rahner provides fresh insight when he states that the attitude by which the martyr 'surrenders himself fully' to God is the diametric opposite of 'the will to die autonomously' (QD2: 44). As he becomes increasingly aware in his more mature writings, there is in Christian death a subtle interplay of action and passivity, and of work and grace. It is a voluntary act, but it is an act of surrendering oneself and one's will and hence it is emphatically to be differentiated from the act of bringing about death.

What differentiates suicide from martyrdom, then, is not only the physical reality of who does the killing (oneself or another), but is also the intentional reality of the attitude from which the action springs. It is precisely because suicide is the autonomous act of bringing about death apart from the command of God (here Rahner is close to Augustine) that it is a failure to surrender oneself to God in the mysterious 'veiledness' of death. The person who attempts suicide does not acknowledge the need to endure death freely, but seems in a curious way to deny the reality of death. It is noteworthy that already in the fourth century Ambrose had recognized this. He speaks of those who commit suicide out of grief and 'by that very means demonstrate their madness in not enduring death, and yet seeking it; in adopting that as a remedy which they flee from as an evil... But this is not common, since nature herself restrains although madness drives men on' (*FR* 11). Nature restrains the impulse to suicide, but, from a theological perspective, the sin of suicide consists not primarily in opposing nature but more fundamentally, in failing to accept death from God. From a theological perspective, suicide can thus be understood as a rejection of the proper acceptance of death. Furthermore, if sickness can rightly be seen, as Rahner argues, as the '*prolixitas mortis*' (QD2: 76), then to commit suicide out of a fear of losing control in progressive terminal disease is, implicitly, to fail to acknowledge the total loss of control that is present in death.

This position offers a possible bridge between philosophers concerned with the ethical analysis of suicide, and psychologists such as Kübler-Ross concerned with the process of dying. If suicide represents a failure to accept death, then ethical criticism of suicide, and concern to prevent suicide, is wholly consistent with the wish to help people acknowledge the reality of their own approaching death. In recent years there has been a growing awareness, both among Christians and in wider society, that those who take their own lives may be subject to internal constraints which prevent them from acting freely. Inasmuch as a particular act of suicide is the product of a distressed and desperate mind, then the person may not be fully culpable for his or her actions and there is reason for those who are left behind to hope in the mercy of God. For this reason the Christian Churches offer prayers for those who have killed themselves (*Catechism* 1999: 2283; *Common Worship* 2000: 360). Nevertheless, it is important to recognize that the action of killing oneself is of itself a failure to accept death from the hand of God and thus amounts to a rejection of God in death.

ASSISTED SUICIDE AND EUTHANASIA

On the basis of what has been said about suicide, what should be said of assisting suicide and of euthanasia? With regard to assisting suicide a key question is what it means to 'assist' someone. If someone is on the brink of a self-destructive project, is it truly assisting that person to facilitate his or her destruction? Would it not be of more assistance to prevent this destruction? If suicide is indeed a self-destructive project, then it seems that facilitating suicide is not assisting anyone. It is important to note that what is at issue here is not only the approach of death, and whether death would ever be welcome, but the issue is precisely the deliberate bringing about of one's own death. What is being facilitated is not simply a death but a suicide (see Wreen 1988). Everyone must die but no one need die by his or her own hands. If, as has been argued above, suicide in itself is an act of self-harm, an act of injustice to society, and a sin against God, then to assist suicide is to encourage someone to commit a terrible deed. Furthermore, after death comes judgment (Hebrews 9: 27), when the creature meets his or her maker.[8] Someone who commits suicide meets God not only spiritually unprepared, but actually with blood on his or her hands. This is why it is good to

---

[8] The idea of judgment at death is not only present in Christianity but in Judaism and Islam and, in a different way in Hinduism and Buddhism. It is present in Plato's myth in the *Phaedo*. The image of God weighing the spirit in a balance (Proverbs 16: 2) echoes ancient Egyptian beliefs about judgment in death.

pray for God's mercy on those who have taken their own lives, but it is better still to try to prevent suicide, to help people to live well to the end, and to accept death when it comes from God.

For some secular strands of thought, beginning with David Hume in the eighteenth century (Fieser 1995), suicide is conceived as a rightful exercise of autonomy. It expresses one's ownership of one's own life. However, even without directly invoking God's sovereignty, the idea of suicide as an act of autonomy does not seem tenable. True autonomy refrains from self-destructive acts and from injustice towards others and also acknowledges the reality of one's situation. Yet suicide is both a form of self-harm, and an injustice against those who would be bereaved and against society as a whole. More fundamentally, it has been argued here that suicide represents a failure to accept the reality of death, a failure to endure death freely (in Rahner's terms). There is no natural or human right to harm oneself, to injure society, or to deny reality. The portrayal of suicide as an act of autonomy is thus a travesty; nor is it a harmless error, for the romanticization of suicide is liable to endanger vulnerable people. It is important to acknowledge that suicide is a failure and a human tragedy and is not a true act of autonomy. Respect for someone's human dignity and rights is not promoted but is undermined by assisting suicide. Rather than having a duty to assist suicide, it seems rather that as human beings we have a general duty to dissuade our neighbours from committing suicide and instead to help them to live.

Closely related to the issue of assisting suicide is that of euthanasia or mercy killing. There are advocates on both sides of the debate who take exception to the term 'mercy killing'. Some object that euthanasia is not properly described as 'mercy' (Oregon and Washington Bishops 1991; John Paul II 1995: 67; *Hansard* 2005, vol. 674, pt. 38, c. 97), whereas others object to the phrase because of the negative connotation of 'killing': 'To say it is "mercy killing" for a physician to give a patient a requested lethal dose to end her suffering is to invest the act with an air of criminality that the word "mercy" does not adequately temper (Bender 1992: 6). Some also object that the term does not sufficiently distinguish voluntary euthanasia from other forms of killing (e.g. South Australian Voluntary Euthanasia Society 1998).

Nevertheless, there are good reasons to retain this term, for two essential features of 'euthanasia' in the modern sense of the term are that it involves intentional killing,[9] and that it is motivated by a desire to end suffering. Reflection on the term 'mercy killing' also helps clarify an important difference between assisting suicide and euthanasia. In the case of assisting suicide it is the person who kills himself or herself. In the case of euthanasia it is the mercy killer who does the killing. The mercy killer is not simply an assistant but he or she is the principal agent. Euthanasia is thus a step further from suicide and a step closer to murder in the ordinary sense. The motivation of the mercy killer is clearly different from that of the common murderer. He or she kills in order to put an end to the suffering of the victim. Nevertheless, the final act and hence the ultimate responsibility lie with the person killing, not with the person killed. One argument put forward in favour of euthanasia is that human beings should not be treated worse that animals, for we 'put an animal out of his misery' (e.g. Haggart 1991, but the sentiment is a common one). This analogy seeks to emphasize the motive of mercy, but at the same time it highlights the disparity between the killer and the one killed, between the human vet and the suffering animal. Even though the desire to alleviate suffering is a noble desire, the act of killing fails to respect the dignity of the human person.

Suicide, assisting suicide, and euthanasia have all been defended on the basis that they express autonomy. However, it is argued here that suicide itself is not a successful act of autonomy but a human failure and indirectly, a social injustice. It is for this reason that there can be no right to suicide just as there is no 'right', for example, to sell oneself into slavery or prostitution, to sell one's vital organs, or to engage in substance abuse.

If suicide is not properly an act of autonomy, then assisting suicide cannot be justified by appeal to autonomy. Furthermore, the person assisting is responsible for his or her own actions and may well have less excuse than the person committing suicide. The suicidal person may well suffer from depression or an unbalanced mind, and so be less culpable for his actions. The person who 'assists' by giving the person

---

[9] '[T]his term is most appropriate because the act involves an intentional killing, no matter how good the intention may be to alleviate suffering' (Saunders 1996).

the means to commit suicide has less excuse. The least excusable facilitator of suicide is the physician, who has a direct duty of care over the suicidal patient and whose professional ethos, exemplified by the Hippocratic Oath, forbids intentional harm (W. H. S. Jones 1924; D. A. Jones 2003, 2006; Kass 1988; Cameron 1991).

Finally, if neither suicide nor assisting suicide is justifiable by appeal to autonomy, then mercy killing certainly cannot be. Whether mercy killing is done at the request of the victim, to someone incapable of requesting, or against the express wishes of the victim, it is the mercy killer who decides and he or she who does the killing. This clarifies a feature that is present also in assisted suicide. Either the mercy killer kills all who request it automatically and indiscriminately, or the mercy killer makes a distinction between those who have a life that is worth living (and who should not be killed) and those who have a life that is not worth living (and who should be killed). Whereas the first approach represents the abnegation of all responsibility, the second involves making value judgments about the worthwhileness of the lives of others (Keown 2002: 76–9). Neither approach involves a true respect of the dignity or the autonomy of the person.

It is reasonable that the law should regard euthanasia (which is closer to common murder) as a more serious offence than assisting suicide (which is closer to suicide). Indeed, this seems to be the status quo in most jurisdictions. Nevertheless, from a theological perspective, it is arguable that assisting suicide is in fact the more terrible sin. For, as the person who commits suicide is directly involved in bringing about his or her own death, he or she goes to judgment with a greater objective burden of guilt. While there can be no certainty of someone's inner dispositions and the judgment of God, suicide, as a deliberate act, is precisely that kind of act which leads to hell, and assisting suicide delivers someone to judgment at the worst possible time. In contrast, the requests of the victim of euthanasia are ambivalent in their significance, and these requests are only indirectly the cause of death. Euthanasia is an act of injustice which threatens the vulnerable, undermines the proper care for the dying, and prejudices the victim's ability to make a good death. Nevertheless, it is suicide that represents the more direct and fundamental contradiction of surrendering oneself to death. Assisting suicide therefore seems to deliver the victim to a worse death and therefore represents a greater failure of Christian charity.

LAW AND PUBLIC POLICY

This work has focused on the theological meaning of death and dying and hence the morality of bringing about death by suicide, assisting suicide, and euthanasia. However, it would be remiss to leave this discussion isolated from matters of law and public policy. In general terms for each issue one could distinguish four possible stances: one may hold that the act is legitimate in itself and hence ought to be legally permitted in certain cases; one may hold the act is never legitimate in itself and hence that it ought to be forbidden; one may hold that the act is never legitimate in itself, but nevertheless that it ought to be tolerated for the sake of some other good; or one may hold that, though the act is legitimate in itself, it should be prohibited because of the harmful effects of tolerating it.

One of the principal conclusions of this work is that suicide, assisting suicide, and euthanasia are inherently destructive, indirectly unjust, and fail properly to acknowledge the reality of human death. They are not legitimate acts to which people could reasonably claim a right in law. Nevertheless, the question remains, even if these acts are destructive, should they be forbidden by law? For the law does not forbid every destructive act. Some have proposed that suicide, assisted suicide, and euthanasia should be tolerated for the sake of individual liberty (Harris 1985). Pursuing this argument further, Ronald Dworkin (1994) has argued that matters concerning the value of life express profoundly religious values, but that for this very reason diversity of view should be tolerated, as a form of respect for religious liberty. Hence, according to Dworkin, neither assisted suicide nor euthanasia should be prohibited by law, even though many people will regard them as inherently wrong. However, while there is certain a sense in which respect for life is a 'religious' value, this involves a very broad sense of religion which would equally apply to concern for liberty, honesty, social welfare, and indeed to autonomy itself.[10] Society should not attempt to refrain from legislating for matters because they are 'religious' in this extended sense, for this would encompass virtually every personal and social value. Furthermore, respect for liberty does not justify actions which are harmful to oneself, to others, or both; and, as has been argued above, suicide, assisting suicide, and euthanasia all fall into this category.

In this context, it is worth briefly rehearsing a case which is made against legalizing euthanasia precisely because it would seriously endanger many people and would have a harmful effect on society as a whole with regard, for example, to provision of palliative care and to attitudes toward disability. Such a case can and is made even by some who think that euthanasia is legitimate in itself, at least in some circumstances (Biggar 2004). Advocates of decriminalizing euthanasia dispute this, arguing instead that such legislation can be regulated in such a way as to avoid the negative consequences (Griffiths 1998). The evidence from those few jurisdictions which have embraced euthanasia or assisted suicide is thus subject to heated debate (Griffiths 1998; Keown 2002; Biggar 2004).

Without prejudice to debates over the effectiveness of regulating euthanasia in the Netherlands or assisted suicide in Oregon, the conclusions of the present study constitute a strong prima facie case for prohibiting these activities.

There is, nevertheless, a distinction to be made between suicide and assisted suicide and there is also a distinction between assisted suicide and euthanasia. Before 1960 suicide and attempted suicide were subject to legal penalties in English law but since the 1960s and 1970s many jurisdictions have decriminalized suicide, while leaving assisting suicide as a serious crime. These changes were generally based not on an appeal to liberty (as though there was a 'right' to suicide) but on a concern that the involvement of the criminal law was interfering with the treatment of suicidal patients (Keown 2002: 65). There was also a growing realization that those attempting suicide often suffered from unbalanced mind and thus had limited culpability for their actions. Furthermore, while assisted suicide and

---

[10] '[The] valuation of personal freedom and authenticity itself rests (whether people realise this fact or not) upon the "religious" sense which we have been trying to express' (Gormally 1994: 45).

euthanasia remained as criminal offences, it should be noted that they are distinct crimes and euthanasia typically attracts heavier penalties. This also seems reasonable given that assisting suicide stands midway, as it were, between suicide and euthanasia.

Those who advocate the decriminalization of assisted suicide generally also support the decriminalization of euthanasia. Nevertheless, as these are distinct acts, and as suicide is no longer a criminal offence, some have proposed that assisting suicide be decriminalized while euthanasia remain criminal.[11] Groups such as Death with Dignity (formally the Voluntary Euthanasia Society) in the United Kingdom and Compassion & Choices (formally the Hemlock Society) in the United States support such proposals as part of a wedge strategy, a staging post on the way to the full legalization of euthanasia. However, others have supported such proposals on the basis that this legislation could be policed more effectively than the widely criticized Dutch model (Mackay 2005). From the perspective of the present study the exclusive concern with effectiveness of legislation, while it expresses a valid concern, seems to presuppose that there is nothing intrinsically wrong with assisting suicide. This presupposition needs to be questioned. Suicide should be recognized for what it is: a destructive act which fails to accept the reality of death. Suicide was decriminalized not in recognition of a supposed right to kill oneself but in recognition of the unbalanced state of those who attempt to do so. However, such concerns do not typically apply to those assisting suicide,[12] and they apply least of all to medical professionals who have care for suicidal patients. Thus, even if Physician Assisted Suicide could be effectively regulated, and this is by no means established (Keown 2002: 174–80), no adequate moral or public policy rationale has been brought forward that would justify the toleration of such a destructive activity.

[11] This is the present legal situation in Oregon, to which the Mackay Report (2005) seemed favourably inclined, though legislation to introduce it in the United Kingdom was rejected by the House of Lords in May 2006.

[12] One possible exception to this is the situation of carers who assist suicide or who kill those in their care. The Law Commission report on the revision of the (2005) homicide act argued that this should be explicitly acknowledged in the law. Nevertheless, it seems that even here, the relevant legal remedy should be a plea of diminished responsibility in the particular case, and not a general rule for all carers who kill (cf. D. A. Jones and Hiscox 2006).

WITHHOLDING AND WITHDRAWING TREATMENT

The Christian tradition, as represented in this study by Ambrose, Augustine, Thomas, and Rahner, is united in arguing that it is never legitimate to kill oneself or to kill another unless under the command of God. What is more complex is the morality of omitting an action which could sustain or lengthen life. Whereas the duty not to kill the innocent is absolute, the duty to save or sustain life is governed by many factors. Someone who volunteers to go as a doctor or a nurse to a country with a shortage of well-trained healthcare workers could save many lives which might otherwise have been lost. Nevertheless, this does not place on everyone the obligation to become a doctor or a nurse and then volunteer for such work. No one can solve the world's problems on his or her own and not everyone has an equal duty to help. In the parable of the Good Samaritan (Luke 10: 30–7) Jesus reminded his disciples that charity places on us some obligation to help those in need whom we come across, but Jesus himself frequently sought refuge in some lonely place to avoid the demands of the crowds (Mark 1: 35, 45, 3: 20, 6: 31, 7: 24). Not acting might amount to callousness or negligence, but this is not so in every case.

One's obligations to others are shaped by the competing demands on one's time and energy, including the obligation to sustain oneself. The measure of what is appropriate is given by the requirements of virtue, especially the virtue of practical wisdom which Thomas terms *prudentia* (*ST* IIaIIae 47) and by the particular vocation to which each person is called. So also the duty to sustain and extend one's own life is not limitless but is shaped by virtue and calling. This is clear in the case of Jesus and of the martyrs. The requirement to be faithful and to witness to the coming kingdom supersedes the duty to extend the length of life. An interesting example is given by Vitoria, of a man who stays with his dying wife, despite the danger of catching the plague himself (Doyle 1997). If his overwhelming duty were to preserve his own life, then it would seem he had a duty to abandon his wife to her fate. This is certainly not the case. Rather, his decision to stay with his wife shows the virtues of marital fidelity and human solidarity and, if he does die as a result, he does not die recklessly but as a kind of martyr.

Neither in the case of one's own life, nor in the case of the life of another, can there be an absolute obligation to preserve or extend life at all costs. This conforms with the theological approach to death which has been set out so far. Death is never a good in itself, and it is never to be brought about deliberately without the command of God. On the other hand, death comes inevitably to every human being and comes as a command from God (hence the words of Jesus, 'this night your soul is required of you' Luke 12: 20, cf. Wisdom 15: 8). The appropriate Christian response to this command is willingly to surrender one's life, following the example of Christ and of the martyrs. To hold on to life 'at all costs' represents a failure to surrender oneself to God, a failure to accept and freely endure death from the hand of God. The apparently opposite sins of bringing about death and of failing to accept death share a common root, the assertion of autonomy regarding life and death over and against God.

These reflections do not resolve the practical issues of how hard to strive to sustain life and at what point to accept the inevitability of death. They point only to the existence of moral/spiritual limits as to striving to live and the moral/spiritual requirement at some point to accept the inevitable. One way these limits have traditionally been discerned, in the context of a general requirement to show human solidarity, is by reference to the deciding whether medical treatment is futile or unduly burdensome. Futile or unduly burdensome treatment was termed 'extraordinary' or 'disproportionate' and was not obligatory. Useful treatment, where the benefits outweighed the burdens, was termed 'ordinary' or 'proportionate' and there was an obligation to provide and to accept such treatment.

The question of whether some treatment is ordinary or extraordinary is relative to the circumstances of a particular person. That is because both the benefits and the burdens of a treatment will vary considerably from person to person. Nevertheless, it is possible to say that some treatments are prima facie ordinary, in the sense that they are useful and not excessively burdensome for most patients. Furthermore, the decision to withhold or withdraw medical treatment is legitimate only if it embodies a legitimate intention. It is never right to withhold or withdraw treatment in order to bring about some-one's death. This would be killing by omission, just as in the case of deliberately starving a child to death or deliberately leaving a prisoner to die of exposure, in order to bring about their deaths. Intentional killing by omission is just as much an offence against the commandment, just as much a destructive and unjust act as killing by a positive act. Intention is not the only element to consider here, but it is an essential element.

In this context, it is important that the phrase 'quality of life', itself innocuous, is not used so as to deny the human dignity of debilitated patients by categorizing their lives as unworthy to be lived. Similarly, while it is legitimate to ask about the financial and emotional costs of maintaining care, there remains a real requirement to show solidar-ity, and not to abandon vulnerable people. The philosopher Bernard Williams astutely observed that ' "He would be better off dead" can be said for many dubious reasons: the most dubious is that we would be better off if he were dead' (Williams 1985: 42).

The question of intention helps distinguish wrongful, homicidal omissions from appropriate omissions. Nevertheless, the lack of suicidal intention is not sufficient to determine the ethical question. As a doctor might be negligent without having any malicious inten-tion to omit the neglected treatment, so also a patient may fail by neglecting to give proper respect to the positive value of his or her own life. This was mentioned above in relation to the fear of death. Death may be feared too little because life is loved too little (*ST* IIaIIae 126. 1). The failure to appreciate the good of extending life, where is occurs, may be due to depression or to the distorted value judgments of society. This is especially so in regard to mental disability. Whatever the cause of such value judgments, they can lead to decisions to withdraw treatment which are flawed and which undermine the culture of life. The right and wrong in such decisions cannot easily be reduced to universal rules. Therefore, while acknow-ledging that there is scope for improvement of the law in many jurisdictions, the question of what is appropriate in a particular case cannot be reduced to the question of what is legal in that case. It is rather through the individual and collective appreciation of the goods of life and the proper acceptance of death that wise and just actions can be supported. For a Christian these actions will be guided by hope in the mysterious plan of God whether in life or in death.

SUSTAINING THE UNCONSCIOUS

As mentioned in the introductory chapter, one of the most contentious examples of the withdrawal of treatment is the withdrawal of tube feeding from patients who are unconscious and who are very unlikely ever to recover consciousness. This issue was played out in the tragic example of Tony Bland in the United Kingdom and, more recently in the United States in the case of Terry Schiavo. When Pope John Paul II made a short declaration on this issue in March 2004, rather than settle the matter he provoked further controversy, both among Catholics and among non-Catholics. The Pope declared that feeding, even by tube, constituted ordinary care which should only be withdrawn or withheld in exceptional circumstances. This contradicted the view of many people that tube feeding was a form of medial treatment which might legitimately be withdrawn, especially in cases where there seemed no hope that the person would recover consciousness.

Some illumination on this most controversial issue can be achieved by a detailed and critical consideration of Rahner's approach to death. This is in part because Rahner directly and indirectly influences the views of many Catholics on death and dying, but also because he expresses important themes that are present in many contemporary thinkers, both Christian and secular.

Before turning directly to withdrawing food from the unconscious, it is necessary to return briefly to the issues of suicide and mercy killing. Karl Rahner, wishing to base his ethic on the value of human freedom, is reluctant to accept the traditional argument (found for example in Ambrose, Augustine, and Thomas) that suicide, as a usurpation of the authority of God, transgresses the proper limits of human freedom. This explanation seems to Rahner to restrict the power of God and to contradict the nature of human creatures as free and responsible for their own lives. Human responsibility clearly extends over many decisions concerning life and death.

For Rahner, a religious view should emphasize the true freedom that human beings possess, and should not construe the commandments as limits to this freedom. Hence, rather than describe suicide and mercy killing as transgressing the due limits of freedom, Rahner argues that these acts are wrong because they fail to give sufficient opportunity for human freedom. They curtail the scope of human freedom.

A consequence of Rahner's account of the relationship between freedom and the morality of killing is that unconscious patients with no hope of recovery are not included in the prohibition against killing. There can be no extending of opportunities for freedom to people who cannot exercise that freedom. It is precisely for this reason that a number of contemporary theologians distinguish people in a persistent vegetative state from other classes of patient. If free acts are no longer possible, then life is no longer thought to be worth preserving. If life is no longer worth preserving, then even the simple act of feeding is futile and excessive. Hence tube feeding should be withdrawn from the comatose, as their lives are no good to them, while continuing to feed them involves ongoing financial and emotional cost to the family or to the state. The Anglican theologian Nigel Biggar also holds this position, accepting the description of persistently unconsciousness as 'biological' life without 'biographical' life (Biggar 2004: 31–47) and stating that such individuals are 'irretrievably inaccessible to human care' (Biggar 2004: 112 quoting P. Ramsey 1970: 162).

The quotation from Biggar helps clarify what is wrong with this approach. If the condition termed persistent vegetative state can be diagnosed reliably,[13] there is no possibility that the person can make further free acts. However, this does not imply that the person is 'inaccessible to human care'. Someone who is unconscious can still be cared for: housed, cleaned, turned, fed, visited. For all care to be withdrawn would be to leave the patient unsheltered, unwashed,

---

[13] The reliability of diagnosis for 'persistent vegetative state' is disputed (John Paul II 2004). An article published in the *British Journal of Medicine* (Andrews *et al.* 1996) found that 43% of 40 patients were misdiagnosed and that only 13% remained vegetative. A more recent study in *NeuroRehabilitation* (Clauss and Nel 2006) showed that the sleeping pill zolpidem could temporarily restore those in a 'permanent [*sic*] vegetative state' to a level of language comprehension.

untouched, unfed, and utterly abandoned. A patient may not be aware of the care that is given, but this does not mean it has no human significance for those who give the care or for society as a whole. As a living human being the unconscious patient can receive care in a variety of ways. What wider role this unconscious life will have in the lives of others is hidden in the plan of God, but it is presumptuous to claim that it could have none.

If Rahner is wrong to exclude the unconscious from all human care, then his claim that the worth of human life rests only on the opportunities for human freedom needs to be re-examined. Rahner is surely right to say that the prohibition of suicide should not be seen as a law that comes from outside (a heteronomy in Kant's terms), as though God's sovereignty were antithetical to the authentic human freedom. On the contrary, as Herbert McCabe states, 'We are not free in spite of God, but because of God' (McCabe 2005: 15). If suicide is wrong, it must be for some reason inherently connected with human freedom, not because of an arbitrary restriction of that freedom. However, Rahner's claim that we have a duty to maximize the opportunity to free actions is unpersuasive. If it were true, then human beings would have an overriding obligation to live as long as possible, and within their lives to make as many decisions as possible, but there does not seem to be any such moral duty.

Rahner would have done better to focus, not on the opportunities for free action, but on the relationship between freedom and truth (as Pope John Paul II does 1993: 54–64). Truth is not an external limit to freedom (of the sort Rahner rightly resists) but is an inherent measure of what constitutes true freedom. What is wrong with self-killing and mercy killing is not primarily that they limit someone's future opportunities for freedom but more fundamentally that they attack the human goods that freedom exists to serve: the valuing of life, the acceptance of death, justice to others, gratitude to God.

The weakness of Rahner's argument for the worthlessness of unconscious human life seems closely related to his conception of death as a free act, which is precisely the area where Rahner is most in danger of reviving the problematic approach of Ambrose towards death. Nevertheless, it has been argued above that Rahner's account of the free acceptance of death in fact provides a strong theological basis for rejecting suicide and mercy killing. Furthermore, his thought also provides a valuable insight as to why people find so troubling the very existence of people in an unconscious state. Why is it that the sustaining of these patients, who themselves seem beyond pleasure and pain, joy and suffering, and who represent no real threat to others, is so strongly rejected by many people, including by many Christians? What makes their continued existence a threat or the prospect of falling into this state more fearful than death itself? It seems to be that their lack of responsiveness and hence lack of control represents a living image of death. This coheres with Rahner's argument that what is frightening about death is precisely its ambiguity and the loss of autonomy, ambiguity and loss which are often anticipated in sickness. The persistent vegetative state is perhaps the ultimate example of *prolixitas mortis*, the anticipation of death in life. However, if this is the case, then the wish to end the life of someone in PVS, either by intervention or by withdrawal of food and fluids, represents not the proper acceptance of death but a failure to accept death. It is another instance of the phenomenon Ambrose describes, of 'not enduring death, and yet seeking it ... adopting that as a remedy which they flee from as an evil' (*FR* 11). The decision to sustain and care for unconscious patients, far from a failure to accept the inevitability death, is better seen as an acceptance of the loss of control that is complete in death.

What has been said so far does not resolve the issue as to whether tube feeding is nursing care which should never be withdrawn, or whether it is medical treatment which should be assessed in terms of its burdens and benefits. There is a good case to be made that providing food and water has an important symbolic value which distinguishes it from medical treatment, and hence that it is part of basic nursing care (Fisher 1993; John Paul II 2004; Meilaender in Meilaender and Orr 2004). However, even if it is to be classified as medical treatment, the giving of food and fluid has a very clear benefit in terms of sustaining life, except in rare circumstances. Furthermore the unconscious patient cannot experience any discomfort from the presence of the tubes. There seems then to be a very strong presumption in favour of providing food and fluid. It is difficult to see how providing food and fluid could generally be thought futile except on the false premise that the lives of these patients are worthless and caring for them is meaningless. It has here been argued that there is no reason to exclude these patients from human care and that the impulse to do so may be bound up with a failure to accept the surrender of human autonomy in death.

MAKING A GOOD DEATH

The approach of death is the approach of loss and exile. Death is the loss of life and the exile of the soul into the shadow world of Sheol. Augustine of Hippo and Thomas Aquinas both reflect a thoroughly scriptural view in claiming that the separation of body and soul is not a liberation but a kind of imprisonment. Even Jesus feared death. However, Jesus was raised from the dead and the message of the Gospel promises redemption from death. The loss of life will then become the gateway to an eternal life. Nevertheless, the transition from grief to joy, from death to resurrection is not necessary or automatic. It is based on the mercy of God and is received by those who surrender themselves to that mercy.

With this is mind, a 'good death' will be one where the person receives the mercy of God, possesses a lively hope of enjoying eternal life with Christ and with all the saints, and surrenders his or her life to God praying 'Lord Jesus, receive my spirit' (Acts 7: 59). The traditional picture of a good death is one where the person is aware up to the very end, in which reconciliation to God and to one's brothers and sisters is explicit and sacramental, and in which the acceptance of death is conscious and peaceful. The martyrs provide a model for a 'good death' in that the voluntary acceptance of death is explicit, though their deaths come as a result of terrible injustice, and often with torture or humiliation. The martyrs die freely but do not reject or flee from life. Despite superficial similarities, martyrdom is in fact the diametric opposite of suicide, as Rahner observed (QD2: 44). Martyrdom involves freely enduring death out of love of God. Suicide involves wilfully bringing death about, out of a wish to flee from this mortal life. It might seem that most people die a death that is neither martyrdom nor suicide, but Rahner argues that, in practice, every death is either martyrdom or suicide. Either death is accepted from God or God is rejected in death.

The link between martyrdom and the everyday experience of decline and loss of control is also evident in a Gospel passage quoted by Augustine and by Thomas Aquinas in their reflections on death.

'When you were young, you girded yourself and walked where you would; but when you are old, you will stretch out your hands, and another will gird you and carry you where you do not wish to go.' This [Jesus] said to show by what death [Peter] was to glorify God. (John 21: 18–19)

This cryptic saying of Jesus seems at first a reflection of the common experience of the loss of independence in later years. Those who are young and strong decide where they walk, those who in old age have become dependent on others have lost the freedom they used to have. Old age can thus mark a return to the status of the very young. The person who cannot look after himself or herself stretches out his or her hands and is girded by someone else. Increasingly that person is carried off not where he or she wants but where others want.[14] Jesus uses this remark, perhaps a commonplace saying, perhaps a saying of his own devising, to show by what death Peter is to die. Jesus does not refer to the method of Peter's execution, but to the surrender of will that is the essence of martyrdom. The loss of autonomy that so often accompanies decline, which is the aspect of sickness and dying that is hardest to bear, is thus an anticipation of the loss that is death, a loss which must be accepted if death is truly to be accepted.

Rahner is at his most profound in describing how the need to surrender oneself to God in death (the need to die like a martyr) is anticipated throughout life. This explains how even when death comes suddenly or to someone who is no longer conscious or aware, it can still be a good death, a death that is freely accepted. If, by the grace of God, the approach of death can be freely endured, and

---

[14] This observation is also echoed in the riddle of the Sphinx (in a famous incident not found in Homer but in a later version of the story given by Apollodorus): 'What is that which has one voice and yet becomes four-footed and two-footed and three-footed?' (Apollodorus 3. 5. 7) Oedipus solves the riddle. It is a human being that first crawls on all four, then walks on two legs, and finally walks with a stick. The last stage thus represents a decline and a partial return to the first.

all that has been said implies that this is no easy task, then the final surrender in death will be the end of death and the preamble to our true end:[15] eternal happiness in which all the faithful departed will be reunited in Christ and in which death will be no more.

Because we die our death in this life, because we are permanently taking leave, permanently parting, looking towards the end, permanently disappointed, ceaselessly piercing through the realities into their nothingness, continually narrowing the possibilities of free life through our actual decisions and actual life until we have exhausted life and driven it into the straits of death...we die throughout life, therefore what we call death is really the end of death, the death of death. (QD2: 85)

---

[15] On heaven as the redemption of the freedom which is so painfully lost in death, see Gaine (2003).

Bibliography

List of Abbreviations

CSEL   *Corpus Scriptorum Ecclesiasticorum Latinorum,* Vienna, 1866.
CCL   *Corpus Christianorum Series Latina,* Turnout, 1953.
EPL   *Super Epistolas S. Pauli Lectura S. Thomae Aquinatis,* ed. Marietti, Rome, 1953.
Leo   *Sancti Thomas Aquinatis Opera Omnia Iussu Leonis XIII P.M.* Rome, 1882.
NPN   *Library of the Nicene and Post-Nicene Fathers,* Grand Rapids, Mich., 1886–.
Opusc. *Opuscula Omnia Sancti Thomas Aquinatis,* ed. Mandonnet, Paris, 1927.
PG   *Patrologia Graeca,* ed. J. P. Migne, Paris, 1857.
PL   *Patrologia Latina,* ed. J. P. Migne, Paris, 1841.
SC   *Sources Chrétiennes,* Paris 1941.
TA   *Thomae Aquinatis Opera Omnia,* ed. Fretté, Paris, 1871.

Patristic and Medieval Texts

Albert of Cologne

Quaestiones de Animalibus, in *Alberti Magni Opera Omnia,* xii. Ashendorf, 1951.
Summae de Creaturis, in *Beati Alberti Magni Opera Omnia,* xxxv. Paris, 1890.

Ambrose of Milan

De bono mortis, CSEL 32, *PL* 14; English trans. by M. P. McHugh, 'Death as a Good', in Peebles et al., 1972.
De excessu fratris sui Satyri, CSEL 73, *PL* 16; English trans. by H. de Romestin, 'On the Death of Satyrus', in *NPN* II vol. 10, 1887.
Expositio Evangelium secundum Lucam, CSEL 32, *PL* 15.
De fide resurrectionis CSEL 73, *PL* 16; English trans. by H. de Romestin, 'On the Belief in the Resurrection', in *NPN* II vol. 10, 1887.
Letters, *CSEL* 82, *PL* 17.

De paradiso, CSEL 32, *PL* 14; English trans. by J. J. Savage, 'Paradise', in Deferrari 1961.

De virginibus, *PL* 16 English translation by H. de Romestin, 'Concerning Virgins', in *NPN* II vol. 10, 1887.

Augustine of Hippo

De bono coniugali, CSEL 41, *PL* 40; English trans. by C. L. Cornish, 'On the Good of Marriage', in *NPN* I vol. 3, 1887.

De civitate Dei, CCL 47–8, *PL* 41; English trans. by H. Bettenson, 1984.

Confessiones, CCL 27, *PL* 32; English trans. by H. Chadwick, 1991.

Contra academicos, CCSL 29, *PL* 32.

Contra adversarium legis et prophetarum, CCL 49, *PL* 42.

Contra duas epistolas Pelagianorum, CSEL 60, *PL* 44.

Contra mendacium, CSEL 41, *PL* 40.

De cura pro mortuis gerenda, CSEL 41, *PL* 40.

De diversis quaestionibus octoginta tribus, CCL 44, *PL* 40.

De doctrina Christiana, CCL 32, *PL* 34; English trans. by J. J. Gavigan, 'Christian Instruction', in Schopp 1947.

Enarrationes in Psalmos, CCL 38–40; English trans. 'Saint Augustin: Expositions on the Pslams' in *NPN* I vol. 8.

Enchiridion, CCL 46, *PL* 40.

De Genesi ad litteram, CSEL 28, *PL* 34; English trans. by J. H. Taylor 1982.

De gestis Pelagii, CSEL 42, *PL* 44; English trans. by P. Holmes, and R. E. Wallis, 'On the Proceedings of Pelagius', in *NPN* I vol. 5, 1887.

De gratia Christi, et de peccato originali, CSEL 42, *PL* 44.

In Joannis evangelium tractatus, CCL 36, *PL* 35.

Letters, CSEL 34, *PL* 33; English trans. by J. G. Cunningham, 'The Letters of St Augustine', in *NPN* I vol. 1, 1886.

De moribus ecclesiae catholicae, CSEL, 90, *PL* 32.

De musica, *PL* 32.

De peccatorum meritis et remissione, et De baptismo parvulorum, CSEL 60, *PL* 44.

De perfectione justitiae hominis, *PL* 44.

Retractationes, CCL 57, *PL* 32.

Sermons, *PL* 38.

De sancta virginitate, CSEL 41, *PL* 40; English trans. by C. L. Cornish, 'On Holy Virginity', in *NPN* I vol. 3, 1887.

De Trinitate, CCL 50, *PL* 42.

De vera religione, CCL 32, *PL* 34.

Bernard of Clairvaux

De gradibus humilitatis PL 182; English trans. in Burch 1940.
Sermones super Cantica Canticorum PL 184.
Sermones de diversis PL 183.

Bonaventure

Commentaria in IV libros Sentiarum in *Sancti Bonaventurae Opera Theologica Selecta*, i–iv, Florence, 1934.

Cyprian

De mortalitate, CSEL 3/1.

Gregory of Nyssa

De anima et resurrectione, PG 46; English trans. in Roth 1993.
De hominis opificio, SC 6, PG 44; English trans. by H. A. Wilson, 'On the Making of Man', in *NPN* II vol. 5, 1892.
De virginitate, SC 119, PG 46; English trans. by H. A. Wilson, and W. Moore, 'On Virginity' *NPN* II vol. 5, 1892.

Origen

'Dialogue with Heraclides', SC 67.
Commentaria in epistolam Beati Pauli ad Romanos, PG 14 (Latin), *Journal of Theological Studies*, 13 (1911–12), 209–24, 357–68; 14 (1912–13), 10–22 (Greek fragments).
De principiis, SC 252, 253, 268, 269, 312, PG 11.

Orosio

Praefatione ad historiarum, CSEL 5, PL 31.

Tertullian

Passio Perpetuae et Felicitatis PL 32; English trans. by R. Wallis, 'Martyrdom of Perpetua and Felicitas', in Roberts and Donaldson 1886.

Thomas Aquinas

Contra errores Graecorum, Leo 40.
De unitate intellectus contra Averroistas, Leo 43.
Super I ad Corinthianos, EPL 1.
Super II ad Corinthianos, EPL 1.

Sententia super De anima, Leo 45, 1.
Lectura super evangelium Johannis (Marietti edn. 1952).
Super ad Philippenses, EPL 2.
Scriptum super libros Sententiarum, TA 9–11.
Collationes super Credo in Deum, Opusc. 4.
Quaestiones disputatae De anima, Leo. 24, 1.
Quaestiones disputatae De potentia (Marietti edn. 1953).
Quaestiones disputatae De spiritualibus creaturi (Marietti edn. 1953).
Quaestiones disputatae De veritate, Leo. 22, 1–3.
Quaestiones Quodlibitales (Marietti edn. 1949).
Summa Contra Gentiles, Leo 13–15.
Summa Theologiae, Leo 4–12; English trans. by the Fathers of the English Dominican Province, *Summa Theologica*, London: Burns, Oates & Washbourne, 1912–36, cf. Durbin 1968; Fearon 1969; Suttor 1970.

Modern Works

AERTSEN, J. A. (1993), 'Aquinas's Philosophy in its Historical Setting', in Kretzmann and Stump 1993.

AMUNDSEN, D. W. (1989), 'Suicide and Early Christian Values', in B. A. Brody (ed.), *Suicide and Euthanasia*, Dordrecht: Kluwer Academic Publishers, 77–153.

ANDREWS, K., L. MURPHY, R. MUNDAY, and C. LITTLEWOOD (1996), 'Misdiagnosis of the Vegetative State: Retrospective Study in a Rehabilitation Unit', *British Medical Journal*, 313: 13–16.

ANSCOMBE, G. E. M. (1961), 'Aristotle', in Anscombe and Geach (1961).

—— (1981*a*), *From Parmenides to Wittgenstein: Collected Philosophical Papers*, i, Oxford: Basil Blackwell.

—— (1981*b*), *Ethics, Religion and Politics: Collected Philosophical Papers*, iii, Oxford: Basil Blackwell.

—— (1981*c*), 'Authority in Morals', in Anscombe 1981*b*.

—— (1981*d*), 'The Principle of Individuation' in Anscombe 1981*a*.

—— (1981*e*), 'On Transubstantiation' in Anscombe 1981*b*.

—— and P. T. GEACH (1961), *Three Philosophers*, Oxford: Basil Blackwell.

ASHLEY, B., and K. O'ROURKE (1997), *Healthcare Ethics: A Theological Analysis*, St Louis: Catholic Health Association of the United States.

ATKINS, M. (1999), 'Could there be Squirrels in Heaven?' *The Ark*, 183.

—— (2000), 'Could there be Squirrels in Heaven?: Part II', *The Ark* 184.

BALTHASAR, HANS URS VON (1956), 'Der Tod in heutigen Denken', *Anima*, 2: 292–9.

Barnes, M. R., and D. H. Williams (1993), *Arianism after Arius: Essays on the Development of Fourth Century Trinitarian Conflicts*, Edinburgh: T. & T. Clark.

Barr, J. (1992), *The Garden of Eden and the Hope of Immortality*, London: SCM Press.

Barth, K. (1960), *Church Dogmatics 3/2*, Edinburgh: T. & T. Clark.

—— (1961), *Church Dogmatics 3/3*, Edinburgh: T. & T. Clark.

Battin, M. P. (1994), *The Least Worst Death*, Oxford: Oxford University Press.

Bazan, B. C. (1991), 'The Highest Encomium of Human Body', in *Littera, Sensus, Sententia. Studi in onore del Prof. Clemente J. Vansteenkiste OP*, Milan: Studia Universitatis S.Thomae de Urbe, 33: 99–116.

Becker, E. (1974), *The Denial of Death*, New York: Free Press.

Bender, L. (1992), 'A Feminist Analysis of Physician-Assisted Dying and Voluntary Active Euthanasia', 59 *Tennessee Law Review* 519: 1–17.

Bettenson, H. (1984), *Augustine: City of God*, London: Penguin.

Biggar, N. (2004), *Aiming to Kill: The Ethics of Suicide and Euthanasia*, London: Darton, Longman & Todd.

Bonner, G. (1963), *St Augustine of Hippo*, London: SCM Press.

Boros, L. (1965), *The Moment of Truth (Mysterium mortis)*, London: Burns & Oates.

Boyle, L. (1982), *The Setting of the Summa of St Thomas Aquinas*, Etienne Gilson Series, 5, Toronto: Pontifical Institute of Mediaeval Studies.

Bradley, D. J. M. (1977), 'Rahner's "Spirit in the World": Aquinas or Hegel?' *The Thomist*, 41: 167–99.

Braine, D. (1993), *The Human Person: Animal and Spirit*, London: Duckworth.

Branson, R. (1975), 'Is Acceptance a Denial of Death? Another Look at Kübler-Ross', *Christian Century*, (7 May), 464–8.

Brown P. (1968), 'Pelagius and his Supporters: Aims and Environment', *Journal of Theological Studies*, 19/1.

—— (1989), *The Body and Society*. London: Faber and Faber.

—— (2000), *Augustine of Hippo: A Biography*, new edn. Berkeley: University of California Press.

Burch, G. B. (1940), *The Steps of Humility by Bernard Abbot of Clairvaux*, Cambridge, Mass.: Harvard University Press.

Burnaby, J. (1938), *Amor Dei*, London: Hodder & Stoughton.

Burnes, M. H. (1994), 'Demythologisation in the Theology of Karl Rahner' *Theological Studies*, 35: 24–45.

Cahill, L. S. (1996), *Sex Gender and Christian Ethics*, Cambridge: Cambridge University Press.

CALLAHAN, D. (2003), *What Price Better Health? Hazards of the Research Imperative*, Berkeley: University of California Press.

CAMERON, N. (1991), *The New Medicine: Life and Death after Hippocrates*, London: Hodder & Stoughton.

Catechism Catholic Church (1999), London: Geoffrey Chapman.

CAVADINI, J. C. (1999), 'Ambrose and Augustine De Bono Mortis', in Klingshirn and Vessey 1999.

CHADWICK, H. (1991), *Saint Augustine's Confessions*, Oxford: Oxford University Press.

CHADWICK, O. (1975), *The Secularization of the European Mind in the Nineteenth Century*, Cambridge: Cambridge University Press.

CHARLTON, W. (1972), 'Aristotle and the Principle of Individuation', *Phronesis*, 17: 239–49.

CLAUSS, R., and W. NEL (2006), 'Drug Induced Arousal from the Permanent Vegetative State', *Neurorehabilitation*, 21/1: 23–8.

Common Worship (2000), London: Church House Publishing.

CROSS, F. L, and A. E. LIVINGSTONE (2005), *The Oxford Dictionary of the Christian Church*, Oxford: Oxford University Press.

CROSS, R. (1999), *Duns Scotus*, Oxford: Oxford University Press.

CULLMAN, O. (1958), *Immortality of the Soul or Resurrection of the Dead?* London: Epworth Press.

DALES, R. C. (1995), *The Problem of the Rational Soul in the Thirteenth Century*, Leiden: E. J. Brill.

DAVIDSON, H. A. (1992), *Alfarabi, Avicenna, and Averroes on Intellect*, Oxford: Oxford University Press.

DAVIES, B. (1992), *The Thought of Thomas Aquinas*, Oxford: Clarendon Press.

DEFERRARI, R., et al., eds. (1961), *Saint Ambrose: Hexameron, Paradise, and Cain and Abel*, The Fathers of the Church, a new translation, 42, New York: Fathers of the Church, Inc.

DENZINGER, H. (1953), *Enchiridion Symbolorum*, Freiburg: Herder.

DE SPELDER, L. A., and A. L. STRICKLAND (1995), *The Last Dance*, Mountain View, Calif.: Mayfield.

DEWAN, L. (1999), 'The Individual as a Mode of Being According to Thomas Aquinas', *The Thomist*, 63: 403–24.

DI NOIA, J. A. (1997), 'Karl Rahner', in D. Ford, ed. (1997), *The Modern Theologians*, Oxford: Blackwell Publishers.

DODARO, R. (1989), ' "Christus Iustus" and Fear of Death in Augustine's Dispute with Pelagius', in A. Zumkeller, ed., *Signum Pietas*, Wurzburg: Augustinus-Verlag.

—— and G. LAWLESS (2000), *Augustine and his Critics*, London: Routledge.

DOYLE, J. P. (1997), *Franciso de Vitoria On Homicide & Commentary on Summa Theologiae IIaIIae Q.64 (Thomas Aquinas)* Milwaukee: Marquette University Press.

DROGE, A. J., and J. D. TABOR (1992), *A Noble Death: Suicide and Martyrdom among Christians and Jews in Antiquity,* San Francisco: Harper.

DUFFY, E. (2004), *Faith of our Fathers,* London: Continuum.

DURBIN, P. T. (1968), *St Thomas Aquinas Summa Theologiae Vol. 12 (Ia 74–89): Human Intelligence,* London: Eyre & Spottiswoode.

DURKHEIM, E. (2002), *Suicide,* London: Routledge.

DWORKIN, R. (1994), *Life's Dominion: An Argument about Abortion, Euthanasia, and Individual Freedom,* New York: Vintage Books.

DYCH, W. (1992), *Karl Rahner,* London: Chapman.

DYSON, R. W. (1998), *The City of God against the Pagans,* Cambridge: Cambridge University Press.

EDWARDS, M. (1992), 'Origen No Gnostic; or On the Corporeality of Man', *Journal of Theological Studies,* 43/1.

ERNST, C. (1959), 'The Theology of Death', *Clergy Review,* 44: 588–602.

—— (1961), Introduction to K. Rahner, *Theological Investigations,* i, London: Darton, Longman & Todd.

FEARON, J. (1969), *St Thomas Aquinas Summa Theologiae Vol. 25 (IaIIae 71–80): Sin,* London: Eyre & Spottiswoode.

FIESER, J., ed. (1995), *David Hume: Essays on Suicide and the Immortality of the Soul: The Complete Unauthorized 1783 Edition,* Internet Release.

FINNIS, J. (1980), *Natural Law and Natural Rights,* Oxford: Clarendon Press.

FIORENZA, F. P. (1968), 'Karl Rahner and the Kantian Problematic' published as the introduction to K. Rahner, *Spirit in the World,* London: Sheed & Ward.

FISHER, A. (1993), 'On Not Starving the Unconscious', *New Blackfriars,* 74: 130–45.

FITZGERALD, A. (1999), *Augustine through the Ages: An Encyclopedia,* Grand Rapids, Mich.: William B. Eerdmans.

FOSTER, D. R. (1991), 'Aquinas on the Immateriality of the Intellect', *The Thomist,* 55: 415–38.

FOSTER, K. (1959), *The Life of Saint Thomas Aquinas: Biographical Documents,* London: Longmans, Green and Co.

FREND, W. H. C. (1985), *The Donatist Church,* Oxford: Clarendon Press.

GAINE, S. (2003), *Will There Be Free Will in Heaven?* London: Continuum (T. & T. Clark).

GARBER, J., and M. E. P. SELIGMAN, eds. (1980), *Human Helplessness: Theory and Applications,* New York: Academic Press.

GARCIA, J. (1994), *Individuation in Scholasticism: The Later Middle Ages and the Counter Reformation 1150–1650*, Albany: State University of New York Press.

GARVEY, M. P. (1939), *Saint Augustine: Christian or NeoPlatonist?* Milwaukee: Marquette University Press.

GEACH, M. and L. GORMALLY, eds. (2005), *Human Life, Action and Ethics: Essays by G. E. M. Anscombe*, St Andrews: Imprint Academic.

GEACH, P. T. (1961), 'Aquinas', in Anscombe and Geach 1961.

—— (1969), *God and the Soul*, London: Routledge & Kegan Paul.

—— (1977), *Providence and Evil*, Cambridge: Cambridge University Press.

GILSON, E. (1957), *The Christian Philosophy of St. Thomas Aquinas*, London: Victor Gollancz.

GLOVER, J. (1990), *Causing Death and Saving Lives*, London: Penguin.

GORMALLY, L., ed. (1994), *Euthanasia, Clinical Practice and the Law*, London: Linacre Centre.

GRIFFITHS, J. (1998), 'The Slippery Slope: Are the Dutch Sliding Down or are They Climbing Up?' in Thomasma et al. 1998.

GRISEZ, G. (1983), *The Way of the Lord Jesus*, i. *Christian Moral Principles*, Quincy, Ill.: Franciscan Press, Quincy University.

—— (1993), *The Way of the Lord Jesus*, ii. *Living a Christian Life*, Quincy, Ill.: Franciscan Press, Quincy University.

GUIGONON, C. B. (1993), *The Cambridge Companion to Heidegger*, Cambridge: Cambridge University Press.

HAGGART, A. (1991), 'A Theological Perspective on Euthanasia', address to Edinburgh branch of the Voluntary Euthanasia Society.

HALDANE, J. (1998), 'A Return to Form in the Philosophy of Mind', *Ratio* 11/3:253–77.

HANSON, R. P. C. (1988), *The Search for the Christian Doctrine of God: The Arian Controversy 318–381*, Edinburgh: T. & T. Clark.

HARRIS, J. (1985), *The Value of Life: An Introduction to Medical Ethics*, London: Routledge.

HARRISON, C. (2000), *Augustine: Christian Truth and Fractured Humanity*, Oxford: Oxford University Press.

HEALEY, N. (1992), 'Indirect Methods in Theology: Karl Rahner as an ad hoc Apologist', *The Thomist*, 56: 613–34.

HEBBLETHWAITE, B. (1979), 'Time and Eternity and Life "after" Death', *Heythrop Journal*, 20: 57–62.

HEIDEGGER, M. (1927), *Sein und Zeit*, Tübingen: Max Niemeyer Verlag; English trans. J. Stambaugh, *Being and Time*, Albany: State University of New York Press, 1996.

HENLE, R. J. (1956), *Saint Thomas and Platonism*, The Hague: Martinus Nijhoff.

HIBBS, T. S., ed. (1999), *Aquinas On Human Nature*, Indianapolis: Hackett Publishing Co.

HOMES DUDDEN, F. (1935), *The Life and Times of St Ambrose*, 2 vols., Oxford: Clarendon Press.

JOHN PAUL II (1993), *Veritatis Splendor*, London: Catholic Truth Society.

—— (1995), *Evangelium Vitae*, London: Catholic Truth Society.

—— (2004), 'Address of John Paul II to The Participants in the International Congress on "Life-Sustaining Treatments and Vegetative State: Scientific Advances and Ethical Dilemmas"', Saturday, 20 March.

JOHNSON, S., and D. J. ENRIGHT, eds. (1977), *The History of Rasselas, Prince of Abissinia*, London: Penguin Classics.

JONAS, H. (1966), 'Cybernetics and Purpose: A Critique', in *The Phenomenon of Life*, Westport, Conn.: Greenwood Press.

JONES, D. A. (1992), 'Do Whales Have Souls?' *New Blackfriars*, 73/866.

—— (2003), 'The Hippocratic Oath I: Its Content and the Limits to its Adaptation', *Catholic Medical Quarterly*, 54/3, August.

—— (2004), *The Soul of the Embryo: An Enquiry into the Status of the Human Embryo in the Christian Tradition*, London: Continuum.

—— (2006), 'The Hippocratic Oath II: Modern Adaptations of the Classical Doctors' Oath', *Catholic Medical Quarterly*, 57/1, February.

—— and W. HISCOX (2006), 'Malice Aforethought: The Proposed Review of the Homicide Act', *Catholic Medical Quarterly*, 57/3, August.

JONES, W. H. S. (1924), *The Doctor's Oath: An Essay in the History of Medicine*, New York: Cambridge University Press.

KASS, L. (1988), *Towards a More Natural Science*, New York: Free Press.

KELSEY, D. H. (1997), 'Two Theologies of Death: Anthropological Gleanings', *Modern Theology*, 13: 347–70.

KENNEDY, L. A. (1988), 'Early Jesuits and the Immortality of the Soul', *Gregorianum*, 69/1.

KENNY, A. J. P., ed. (1969), *Aquinas: A Collection of Critical Essays*, London: Macmillan.

—— (1984), 'Intentionality: Aquinas and Wittgenstein', in *The Legacy of Wittgenstein*, Oxford: Basil Blackwell.

—— (1989), *The Metaphysics of Mind*, Oxford: Oxford University Press.

KEOWN, J. (2002), *Euthanasia, Ethics and Public Policy: An Argument against Legalization*, Cambridge: Cambridge University Press.

KERR, F. (1980a), 'Rahner's *Grundkurs* Revisited', *New Blackfriars*, 61: 148–57.

—— (1980*b*), 'Rahner Retrospective I: Rupturing "*Der Pianische Monolithismus*"', *New Blackfriars* 61: 224–33.

—— (1980*c*), 'Rahner Retrospective II: Historicity of Theology', *New Blackfriars*, 61: 331–41.

—— (1981), 'Rahner Retrospective III: Transcendence or Finitude', *New Blackfriars*, 62: 370–9.

—— (1997a), *Theology after Wittgenstein*, 2nd edn., London: SPCK.

—— (1997b), *Immortal Longings*, London: SPCK.

—— (2002), *After Aquinas: Versions of Thomism*, Oxford: Blackwell Publishing.

KILBY, K. (1997), *Karl Rahner*, London: Fount (HarperCollins).

KLIMA, G. (1997), 'Man = Body + Soul: Aquinas's Arithmetic of Human Nature', in T. Koistinen and T. Lehtonen, eds., *Philosophical Studies in Religion, Metaphysics, and Ethics: Essays in Honour of Heikki Kirjavainen*, Helsinki: Luther-Agricola-Society.

KLINGSHIRN, W. E., and M. VESSEY, eds. (1999), *The Limits of Ancient Christianity*, Ann Arbor: University of Michigan Press.

KRETZMANN, N. (1993), 'Philosophy of Mind', in Kretzmann and Stump 1993.

KRETZMANN, N., and E. STUMP, eds. (1993), *The Cambridge Companion to Aquinas*, Cambridge: Cambridge University Press.

KÜBLER-ROSS, E. (1969), *On Death and Dying*, London: Macmillan.

LAMBERIGTS, M. (2000), 'A Critical Evaluation of Critiques of Augustine's View of Sexuality', in Dodaro and Lawlesss 2000.

LANCEL, S. (2002), *St Augustine*, London: SCM Press.

LASH, N. (1978), 'Eternal Life, Life "After" Death?' *Heythrop Journal*, 19: 271–84.

LAWRENCE, C. H. (1994), *The Friars*, London: Longman.

Law Commission (2005), *A New Homicide Act for England and Wales?* Consultation Paper 177.

LE GOFF, J. (1984), *The Birth of Purgatory*, London: Scolar Press.

LEWIS, C. S. (1984), *Mere Chrsitianity*, New York: Macmillan.

LONERGAN, B. (1963), 'Metaphysics as Horizon', *Gregorianum*, 44: 307–18.

McCABE, H. (1969), 'The Immortality of the Soul', in Kenny 1969.

—— (1987), 'Death' in H. McCabe, *Hope*, London: Catholic Truth Society.

—— (2005), *God Matters*, London: Continuum.

McCOOL, G. A. (1975), *A Rahner Reader*, London: Darton, Longman & Todd.

—— (1992), *From Unity to Pluralism: The Internal Evolution of Thomism*, New York: Fordham University Press.

—— (1994), *The Neo-Thomists*, Milwaukee: Marquette University Press.

McCool, G. A. (2000), 'The Christian Wisdom Tradition and Enlightenment Reason', in A. J. Cernera and O. J. Morgan, eds. *Examining the Catholic Intellectual Tradition*, Fairfield, Conn.: Sacred Heart University Press.

McCormick, R. (1984), *Health and Medicine in the Catholic Tradition*, New York: Crossroad.

MacIntyre, A. (1981), *After Virtue: A Study in Moral Theory*, London: Duckworth.

—— (2001), *Dependent Rational Animals: Why Human Beings Need the Virtues*, Chicago: Open Court.

Mackay, J. (chair) (2005), *House of Lords Select Committee Report on the Assisted Dying for the Terminally Ill Bill*, London: HMSO.

McLeod, H. (2000), *Secularisation in Western Europe, 1848–1914*, London: Macmillan.

McLynn, N. B. (1994), *Ambrose of Milan*, Berkeley: University of California Press.

Macquarrie, J. (1984), 'The Anthropological Approach to Theology', *Heythrop Journal*, 25: 272–87.

Mahoney, J., G. E. M. Anscombe, et al. (1982), 'Euthanasia and Clinical Practice: Trends, Principles and Alternatives', in Gormally 1994.

Martin, C., ed. (1988), *The Philosophy of Thomas Aquinas: Introductory Readings*, London: Routledge.

Martin, J. T. (1993), 'Aquinas as a Commentator on De Anima 3.5', *Thomist*, 57: 621–40.

Masson, R. (1973), 'Rahner and Heidegger: Being, Hearing and God', *Thomist*, 37: 455–88.

Mauer, A., et al., eds. (1974), *St. Thomas Aquinas 1274–1974 Commemorative Studies*, Toronto: Pontifical Institute of Mediaeval Studies.

Meilaender, G., and R. Orr (2004), 'Ethics & Life's Ending: An Exchange', *First Things*, 145 (August/September), 31–7.

Meynell, H. (1980), 'Rahner's *Grundkurs*', *New Blackfriars*, 61: 77–89.

Midgely, M. (1980), *Beast and Man*, London: Methuen.

Moorhead, J. (1999), *Ambrose*, London: Longman.

Murphy, M. (1988), *New Images of the Last Things: Karl Rahner on Death and Life after Death*, New York: Paulist Press.

Murray, Alexander (2000), *Suicide in the Middle Ages*, ii. *The Curse on Self-Murder*, Oxford: Oxford University Press.

Nagel, T. (1970), 'Death', *Nous*, 4/1: 73–80.

Nelson D. M. (1987), 'Karl Rahner's Existentialist Ethics: A Critique Based on St Thomas's Understanding of Prudence', *Thomist*, 51: 461–79.

Nichols, A. (1990), *From Newman to Congar*, Edinburgh: T. & T. Clark.

O'DALY, G. (1999), *Augustine's City of God: A Reader's Guide*, Oxford: Clarendon Press.

O'DONNELL, J. J. (1992), *Augustine Confessions*, 3 vols., Oxford: Clarendon Press.

—— (1999), 'The Next life of Augustine', in Klingshirn and Vessey 1999.

O'DONNELL, R. A. (1959), 'Individuation: An Example of Development in the Thought of St Thomas Aquinas', *New Scholasticism*, 33.

OMBRES, R. (1981), 'The Doctrine of Purgatory according to St Thomas Aquinas', *Downside Review*, 99: 279–87.

O'MEARA, J. J. (1997), *Understanding Augustine*, Dublin: Four Courts Press.

Oregon and Washington Bishops (1991), 'Living and Dying Well', *Origins*, 21–22 (7 November).

OWENS, J. (1974), 'Aquinas as Aristotelian Commentator', in Mauer et al. 1974.

—— (1988), 'Thomas Aquinas: Dimensive Quantity as Individuating Principle', *Medieval Studies*, 50: 279–310.

—— (1993), 'Aristotle and Aquinas', in Kretzmann and Stump 1993.

—— (1994), 'Thomas Aquinas', in Garcia 1994.

PARK, K. (1980), 'Albert's Influence on Late Medieval Psychology', in J. A. Weisheipl, ed., *Albertus Magnus and the Sciences: Commemorative Essays 1980*, Toronto: Pontifical Institute of Mediaeval Studies.

PARKER, M. G. (1999), 'Rahner's Transcendental Theology', *Thomist*, 63: 191–216.

PASCAL, B. (1966), *Pensées*, trans. A. J. Krailsheimer, Harmondsworth: Penguin Classics.

PAUL, J. (2004), 'Salt that has Lost its Saltiness: Towards the Recovery of the a Distinctive Christian Bioethic in the Culture of Pluralism' MA thesis, St Mary's University College, Twickenham.

PEDLEY, C. J. (1984), 'An English Bibliographical Aid to Karl Rahner', *Heythrop Journal*, 25: 319–60.

PEEBLES, P. M., et al., eds. (1972), *Saint Ambrose: Seven Exegetical Works*, The Fathers of the Church: A New Translation, vol. 65, Washington: Catholic University of America Press.

PEGIS, A. C. (1934), *St Thomas and the Problem of the Soul in the Thirteenth Century*, Toronto: St Michael's College.

—— (1974), 'The Separated Soul and its Nature in St. Thomas', in Mauer et al. 1974.

PHAN, P. C. (1994), 'Contemporary Context and Issues in Eschatology', *Theological Studies*, 35: 507–36.

PHILLIPS, W. G. (1992), 'Rahner's Transcendental Deduction of Vorgriff', *The Thomist*, 56: 257–90.

PIEPER, J. (1957), *The Silence of St. Thomas: Three Essays*, London: Faber and Faber.

—— (1969), *Death and Immortality*, London: Burns & Oatcs.

PINCKAERS, S. (1995), *The Sources of Christian Ethics*, Edinburgh: T. & T. Clark.

Pontifical Biblical Commission (1994), 'The Interpretation of the Bible in the Church', *Origins*, 6 January 1994.

PORTER, J. (1995), *Moral Action and Christian Ethics*, Cambridge: Cambridge University Press.

POTTS, M. (1995), 'The Spatio-Temporal Theory of Individuation', *The Thomist*, 59: 59–68.

PRÜMMER, D., and M.-H. LAURENT, (1911–37), *Fontes Vitae Thomae Aquinatis*, published in fascicles attached to *Revue Thomiste*.

RADICE, R., and RUNIA, D. (1988), *Philo of Alexandria: An Annotated Bibliography 1937–1986*, Leiden: Brill.

—— —— (2000), *Philo of Alexandria: An Annotated Bibliography 1987– 1996*, Leiden: Brill.

RAHNER, K. (1939), *Geist in Welt*; English trans. (of 2nd German edn.), *Spirit in the World*, London: Sheed & Ward, 1968.

—— (1957), 'Abgestiegen in Totenreich', in *Schriften zur Theologie*, vii, Einsiedeln: Benziger Verlag, 1966 (*SZT* vii); English trans. 'He Descended into Hell', in *Theological Investigations* vii, London: Darton, Longman & Todd, 1971 (*TI*, vii).

—— (1958), *Zur Theologie des Todes*, Quaestiones Disputatae 2; English trans. *On the Theology of Death*, Quaestiones Disputatae 2, New York: Herder and Herder, 1961.

—— (1959*a*), 'Über die christlich Sterbens', *SZT* vii; English trans. 1971, 'On Christian Dying' *TI* vii.

—— (1959*b*), 'Das Leben der Toten', *SZT* iv, English trans. 1965, 'The Life of the Dead', *TI* iv.

—— (1959*c*), 'Über die Frage einer formalen Existentialethik', *SZT* ii; English trans. 1965, 'On the Question of a Formal Existential Ethics' *TI* ii.

—— (1960), 'Theologische Prinzipien der Hermeneutik eschatologischer Aussagen', *SZT* iv; English trans. 1965, 'The Hermeneutics of Eschatological Assertions', *TI* iv.

—— (1961), 'Tod', in *Kleines theologisches Wörterbuch*; English trans. 1965, 'Death' in *Concise Theological Dictionary*, London: Burns & Oates.

—— (1965*a*), 'Tod' *Lexikon für Theologie und Kirche*, x.

—— (1965*b*), *Betrachtungen zum ignatianischen Exerzitienbuch*; English trans. *Spiritual Exercises*, London: Sheed & Ward, 1967.

—— (1966) 'Das Ärgernis des Todes', *SZT* vii; English trans. 1971, 'The Scandal of Death', *TI* vii.

—— (1967), 'Tod', *Sacramentum Mundi*; English trans. 'Death' in *Sacramentum Mundi*, London Burns & Oates, 1969.

—— (1968*a*) 'Theologische Erwägungen über den Eintritt des Todes', *SZT* ix; English trans. 1974, 'Theological Considerations of the Moment of Death', *TI* xi.

—— (1968*b*) 'Zur Enzyklika "Humanae Vitae"', *SZT* ix; English trans. 1974. 'On the encyclical "Humanae Vitae"' *TI* xi.

—— (1968*c*) 'Die Zukunft des Menschen. Zum Problem der genetischen Manipulation', *SZT* viii; English trans. 1972, 'The Problem of Genetic Manipulation', *TI* ix.

—— (1970), 'Zu einer Theologie des Todes', *SZT* x; English trans. 1975, 'Ideas for a Theology of Death', *TI* xiii.

—— (1973), 'Tod', *Theologisches TaschenLexican*.

—— (1975*a*), 'Über den "Zwischenzustand"', *SZT* xii; English trans. 1981, 'The Intermediate State', *TI* xvii.

—— (1975*b*), 'Death', *Encyclopaedia of Theology*, London: Burns & Oates.

—— (1976*a*), 'Das christliche Sterben', in *Mysterium Salutis*; English trans. 1981, 'Christian Dying', *TI* xviii.

—— (1976*b*), *Grundkurs des Glaubens: Einführung in den Begriff des Christentums*; English trans. *Foundations of Christian Faith*, London: Darton, Longman & Todd, 1978.

—— (1977), 'Die Freiheit des Kranken in theologischer Sicht', *SZT* xii; English trans. 1981, 'The Liberty of the Sick, Theologically Considered', *TI* xvii.

—— (1983*a*), 'Theologie des Todes und christlicher Skeptizismus', in *Im Gespräch II*, Munich: Kösel.

—— (1983*b*), 'Dimensions of Martyrdom: A Plea for the Broadening of a Classical Concept', *Concilium*, 163: 9–11.

—— (1984), *Erinnerungen im Gespräch mit Meinold Krauss*; English trans., *I Remember*, London: SCM, 1985.

RAMSEY, B. (1997), *Ambrose*, London: Routledge.

RAMSEY, P. (1970), *The Patient as Person: Explorations in Medical Ethics*, New Haven: Yale University Press.

—— (1974), 'The Indignity of "Death with Dignity"', *Studies—Hastings Center*, 2/2, May: 47–62.

RATZINGER, J. (1977), *Eschatologie—Tod und ewiges Leben*; English trans. A. Nichols, *Eschatology: Death and Eternal Life*, Washington: Catholic University of America Press, 1998.

REES, B. R., ed. (1991), *The Letters of Pelagius and his Followers*, Woodbridge: Boydell.

REYNA, R. (1972), 'On the Soul: A Philosophical Exploration of the Active Intellect in Averroes, Aristotle, and Aquinas', *The Thomist*, 36: 131–49.

RIST, J. M. (1994), *Augustine*, Cambridge: Cambridge University Press.

ROBERTS, A., and J. DONALDSON eds. (1886), *Ante-Nicene Fathers*, iii. *Latin Christianity: Its Founder, Tertullian*, Grand Rapids, Mich.: Eerdmans.

ROBERTS, L. (1967), *The Achievement of Karl Rahner*, New York: Herder and Herder.

ROTH, C. P. (1993), *Gregrory of Nyssa: On the Soul and the Resurrection*, Crestwood, NY: St Vladimir's Seminary Press.

ROUSSEAU, M. (1979), 'Elements of Thomistic Philosophy of Death', *The Thomist*, 43: 581–602.

ROUSSELOT, P. (1935), *The Intellectualism of St Thomas*, London: Sheed & Ward.

RYLE, G. (1949), *The Concept of Mind*, London: Hutchinson.

SAUNDERS, W. (1996), 'Mercy Killing or Euthanasia?' *Arlington Catholic Herald*, 5 December <http://www.catholicherald.com/saunders/96ws/fs961205.htm>

SCHILLEBEECKX, E. H. (1962*a*), 'The Death of a Christian I: The Objective Fact', *Life in the Spirit*, 16: 270–9.

—— (1962*b*), 'The Death of a Christian II: Our Personal Approach', *Life in the Spirit*, 16: 335–45.

SCHOPP, L. et al., eds. (1947), *Writings of Saint Augustine*, iv, New York: CIMA Publishing Co.

SILVER, R. L., and C. B. WORTMAN (1980), 'Coping with Undesirable Life Events', in Garber and Seligman 1980.

SINGER, P. (1994), *Rethinking Life and Death*, Melbourne: text publishing.

SOLOMON, R. C., and J. MALPAS (1998), *Death and Philosophy*, London: Routledge.

South Australian Voluntary Euthanasia Society (1998), *The Right to Choose: The Case for Legalising Voluntary Euthanasia*, Kent Town, Australia: South Australian Voluntary Euthanasia Society.

STITH, R. (1987), 'Towards Freedom from Value', in S. Lammers and A. Verhey, *On Moral Medicine*, Grand Rapids, Mich.: Eerdmans, 1987.

SUTTOR, T. (1970), *St Thomas Aquinas Summa Theologiae Vol. 11 (Ia 75–83): Man*, London: Eyre & Spottiswoode.

TANNER, N., ed. (1990), *Decrees of the Ecumenical Councils*, London: Sheed and Ward.

TAYLOR, C. (1964), *The Explanation of Behaviour*, London: Routledge and Kegan Paul.

TAYLOR, J. H. (1982), *Augustine: The Literal Meaning of Genesis*, Ancient Christian Writers 41–2, New York: Newman Press.

TAYLOR, M. J., ed. (1973), *The Mystery of Suffering and Death*, New York: Alba House.

TESELLE, E. (1970), *Augustine the Theologian*, London: Burns & Oates.

THOMASMA, D., T. KIMBROUGH-KUSHER, G. KIMSA, and C. CIESEIELSKI-CARLUCCI, eds. (1998), *Asking to Die: Inside the Dutch Debate about Euthanasia*, Dordrecht: Kluwer Academic Press.

TONER, P. (1913), 'Limbo', in *The Catholic Encyclopedia*, New York: Encyclopedia Press.

TORRELL, J.-P. (1996), *Saint Thomas Aquinas: The Person and his Work*, Washington: Catholic University of America Press.

TRELOAR, J. L. (1990), 'Pomponazzi's Critique of Aquinas's Arguments for the Immortality of the Soul', *The Thomist*, 54: 453–70.

TUGWELL, S., ed. (1982), *Early Dominicans: Selected Writings*, Mahwah, NJ: Paulist Press.

—— ed. (1988), *Albert and Thomas: Selected Writings*, Mahwah, NJ: Paulist Press.

—— (1990), *Human Immortality and the Redemption of Death*, London: Darton, Longman and Todd.

VAN EVRA (1971), 'On Death as a Limit', *Analysis*, 31: 170–6.

VASS, G. (1989*a*), *Understanding Karl Rahner*, i. *A Theologian in Search of a Philosophy*, London: Sheed and Ward.

—— (1989*b*), *Understanding Karl Rahner*, ii. *The Mystery of Man and the Foundations of a Theological System*, London: Sheed and Ward.

VEATCH, R. M. (1974), 'Essentialism and the Problem of Individuation', *Proceedings of the American Catholic Philosophical Association*, 48: 64–73.

VICAIRE, M.-H. (1964), *Saint Dominic and his Times*, Green Bay, Wis.: Alt Publishing.

VORGRIMLER, H. (1965), *Karl Rahner: His Life, Thought and Works*, Montreal: Palm.

—— (1986), *Understanding Karl Rahner: An Introduction to his Life and Thought*, London: SCM Press.

WALLACE, W. (1963), 'Existentialist Ethics: A Thomist Appraisal', *The Thomist*, 27: 493–515.

WALTON, J. (chair) (1994), *Report of the House of Lords Select Committee on Medical Ethics*, London: HMSO.

WATT, H. (2000), *Life and Death in Healthcare Ethics*, London: Routledge.

WEGER, K.-H. (1980), *Karl Rahner: An Introduction to his Theology*, London: Burns & Oates.

WEISHEIPL, J. A. (1983), *Friar Thomas D'Aquino: His Life, Thought & Works,* Washington: Catholic University of America Press.

WESTBERG, G. (1962), *Good Grief,* Philadelphia: Augsburg Fortress Press.

WHITE, V. (1956), *God the Unknown and Other Essays,* London: Harvill Press.

WIGGINS, D. (1980), *Sameness and Substance,* Oxford: Basil Blackwell.

WILLIAMS, A. N. (1997), 'Mystical Theology Redux: The Pattern of Aquinas' *Summa Theologiae', Modern Theology,* 13/1: 53–74.

WILLIAMS, B. (1973), 'The Makropolus Case', in B. Williams, *Problems of the Self,* Cambridge: Cambridge University Press.

—— (1985), *Ethics and the Limits of Philosophy,* London: Fontana.

WILLIAMS, D. H. (1993), 'Ambrose, Emperors and Homoians in Milan: The First Conflict over a Basilica', in Barnes and Williams 1993.

WILLIAMS, G. (1957), *The Sanctity of Life and the Criminal Law,* New York: Alfred A Knopf.

WILLIAMS, J. R. (1971), 'Heidegger and the Theologians', *Heythrop Journal,* 12: 258–80.

WITTGENSTEIN, L. (1953), *Philosophical Investigations,* Oxford: Basil Blackwell.

WRIGHT, N. T. (2003), *The Resurrection of the Son of God,* London: SPCK.

WREEN, M. (1988), 'The Definition of Suicide', *Social Theory and Practice,* 14: 1–23.

ZEDLER, B. H. (1968), *Saint Thomas Aquinas On the Unity of the Intellect against the Averroists,* Milwaukee: Marquette University Press.

Index

Scriptural Index